BOMBING 1939–45

BOMBING 1939-45

*The Air Offensive against Land
Targets in World War Two*

KARL HECKS

ROBERT HALE · LONDON

Copyright © Karl Hecks 1990
First published in Great Britain 1990

Robert Hale Limited
Clerkenwell House
Clerkenwell Green
London EC1R 0HT

British Library Cataloguing in Publication Data

Hecks, Karl
  Bombing 1939 – 1945: the air offensive against land
  targets in World War Two.
  1. World War 2. Air operations by bomber aeroplanes
  I. Title
  940.54′4

ISBN 0–7090–4020–2

Photoset in Times by
Derek Doyle & Associates, Mold, Clwyd.
Printed in Great Britain by
St Edmundsbury Press, Bury St Edmunds, Suffolk.
Bound by Woolnough Limited.

Contents

Illustrations

PICTURE CREDITS

All photographs are reproduced courtesy of the Imperial War Museum, London.

Introduction

As befits the large and much-publicized role played by
bombing against land targets during World War Two, it has
been the subject of many books since that time. The
majority of these have been concerned with strategic
bombing, and most have dealt at length with the actions of a
particular bomber force, or one bombing campaign, or
bombing in one war theatre. Others have given a detailed
treatment of a single important raid.

This present book differs in that it attempts to bring into
one volume a concise but wider coverage of the subject. It
deals with tactical as well as strategic bombing. It covers all
of the combatant powers, and operations in all the main
theatres of the air/land war. The major bombing campaigns,
and the key raids, are all included in summary form. Also it
gives most emphasis to innovations in the weapons,
techniques and tactics devised and used, those that worked
and many that didn't. Since strafing and rocket attacks are
not readily separable from bombing in tactical actions, they
have been included. But space limitations have allowed only
passing mention of other related subjects: strategic missiles
for use against land targets, bombing in the maritime war,
and defence against bombing, which are major subjects in
their own right.

The form of presentation adopted is perhaps unusual.
Given the diversity of the material covered, it was found
convenient to subdivide it into individual or related topics,
which are then grouped under appropriate headings. The
work is mostly presented in approximate chronological
order – year by year – to help show the various technical and
operational developments as the war progressed. While the
basics of bombing remained much the same throughout the
war, six years of intensive development, of responding to the
enemy's capability, and of learning from one's own
mistakes, produced many, many changes.

Much of the information compiled in the text relies on research spadework performed by many writers, for which this author is very grateful. All of the main sources used are listed in the bibliography, but books found particularly valuable include the writings of: Chaz Bowyer, Michael J.F.Bowyer, Roger Freeman, William Green, Bill Gunston, von Hardesty, Max Hastings, Ian V.Hogg, R.V.Jones, Norman Longmate, Martin Middlebrook, Kenneth Munson, Gordon Musgrove, Roderic Owen, Janus Pie-kalkiewicz, Alfred Price, Winston Ramsey, Dennis Richards and Hilary St.George Saunders, Christopher Shores, Peter C.Smith, Martin Streetley, John Sweetman, John Terraine, Anthony Verrier, Kenneth Wakefield, and Charles Webster and Noble Frankland. The staff of the Imperial War Museum (photographic) and Royal Air Force Museum (library) were very helpful in finding material.

In the text, place names have been left anglicized (Cologne, rather than Köln, etc.), while imperial and metric units have been retained as appropriate for the country of origin. A further small point: throughout the text, reference to some night action say 'on 17 May' means 'during the night of 17/18 May'.

The various published accounts of war events are not always free from discrepancies. While much care has gone into checking to minimize errors and omissions for this present work, given the scope of the book it would be overly optimistic to expect there to be none. Nevertheless, it is hoped that the errors (transcribed or home grown) and omissions remaining are few and relatively small.

Abbreviations

AA	Anti-Aircraft
AAF	Army Air Force
A&AEE	Aeroplane and Armament Experimental Establishment, Boscombe Down (Br.)
AB	*Abwurf Behalter* (Jettisoning container, for bombs, Ger.)
ABB	*Abwurf Behalter Brandbomben* (As above, for incendiaries, Ger.)
ACC	Army Cooperation Command (Br.)
ACIU	Allied Central Interpretation Unit, Medmenham
ACM	Air Chief Marshal (Br.)
ADD	*Aviatsiya Dal'nevo Deystviya* (Long Range Aviation, Sov. long range bomber force)
ADGB	Air Defence of Great Britain (RAF Fighter Command)
AF	Air Force
AFV	Armoured Fighting Vehicle
AI	Air Interception (Night fighter radar)
ALO	Air Liaison Officer (Br.)
AMES	Air Ministry Experimental Station (Cover name for Br. radio/radar stations)
AN/APS	Army-Navy/Air Pulsed Search (US airborne radar)
AP	Armour Piercing (Shell, bomb); Aiming Point
ASM	Air-to-Surface Missile
ASR	Air-Sea Rescue
ASSU	Air Support Signals Unit (Br.)
AVG	American Volunteer Group
AVM	Air Vice Marshal
BAF	Balkan Air Force
BATDU	Blind Approach Technical and Development Unit, Wyton (Br.)
BBC	British Broadcasting Corporation
BC	Bomber Command
BG	Bombardment Group (US); Bomb-Glider (US)
BK	*Bordkanone* (Externally mounted cannon, Ger.)

BLC	*Blitzlichtcylindrische* (Photo-flash bomb, Ger.)
Br.	British
BS	Bombardment Squadron (US)
BSDU	Bomber Support Development Unit, Foulsham (Br.)
BTO	Bomb Through Overcast (Ground-imaging radar, US)
BW	Biological Warfare; Biological Weapons
BZA	*Bombenziel Automatik* (Automatic dive-bombing sight, Ger.)
Can.	Canadian
CAP	Combat Air Patrol
CB	Construction Battalion (US)
CBI	China/Burma/India war theatre
CBW	Chemical/Biological Warfare
CEP	Circular Error Probable (Measure of bombing accuracy)
c.g.	Centre of Gravity
CH	Chain, Home (Early warning radar, Br.)
CHEL	Chain, Home, Extra Low (Early warning radar, Br.)
CHL	Chain, Home, Low (Early warning radar, Br.)
C.in C	Commander-in-Chief
CIU	Central Interpretation Unit, Medmenham (Br.)
CO	Chain, Overseas (Early warning radar, Br.)
COW	Coventry Ordnance Works (Br.)
CP/RA	Concrete Penetration/Rocket Assisted (Terrel bomb, Br.)
CRT	Cathode Ray Tube
CSBS	Course Setting Bomb Sight (Br.)
CVE	Escort Carrier Designation (US Navy)
CW	Chemical Warfare, Chemical Weapons
CWR	Charge-weight ratio (Bomb explosive content)
DA	*Dal'nyaya Aviatsiya* (Long Range Air Force, Sov.)
DAF	Desert Air Force (Br.)
DDT	DichloroDiphenylTrichloroethane (Insecticide)
D/F	Direction Finding
DFS	*Deutsche Forschungsinstitut für Segelflug* (Ger. Institute for Glider Research)
DLH	Deutsche Lufthansa (Ger. state airline)
DP/HE	Deep Penetration/High Explosive (British 'Wallis' bombs)
DT	*Dezimeter Telegraphie* (Decimetric Telegraphy, cover name for radar, Ger.)

DVL	*Deutsche Versuchsanstalt für Luftfahrt* (Ger. Aviation Experimental Establishment)
ECM	Electronic CounterMeasures
ELG	Emergency Landing Ground
ETA	Estimated Time of Arrival
ETO	European Theatre of Operations
EW	Electronic Warfare, Early Warning
FAC	Forward Air Controller
FCP	Forward Control Post
FFO	*Flugfunk Forschungsanstalt, Oberpfaffenhofen* (Electrical Research Institute for High Frequency, Ger.)
FIDO	Fog Investigation and Dispersal Operation (Br.)
FIU	Fighter Interception Unit, Ford (Br.)
FRAS	Fuel Research Aluminium Stearate (Gelled fuel, Br.)
FuG	*Funk Gerät* (Radio/radar equipment, Ger.)
FuMG	*Funk Mess Gerät* (Ground radar, Ger.)
GB	Glide-Bomb (US)
GCI	Ground Control of Interception
GE	General Electric Co. (US)
Gee	Radio navigational aid ('G' system, Br.)
Gee-H	Blind bombing aid (Combined 'G' and 'H' systems, Br.)
Ger.	German
GGS	Gyro Gun Sight
GL	Gun Laying (Radar for AA guns)
GLOMB	Glider-Bomb (US)
G/O	*General-Oberst* (Ger.)
GP	General Purpose (Bomb)
GPO	General Post Office (Br.)
H2S,H2X	Code names for ground-imaging radar (Br./US)
h/c	Hollow charge
HC	High Capacity (Bomb, Br.)
HE	High Explosive
HQ	Headquarters
HVAR	High Velocity Aircraft Rocket (US)
IFF	Identification Friend or Foe
IJA	Imperial Japanese Army
IJAAF	Imperial Japanese Army Air Force
IJN	Imperial Japanese Navy
IP	Initial Point (for bombing run)
IR	Infra Red

JATO	Jet Assisted Take-Off (US, rocket)
JG	*Jagdgeschwader* (Fighter wing, Ger.)
KB	*Konstruktorskoye Byuro* (Design Bureau, Sov.)
KC	*Kampstoff Cylindrisch* (Chemical cylinder, Ger. CW bomb)
KG	*Kampfgeschwader* (Bomber wing, Ger.)
KGr	*Kampfgruppe* (Bomber group, Ger.)
LC	Light Case (Bomb, Br.); *Leuchtcylindrische* (Parachute flare, Ger.)
LCHE	Light Case High Explosive (Bomb, US)
LEK	*Lehr und Erprobungskommando* (Instruction and Proving Detachment, Ger.)
LM	*Luftmine* (Air-dropped mine, Ger.)
LNB	*Legkii Nochnoi Bombardirovshchik* (Light night bomber, Sov.)
LNSF	Light Night Striking Force (Br.)
LOX	Liquid Oxygen
LP	Liquid Propellant (Rocket)
MAD	Magnetic Anomaly Detector
MAP	Ministry of Aircraft Production (Br.)
MC	Medium Capacity (Bomb)
Mc/s	Megacycles/second (Hz), radio frequency
MEW	Microwave Early Warning (Radar, US)
MF	Medium Frequency (Radio)
MG	*Maschinengewehr* (Machine gun, Ger.)
MIT	Massachusetts Institute of Technology (US)
MK	*Maschinenkanone* (Cannon, Ger.)
MPI	Mean Point of Impact
MTB	Motor Torpedo Boat
NACA	National Advisory Committee for Aeronautics (US)
NAF	Naval Aircraft Factory (US)
NDRC	National Defense Research Committee (US)
NITI	Nose instantaneous, tail instantaneous (Bomb fusing)
NJG	*Nachtjagdgeschwader* (Night fighter wing, Ger.)
NRC	National Research Council (Can.)
NRL	National Research Laboratory (US)
OSS	Office of Strategic Services (US)
OTU	Operational Training Unit (Br.)
PC	*Panzerbombe-Cylindrisch* (Armour-piercing bomb, Ger.)
PDE	Projectile Development Establishment, Westcott (Br.)

PFF	Pathfinder Force (Br.)
PI	Photo-Interpretation, Photo-Interpreter
POW	Prisoner of War
PPI	Plan Position Indicator (Scanning radar display screen)
PR	Photo-Reconnaissance
PTAB	*Protivotankovaya Aviatsionna Bomba* (Anti-tank bomb, Sov.)
PWD	Petroleum Warfare Dept. (Br.)
PZL	*Panstwowe Zaklady Lotnicze* (Aircraft manufacturer, Poland)
RA	*Regia Aeronautica* (Italian Air Force)
RAAF	Royal Australian Air Force
R&D	Research and Development
RAE	Royal Aircraft Establishment, Farnborough (Br.)
RAF	Royal Air Force (Br.)
RATOG	Rocket Assisted Take-Off Gear (Br.)
RCAF	Royal Canadian Air Force
RCM	Radio CounterMeasures
RDF	Radio Direction Finding (Cover name for radar, Br.)
RDX	Research Department Explosives (Br./Can.)
RLM	*Reichsluftfahrtministerium* (Ger. Air Ministry)
RN	Royal Navy (Br.)
RNZAF	Royal New Zealand Air Force
RP	Rocket Projectile
RR	Rolls Royce Co. (Br.)
RS	*Reactivnii Snaryad* (Jet missile; Sov. RP)
RSHA	*Reichssicherheitshauptamt* (Ger. Central Security Dept.)
R/T	Radio Telephony (Radio communication by voice)
RWR	Radar Warning Receiver
SAAF	South African Air Force
SABS	Stabilized Automatic Bomb Sight (Br.)
SAP	Semi-Armour Piercing (Shell, bomb)
SARAH	Search and Rescue and Homing (Emergency radio beacon, Br.)
SB	*Spreng Behalter* (Explosive container, Ger.); *Sprengbombe* (Parachute bomb, Ger.); *Skorostnoi Bombardirovshchik* (High speed bomber, Sov.)
SBA	Standard Beam Approach (Blind approach system, Br.)
SBC	Small Bomb Container (Br.)
SBX	Slow Burning Explosive

SC	*Sprengbombe Cylindrisch* (Explosive cylinder; Ger. GP HE bomb)
SCI	Smoke Curtain Installation (Br.)
SCR	Signals Corps Radio (US Army)
SD	*Sprengbombe Dickwandig* (Explosive, thick-walled; Ger. fragmentation bomb)
ShkAS	*Shpitalny Komaritsky Aviatsionny Skorostrelny* (Shpitalny rapid-fire aircraft gun, Sov.)
ShVAK	*Shpitalny Vladimirov Aviatsonnaya Krupno Kalibernaya* (Shpitalny Vladimirov large calibre aircraft gun, Sov.)
SLC	SearchLight Control (Radar, Br.)
SOE	Special Operations Executive (Br.)
Sov.	Soviet
SP	Solid Propellant (Rocket)
St.G	*Sturzkampfgeschwader* (Dive Bomber Group, Ger.)
SWF	Special Window Force (Br.)
SWOD	Special Weapon Ordnance Device (US guided weapon)
Tac/R	Tactical Reconnaissance (Br.)
TAF	Tactical Air Force
TB	*Tyazhyoly Bombardirovshchik* (Heavy bomber, Sov.)
TI	Target Indicator (Pyrotechnic marker bomb, Br.)
TNT	Trinitrotoluene
TRE	Telecommunications Research Establishment (Br.)
TV	Television
UBS	*Universalny Berezina Skorostrelny* (Beresin universal rapid-fire gun, Sov.)
u/c	Undercarriage (Landing gear)
UHF	Ultra High Frequency (Radio)
UP	Unrotated Projectile (Fin-stabilized RP, Br.)
USAAC	United States Army Air Corps
USAAF	United States Army Air Force
USMC	United States Marine Corps
USN	United States Navy
VB	Vertical Bomb (US)
VC	Victoria Cross (Medal, Br.)
VCP	Visual Control Post
VHF	Very High Frequency (Radio)
VIT	*Vozdushny Istrebitel' Tankov* (Anti-Tank Aircraft, Sov.)
VNOS	*Vozdushnovo Nablyudeniya Opoveshcheniya i Svyazi*

	(Air Observation, Alert and Communications; service, Sov.)
VVS	*Voyenno-Vozdushnyye Sily* (Air Forces, Sov.)
WAAF	Women's Auxiliary Air Force (Br.)
WDAF	Western Desert Air Force (Br.)
Wfr.Gr	*Werfer-granate* (Rocket mortar, Ger.)
WI	Wireless Investigation
WIDU	Wireless Intelligence Development Unit (Br.)
W/T	Wireless Telegraphy (Radio communication by Morse code)
ZG	*Zerstorergeschwader* (Long range fighter wing, Ger.)
ZOS	*Zemnogo Obespecheniya Samoletovozhdeniya* (Ground Assistance to Air Navigation, Sov.)

I   Pre-World War Two

Bombing Concepts and Techniques

Bombing: the New Factor
In the late 1930s, bombing, and particularly strategic bombing, was seen as the new and frightening factor in war. The bombing by Japan in China, by Italy in Abyssinia, and by the USSR, Italy, and especially Germany in Spain, filled the World with foreboding. Tactical bombing in support of ground troops was now joined by long-range bombing of towns as a weapon and a threat. A future war promised to be a people's war. Fleets of bombers could now rain explosive, incendiary and poison gas bombs down upon populations far from the front. The fear, combined with the rise of the totalitarian powers, brought variously new alliances, isolationism, pacifism, declarations of neutrality; and appeasement – the threat of Hitler's bombers brought him the coup at Munich. But the bombing which had taken place, largely by the totalitarian powers, had been either against ill-equipped adversaries or limited in scale. Some lessons drawn were not wholly valid, others not widely appreciated. In the main, whether against troops and tanks, or factories, towns and cities, bombing remained largely an untried quantity. Mostly its effectiveness was overestimated by the general public (fearing huge casualties), by governments (anticipating a severe decline in civilian morale) and by air forces (predicting air power to be the decisive element in future military action); but it was often underestimated by armies (tending to regard air power as peripheral).

Bombing Categories
Pre-war theories of air attacks against land targets envisaged three main categories, two tactical and one strategic:

(1) Close support to ground forces at the front line, attacking local concentrations of enemy troops and supplies, vehicles, strong points, etc., using mainly light bombers or purpose-built ground attack aircraft.

(2) Interdiction at longer range to isolate the enemy on the battlefield from reinforcement and supply, by attacking his airfields, storage dumps, convoys and communications (railways, bridges, road junctions) beyond the front line, using mainly medium bombers.

(3) Strategic, long-range heavy bombing of the enemy's heartland, against the main sources of his military power – factories, shipyards, steelworks, power stations, rail centres, docks, etc. – and his civilian population centres, to destroy morale (it was imagined) and hence the will to wage war.

Horizontal Bombing and Dive-bombing

For bombing at speed in horizontal flight, the bomb had to be released well short of the target, using appropriate bomb-sight settings for aircraft speed and altitude, the ballistic characteristics of the bomb, and local wind. Bombing from medium/high altitude to avoid AA fire, small targets were difficult to hit, a factor which made conventional bombing questionable for close support, while also favouring the 'area bombing' of towns as against 'precision bombing' of key strategic targets. But while the British briefly contemplated requiring crews to reduce speed over the target [Terraine, 1985:90], the problem was pushing the Germans towards dive-bombing as the alternative. Release of bombs during a very steep dive offered much greater accuracy, by removing the dependence on aircraft speed and altitude and the weight/ drag of the bomb. Tried in World War One, it had been adopted afterwards by the US Navy as the most promising way of hitting moving ships at sea. But the dive-bomber had acquired few air force advocates, mainly because the dive and braked pull-out robbed it of both speed and altitude, giving greater vulnerability to fighters, and to AA and barrage balloons if it dived low. But a US Navy public display of dive-bombing had greatly impressed Germany's Ernst Udet, who advocated its adoption for the new Luftwaffe. This led first to the Ju87 *Stuka* and then to larger, longer range dive-bombers.

Close Air Support

Ground attack in support of front line troops needed low-level bombing and strafing attacks against small targets. In the interwar period, light bombers had been used in 'air control' or 'air policing' operations against tribesmen equipped with small arms. But attacks against modern armoured ground forces were a tougher proposition. Although the time spent over enemy airspace was short, the bombers could be exposed to severe AA fire. But although 'attack' or 'assault' aircraft had appeared, in the late 1930s close support to ground troops often received little air force priority, indeed some air forces opposed it for political reasons – to distance themselves from possible subordination to army control. On the army side, even progressive tacticians, advocating highly mobile armoured warfare, saw little need for close air support. Thus Liddel Hart's writings made little mention of it; and de Gaulle saw air support only as a means of laying a smokescreen to cover troop/tank movements. [Messenger, 1976:90]

Effective close support required: firstly, an air force commitment to provide it; secondly, aircraft able to perform accurate attacks in an intense AA environment; and thirdly, the necessary liaison and communications between ground troops and the air units. But at the outbreak of the European War, only the Germans had all three; no other forces had the communications. The Italians and Japanese had only the commitment; the Soviets had the commitment and were developing a new aircraft; the RAF had an aircraft but not the commitment to use it; the USAAC had no recent aircraft, and a declining commitment.

Yet close ground attack had shown its value in Spain, first to the Italians and especially the Soviets, who used Ro37 and R–Z biplanes respectively. Then, despite official opposition [Murray, 1985:37], Lt.-Col. W. von Richthofen, using He51s as fighter-bombers then Hs123 and Ju87 dive-bombers, began developing the revolutionary close-support system that would be used with devastating effect in the German blitzkrieg offensives early in the Second World War. Other nations took little interest in these developments.

The German, Soviet and British Positions on Close Air Support

By 1939, the Germans had adopted close air support to aid the Army in its Blitzkrieg offensives, via pinpoint attacks on the enemy positions by Ju87 *Stuka* dive-bombers. To ensure rapid response, liaison and communications were established between the Army units in the field and the Luftwaffe's Ju87 units. To minimize the risk from fighters and AA, the intended use would be in surprise strikes with heavy fighter cover, releasing the bombs from higher altitude if the AA was severe. Just as the Germans were the best equipped for close support, so they were the best equipped to oppose its use by the enemy, the Army having a formidable light AA capability.

The Soviets, soon to be at war with Finland, were also committed to close air support although the aircraft, techniques and tactics were still experimental, and effective communications had not been devised. The *Shturmovik* heavily armoured ground attack aircraft was under development for low-level and shallow-dive attacks. The armour would make the *Shturmovik* less vulnerable to fighters or flak, and it was to prove a valuable tool against German forces who were well equipped with both.

In Britain, there was RAF/Air Ministry opposition to providing close air support to the Army, which continued well into the war. There was no real framework of Army/RAF communications, and no system for directing fighters in an air cover role. No thought had been given to providing an armoured ground attack aircraft, and although the Henley dive-bomber was available, it had been diverted to target towing. The types which would be used over the battlefield were the Battle and Blenheim tactical light bombers, which were to prove highly vulnerable to both AA and fighters.

In 1939, the US and Japan still had some time to review their positions. For the present, although its Air Corps was formally part of the Army, the US was not well placed for effective close support. The Japanese Army, however, was already at war in China, and had adopted close support using strafing and shallow dive-bombing by light bombers, albeit against the poorly-equipped Chinese forces.

Interdiction

The intermediate bombing category was also the least controversial, although, again, the degree of air force integration with army direction varied markedly, from close co-operation (USSR, Germany) to determined independence (RAF). Interdiction involved tactical strikes against targets beyond the front line, mostly using twin-engined medium bombers. The French and Soviets planned attacks close to the front, the Germans, British and Japanese expected to use wider ranging attacks.

The RAF, at least, had made limited exercises with night bombing at relatively low level. But it was generally assumed that attacks would be made by small groups of bombers, in daylight, using horizontal bombing from low/medium altitude, i.e. high enough to be above any light flak. The risk from fighters was not thought to be great because, compared with strategic bombing, the bombers themselves were mostly smaller and faster, the time spent in enemy airspace was less, and the range was more likely to be within the capacity of single-engine fighters to provide escort. But overall, there was a tendency to overestimate the ability to achieve decisive, accurate bombing of what were mainly relatively small targets.

Strategic Bombing

Long-range strategic bombing had appeared in World War One with raids on Britain by German Zeppelins and Gotha bombers. In the 1920s, preparation for strategic bombing had been strongly advocated by Maj. W. Mitchell in the USA, by Maj. Gen. Sir Hugh (later Lord) Trenchard in Britain, and to the exclusion of all else, by Gen. G. Douhet in Italy [Murray, 1985:9]. It was argued that strategic air power could by itself win a war, that there was no adequate defence against bombing, and hence that the best form of defence was the threat of retaliation in kind. In the 1930s only the USSR maintained a large fleet of four-engined bombers. But most of the other major powers gave emphasis to bombers rather than fighters; and most made moves towards a strategic bombing capability, with the development of new large four-engined bombers in the USA, Britain, France, Germany, Italy, and the USSR. But some rethinking then followed, not least because heavy bombers were so expensive to build and to operate.

In the Spanish Civil War, both the Germans and the Soviets had engaged in limited bombing operations with a strategic element, including attacks on civilian populations, using medium bombers. But both were land powers, aware that diversion of huge resources for a strategic bombing force would leave the Army weakened, and that an early Army defeat could lose them a war before a strategic bombing campaign could become decisive. [Murray, 1985:15] Nations with sea protection (Japan, Britain, USA) had more freedom to emphasize strategic bombing. But the experience in Spain led the Germans and the Soviets to conclude that for them, tactical support to the Army should come first. Medium bombers could be built in larger numbers, were more versatile, and could be used for strategic bombing if required. In Japan, the Navy rather than the AAF advocated strategic bombing, and on 14 August 1937, it carried out the World's first transoceanic bombing raid, Mitsubishi G3M2 twin-engined bombers from Taipei flying 1,250 miles overwater to strike targets near Hangchow and Kwangteh.

The RAF and USAAC remained the principal advocates of strategic bombing. But whereas the RAF was building largely for area bombing as a deterrent, the USAAC saw precision bombing of oil and power plants, etc. as an economical approach to war; a relatively small force could quickly disrupt the enemy's war capacity. But generally in 1939, the strategic bombing capability that had been achieved was less than it appeared, and most of it resided with the Germans. Moreover, there was little unanimity with regard to the question of daylight versus night bombing.

Daylight Strategic Bombing

Despite opinions that 'the bomber will always get through' (British Prime Minister Stanley Baldwin's phrase, in 1932), there were indications that in daylight the bomber was becoming increasingly vulnerable, particularly to fighters. 'Getting through' might only be achieved with a loss rate which could not be sustained. This had been true even in the First World War, when the Germans had changed to night bombing against Britain in order to conserve aircraft and crews. Now, the vulnerability of even modern bombers in unescorted daylight raids was shown in August 1937 when in three raids over China, the Japanese lost 54 of their newest Navy bomber, the Mitsubishi G3M. Meanwhile, in Europe and the USA especially, new radiolocation devices were being developed which would enable detection of bombers 70 or more miles away, giving ample time for fighters to be scrambled to climb to meet them. Also it was evident that the new monoplane fighters were well armed and outperforming even the very latest bombers.

Under these circumstances, there were three main approaches to achieving deep penetration in daylight. Some authorities, notably in the USA with the B-17, advocated heavily armed and armoured high-flying bombers in self-defending formations. Others, e.g. in Germany and France, expected to provide bomber defence via long-range heavy escort fighters if necessary. Finally, there were a very few advocates for high speed bombers in which everything, including armament and armour, was sacrificed to give the bomber the performance needed to evade and outstrip enemy fighters. None of these approaches held universal favour in 1939. To most perhaps, the escort fighter looked the most promising, even though there was scepticism that typical heavy twin-engined long-range fighters would be able to counter the small and manoeuvrable interceptors sent aloft by the defence; only in Japan, with the A6M *Zero-sen*, was a long-range single-engine fighter considered a serious possibility.

Night Strategic Bombing

Deep penetration raids made under the cloak of darkness were likely to be much safer than by daylight, and the bombers could fly both at lower altitude and with less defensive armament, and hence with a greater bomb load. But accurate navigation, and especially finding a specific target at night was much more difficult. Visual night navigation over areas in wartime 'blackout' conditions needed a clear moonlit night, and an absence of searchlight dazzle, although flak and searchlight concentrations could themselves indicate the location of towns. Conventional night navigation was by radio DF (direction finding) from available beacons, and 'dead reckoning' updated by astronavigation using a bubble sextant sighted on the stars. But the absence of blackout conditions made realistic wartime night navigation difficult to practise in peacetime, and limited studies on the likely accuracy achievable at night by these methods gave little cause for optimism. The advantage of moonlight in enabling landmarks to be identified led to interest in the dropping of flares as an alternative means of obtaining a visual fix. In Britain this interest increased after a report that the Germans were using flares in Spain; limited tests with towed and parachute-dropped flares were made but no operational technique was established. Also in Britain, in 1937 the then Grp Capt.A.T.Harris advocated development of a 'long-burning incendiary' which could be dropped by lead aircraft onto a target after they had found it, to mark it for succeeding aircraft. But no such development was undertaken. Only in Germany was any serious work done on aids to achieve accurate night navigation by bombers, with the development of blind bombing radio systems.

German Strategic Dive-bombing

Late pre-war, the German Air Staff saw precision dive-bombing as a means of striking against rear and strategic targets, as well as for close support. [Smith, 1981:16] Dive-bombing was a force multiplier: more accurate bombing required fewer bombs, allowing mostly medium rather than heavy bombers, and these could be built in far greater numbers. So, whereas it was largely ignored by other land-based air forces, dive-bombing became a requirement in German bomber specifications, e.g. for the Dornier Do217 and Junkers Ju88 medium bombers and – extraordinarily – for the Heinkel He177 four-engined heavy bomber. Critics would argue later that the policy was unrealistic. Use of small dive-bombers in front-line operations was one thing; sending larger ones deep into well-defended air space was quite another. A diving attack would take the bomber away from both the mutual defence of the formation, and the protection of the accompanying escort fighters. Dive-bombing at night could remove that vulnerability, but introduced new risks as well as the usual difficulties in locating the target in darkness.

The US, German and British Positions on Strategic Bombing

Three air forces were to engage in strategic bombing on any scale during the War, those of Germany, Britain and the USA, but their positions at the start of the war were very different.

The USAAC was committed to precision daylight bombing of key targets, using high-flying heavily armed and armoured B-17 bombers, although as yet it had very few of them and they did not yet have powered gun turrets. Turbosupercharged engines would achieve the high altitudes to place the bombers above the flak, and make them difficult for fighters to reach. To counter fighters that did manage to reach them, the bombers would fly in precise, tight groups, enabling their combined fire power to provide mutual defence. In addition, the US was developing a long-range fighter, the Lockheed P-38. High altitude flight, plus the weight of armour, armament and gunners, implied a small bomb load as well as greater difficulty in hitting the target because of the height. But to offset this, US bombers would have the most advanced bomb-sight in the World, the Norden sight.

In Germany, although Göring retained an inactive plan for a force of 2,000 heavy bombers by 1944 [Overy, 1981:85], following the death of Gen. W. Wever in 1936 the Luftwaffe had lessened its emphasis on strategic bombing. Future prospects were also being compromised by pursuing dive-bombing as the preferred mode of attack. Nevertheless, the Luftwaffe's large force of twin-engined medium bombers, usable for tactical support to the Army, also had a significant strategic bombing capability. The bombers had inadequate armament but were relatively fast, and for long-range daylight operations the Bf110 heavy fighter was already available and was expected to be adequate for escort duty if needed. For night operations, three secret blind bombing radio aids were well advanced.

In Britain, although the RAF had definite aims towards strategic bombing, especially heavy attacks to undermine the enemy's morale, the necessary plans had not been thought through. It was hoped to use daylight bombing; but the twin-engined bombers in service and the heavy bombers under development had unsupercharged engines, rifle-calibre guns (albeit with powered turrets) and no armour. Even so, escort fighters were thought unnecessary, and the two apparently likeliest long-range ones – the Whirlwind and Beaufighter – were not really recognized as such, and were not yet available. Further, if daylight bombing were to prove to give unacceptable losses, Britain was making no effort to develop blind bombing aids to facilitate night operations as the alternative.

Airfields and Catapults

One problem with strategic bombing for the British with their inclement weather was that large bombers needed hard runways for all-weather operation. As elsewhere, British airfields of the 1930s were grass fields without runways. Night operations were carried out with improvised flare paths marked out by manually-positioned and -lit gooseneck paraffin flares. The Air Ministry believed hard runways to be vulnerable to enemy air attack, while a pair of catapults per aerodrome was thought to be cheaper than a concrete or tarmac runway. In 1936, development work was authorized at RAE on a hydro-pneumatic 'Frictionless Take-off' catapult for getting heavily laden bombers airborne. The Avro Manchester bomber was stressed for catapult take-off, and projected versions of the Stirling and Halifax were considered for catapult use. [Lewis, 1980:292] Work on the catapult continued into the war but the Air Ministry had by then sanctioned hard runways.

The German Luftwaffe had far more airfields than the RAF, and paved runway construction was begun in 1939 at some of the main ones.

Bomber Types

The Anatomy of the Bomber

The conventional bomber had been evolving rapidly during the 1930s. By the outbreak of war, although there were many of obsolete design in service, most front-line bombers were now of cantilever monoplane configuration, with all-metal stressed skin construction (apart from fabric-covered control surfaces), electrical and hydraulic power systems, enclosed cockpit, fuselage internal bomb bay, high-lift wing flaps for take-off and landing, and defensive gun positions protected from windblast; some powered gun turrets were in service. Undercarriages were now retractable, mostly tailwheel type but with the nosewheel type coming into favour in the USA. Flying controls were still manually operated. The wing flaps varied from none at all (Whitley) to plain (most), split (B-17) and more advanced area-increasing Fowler (Hudson) and slotted flaps (Ju88). The engines were almost all four-stroke spark ignition type, in liquid (glycol)-cooled inline and air-cooled radial form. Fuel was mostly carried in internal wing tanks, which helped minimize structure weight.

The newer bombers were receiving: variable pitch propellers to improve take-off and climb; a crew oxygen system for flight at altitude; a three-axis automatic pilot (like the RAF's 'George') to relieve workload; and radio for W/T (Morse) communications, using a long trailing aerial wound out then in again during flight. Few bombers had much de-icing; only the Soviet SB-2 (a single plate behind the pilot) had any armour plate protection, although it was also in train for the B-17; and only German bombers had the vitally important self-sealing fuel tanks, having a layer of unvulcanized rubber to swell up and seal bullet holes. Few bombers had much specialization for either day or night operations, although for night bombing the changes required were largely limited to a dark paint scheme, blackout curtains for the navigator's compartment, subdued cockpit/instrument lighting, flash eliminators on the guns, and flame dampers on the engine exhausts to make them less visible both to enemy night fighters and to the crew who were trying to see the ground to navigate. Survival on overwater missions had been little thought of; the war was to force much more attention to ditching behaviour and the provision of sea survival equipment. But Italian and British bombers were operating in the desert, and 'tropicalization' measures (desert camouflage, engine sand filters, cockpit sunblinds, water containers and survival kits) were in use.

Many new types of bomber were to be designed and flown during the war, but few of these were put into production and fewer saw service in substantial numbers. The cost and delays in re-tooling and in pre-operational training were such that once an initial requirement was satisfied the emphasis was usually one of improving existing designs instead of introducing new ones.

Light Single-engined Bombers

Despite their limited potential compared with larger and faster twin-engined machines, in 1939 there were a number of single engine monoplane light bombers in service. Typically they featured a crew of two or three in tandem, a small internal bombload, minimal defensive armament (one or two light machine guns), and no armour even though some were expected to be used for ground attack. Examples include: the PZL P-23 *Karas* (Poland, 1934); Vickers Wellesley and Fairey Battle (Britain, 1935 and 1936, respectively); and the Mitsubishi Ki-30 and Kawasaki Ki-32 (Japan, 1937). The Fairey Battle, of which the RAF had over 1,000 on strength at the start of the war, epitomized the inadequacy of these aircraft. Although of clean design and with the same engine as the Hurricane fighter, it had a crew of three and was much bigger, heavier and less manoeuvrable than a Hurricane. It was vulnerable to light AA, while the 0.303-inch gun on a flexible mount in the rear cockpit offered little defence against a modern fighter.

Ground-attack Aircraft

Low-level attacks against troops, tanks, etc. by bombing and strafing were the province of the 'Attack' or 'Assault' aircraft, but there was little agreement on the need for such aircraft, or their size and configuration, or the importance of speed of attack versus manoeuvrability and precision. Interest in purpose-built aircraft in the USA (Curtiss A-12 Shrike, Northrop A-17) and Italy (Breda 65) had declined in favour of more conventional bombers. Mostly the role was now expected to fall to light bombers having little forward-firing armament (one token machine gun on the Battle) or to better-armed heavy fighters (eight machine guns or four 20mm cannon on the Fokker G.I) but still with little or no tank's armour. Fitting bomb-racks to single-engine fighters had been tried, including in Spain, but not adopted; and the term 'fighter-bomber' tended to be applied to heavy fighters having a bomb bay rather than to a ground-attack aircraft as such.

Probably the Soviets had devoted the most effort to ground-attack aircraft and techniques, although they had little to show for it in 1939. Their developments had included: the 8-gun Polikarpov R-2 armoured biplane; large-calibre recoilless cannon, (76mm DRP-76, and 102mm APK-100); the Archangelskii/TsAGI ANT-29 ground-attack aircraft of 1935 with two APK-100s; the Polikarpov TsKB-48/VIT-2 anti-tank aircraft of 1938, with four 37mm cannon; and several experimental *Shturmovik* ground-attack aircraft with armour-plate protection for crew, engines and fuel. The BSh-1 1937 armoured version of the US Vultee V-11GB light bomber reached limited service, but by 1939 development was well advanced on what would become one of the most successful ground-attack aircraft of the war, the Ilyushin Il-2 *Shturmovik*. The Soviets had also introduced the RS-82 rocket projectile, primarily as an air-to-air weapon but it had potential for ground attack.

From 1936 onwards the Germans had been developing large-calibre recoilless aircraft weapons, usable against ground targets. This Rheinmettal Borsig work on the Düsen *Kanone* guns of 37, 75, and finally 88mm calibre, was cancelled in September 1939 due to other priorities. Meanwhile, a 1937 requirement for a small, heavily armoured twin-engined *Schlachtflugzeug* ground-attack aircraft resulted in the Hs129 which flew in the Spring of

1939, and the Fw189C variant. But the Germans also had the Ju87 *Stuka* dive-bomber. Elsewhere, the Japanese Mitsubishi Ki-51 attack aircraft flew in 1939. The British had paid little attention to ground-attack developments, reflecting the Air Staff's view that close support represented 'a gross misuse of air forces' [Terraine, 1985:64].

Dive-bombers

While many bombers could release bombs in a shallow dive, a true dive-bomber was a specialized aircraft, with: dive brakes or even reversible-pitch propellers to reduce speed build-up; a dive-bombing sight for accurate bomb release at angles less than vertical; an extra-strong airframe to withstand the pull-out; and on single-engine aircraft, a bomb crutch which swung downwards and forwards so that a fuselage-mounted bomb cleared the propeller. Most dive-bombers were manually controlled; but the Germans had devised an automatic bomb release and pull-out system, with the BZA-1 dive-bombing sight integrated with the aircraft flight controls. At the required point in the dive, the system operated elevator tabs to effect pull-out, releasing the bombs a little way into the pull-out.

The first dedicated land-based dive-bomber, the German two-seat single-engined Junkers Ju87 *Sturzkampfflugzeug* or *Stuka* was in service in numbers. Tried out in Spain, including against ships and dock installations, the Ju87 with its fixed spatted u/c was already obsolescent, but able to perform impressively under an air umbrella. The larger, twin-engined Ju88 was just entering service. Outside Germany, there was limited interest in land-based dive-bombers. Those in production – not all of them able to dive vertically – included the Loire-Nieuport LN-411 (France, 1938), the Savoia SM85 and 86 (Italy, 1938 and 1939 respectively), the multi-role Fokker G.I (Netherlands, 1937), and the Archangelskii SB-RK (later Ar-2) version of the SB-2 bomber (USSR, 1939). In Sweden, the *Flygvapnet* used the Hawker Hart as a dive-bomber, and was developing the SAAB 17 dive-bomber. In Britain, the Hawker Henley dive-bomber of 1937 had been relegated to target towing. The USAAC would be able to adapt Navy dive-bombers.

Twin-engined Bombers
The twin-engined light/medium bomber was one of the major military aircraft categories of the period, but types varied considerably in size, crew, load, performance and armament.

The German Luftwaffe's medium bombers included the diesel-powered Junkers Ju86 of 1934, which had not performed well in Spain; and a fleet of more advanced bombers that would play major rôles in the coming war. Of these, the robust dual-role Heinkel He111 of 1935 had appeared first as a ten-passenger transport for DLH, with separate cabins fore and aft of the wings, and the bomb-bay serving as a four-passenger 'smoking compartment'. The slim Dornier Do17 of 1934 had been designed originally as a high-speed light transport, again with two tiny cabins. The Do217 of 1938 was a scaled-up Do17. The Junkers Ju88 of 1936 was still having development problems, but was to become one of the most formidable and versatile aircraft of the War. More than anywhere else, design emphasis on the German bombers was on suitability for mass production and adaptability to different rôles, and different engines and armaments. A particular feature was the close grouping of crew members for mutual assistance and morale.

Aside from the Blenheim light bomber of 1936, Britain's major twin-engined bombers in service were: the utilitarian Armstrong Whitworth Whitley of 1936, the RAF's first bomber with a retractable u/c and turret armament (in 1937); the faster Handley Page Hampden of 1936, with its slim fuselage, tail boom and slotted wings and flaps; and the portly Vickers Armstrong's Wellington of 1937, which featured Barnes Wallis's geodetic construction, employing a fabric covering over a convex latticework of diagonal light alloy stringers. Entering service in 1939, the relatively large Wellington (regarded, in fact, as a heavy bomber) was the RAF's most important bomber at the start of the war, with six squadrons in service.

The principal Soviet VVS medium bombers in 1939 were: the Tupolev SB-2 of 1934, which had been used in Spain, and which the Japanese had found difficult to intercept over China in 1937; and the Ilyushin DB-3 of 1936 (later Il-4), which had made several record-breaking long distance flights, and was the only Soviet medium bomber with the range for much strategic bombing. The most important Soviet bomber of the war, the Petlyakov Pe-2 had just flown as the VI-100 (May 1939).

In Italy, twin-engined bombers in service with the *Regia Aeronautica* included the Caproni Ca309 and variants, mostly already relegated to transport duties; and the Fiat BR20 *Cicogna* of 1936, used in Ethiopia and Spain, and by the Japanese in China. The French *Armée de l'Air* had a variety of twin-engined bombers, mostly in small numbers: the obsolescent Amiot 143 and Bloch 210, the Breguet 693 and Potez 63 light bombers; the fast Bloch 174 light bomber of 1938, and the fast but still troubled SNCASE Lioré et Olivier 451 of 1937, were both about to enter service. The Polish Air Force (*Polskie Lotnictwo Wojskowe*) had a number of ungainly and unsuccessful LWS6ZUBR bombers, plus around 40 of the PZL P-37 *Los* of 1936, one of the more impressive bombers of the day. The Netherlands *Luchtvaartafdeling* had a few Fokker Type T.V and twin-boom Type G.IA twin-engined bombers. The Czech Army Air Force had some Aero A304 light bombers.

The principal USAAC medium bombers in 1939 were the Martin B-10 of 1934; and the Douglas B-18 Bolo of 1935, derived from the DC-3 airliner. Newer aircraft available included: the Douglas A-20, flown as the Model 7B in 1938; the Martin 167 Maryland (March 1939), in production for France; the 1938 Lockheed Hudson derivative of the Model 14 airliner, in production for Britain; the North American NA-40 forerunner of the B-25 (January 1939); and the Douglas B-23 Dragon derivative of the B-18 (July 1939).

The main Japanese Army and land-based Navy medium bombers in 1939 were the Mitsubishi G3M of 1935 and Ki-21 of 1936. Both were in use in the war against China. Newer bombers included the Kawasaki Ki-48 (July 1939), inspired by the Soviet SB-2; and the Nakajima Ki-49 (August 1939). The Mitsubishi G4M was under development. Japanese bomber design emphasized lightness for long range, and the vulnerability of the bombers was to become a major problem.

Tri-motor Bombers
In Italy especially, a lack of high-powered aero-engines led designers to adopt a nose-mounted third engine for

increased installed power without an increase in frontal area. For a bomber, the penalty paid was the loss of a nose gun and/or bomb-aiming position. Italy's tri-motor bombers and bomber-transports included the Caproni Ca133 and Savoia-Marchetti SM81 *Pipistrella* of 1935, the reliable and successful Savoia-Marchetti SM79 *Sparviero* of 1936, and the Cant Z.1007 *Alcione* of 1937. Elsewhere, the German tri-motor Junkers Ju52/3m bomber-transport was already obsolete as a bomber.

The High-speed Unarmed Bomber

Conventional thinking in the 1930s was that a bomber fast enough to need little or no defensive armament would have to be very small, with short range and a tiny bomb load. But a few designers disagreed. In Germany, the Heinkel He119 of 1937 twin-engined unarmed light bomber achieved very high performance with coupled engines driving a single large nose propeller, and wing surface steam/evaporation cooling. But the RLM insisted on the introduction of dorsal and ventral gun positions which degraded its performance, and it was not adopted. In the USSR, the twin-engined Yakovlev Ya-22 flew in 1939 as an unarmed high-speed bomber, but eventually entered service as the Yak-2 and -4, with armament and degraded performance. In Britain in 1938, a De Havilland proposal to adapt the DH91 Albatross airliner as a bomber gave way to a projected small but powerful high-speed unarmed bomber. The resulting twin-engined DH98 Mosquito was conventional if exceptionally clean, and acceptability was enhanced by the use of non-strategic materials for its construction. However, few people foresaw the success the Mosquito would have.

High-altitude Bombers

A stratospheric bomber offered reduced vulnerability to flak and fighters. But it needed major developments in superchargers, pressurization systems, lubrication and de-icing. In Germany, the experimental twin-engined Junkers EF61 of 1936, the first bomber with a pressure cabin, was abandoned after both prototypes crashed. In the USA where turbosupercharger development was most advanced, one twin-engined high-altitude bomber (Martin XB-27) was cancelled in 1939, another (Martin XB-33) was to be cancelled in 1940. In the USSR, an experimental pressure cabin was incorporated into an ANT-25 airframe, *c*.1937. Also in 1937 the Tupolev/Petlyakov ANT-42 (TB-7) bomber was fitted with a fifth engine, mounted in the fuselage to supply compressed air to the four main engines, but this concept was not pursued. The VI-100 experimental high-altitude bomber appeared in 1939, but it gave many technical problems and was stripped of its turbochargers and pressurization to become the conventional but successful Petlyakov Pe-2.

Heavy Bombers

During the 1930s there was some work on very large intercontinental strategic bombers. In the USA, a BLR (Bomber, Long Range) requirement led to prototypes of the Boeing XBLR-1 and Douglas XBLR-2, flying as the XB-15 and XB-19 respectively in 1937 and 1941, but neither was adopted. In the USSR, the 1930s saw several projects for very large bombers. The last was the 70-ton, 12-engined Tupolev ANT-26, cancelled under a 1936 decision to discontinue all work on superheavy aircraft.

Most interest in strategic bombers concentrated on four-engined types of more modest dimensions. In Germany, the *Langstrecken-Grossbomber* or 'Ural bomber' four-engined Dornier Do19 and Junkers Ju89, were cancelled in 1937; Germany's aim was the rapid expansion of the Luftwaffe, with medium/dive-bombers which were quicker and cheaper to build. Elsewhere, heavy bomber programmes continued, but with no great urgency. At the start of the war in Europe, only the USSR, France and the USA had any four-engined heavy bombers in service. The Soviets had built over 800 Tupolev TB-3s, but with open cockpit, fixed u/c and low speed, they were now obsolete and being relegated to a transport rôle. The French had a few of the Farman 222 series bombers of 1935, with engines paired in push-pull strut-mounted nacelles. Only the US had modern all-metal heavy bombers, with just 23 early model Boeing B-17 Fortresses of 1935. But prototypes of other modern four-engined bombers were already flying, notably the ANT-42 (TB-7) of 1936 which would become the Petlyakov Pe-8 (USSR), and the Short Stirling (Britain) and

Piaggio P.108 (Italy), both of 1939. The Avro Manchester (Britain) of 1939 with its Rolls Royce Vulture coupled engines could also be regarded as four-engined. In addition, other heavy bombers were under development, including the Handley Page Halifax (Britain), the CAO 700 (France), the Heinkel He177 (Germany), the Consolidated B-24 (USA), and the Nakajima G5N-1 (Japan). So, although the way it would be used was not well established, the four-engined heavy bomber was already a reality.

The Boeing B-17 was the first heavy bomber to be evolved for a specialist day bomber rôle, and was to become the war's archetypal day bomber, with its turbo-supercharged engines and progressively increasing armour plate protection and defensive fire power. The Short Stirling was the RAF's first monoplane four-engined bomber, with large-chord Gouge flaps for take-off and landing, but with cruise speed and altitude performance compromised by short span wings to fit hangar dimensions.

Escort Fighters and Bomber-support Aircraft
At various times in the 1930s, approaches envisaged for countering defence interceptors for bomber formations on deep penetration daylight raids included the use of other aircraft in support:

The 'battlecruiser': considered by the British as a large, heavily armed aircraft (Vickers Type 163 four-engined bomber with three 37mm COW guns) flying ahead of the bombers to clear the airspace of fighters; it was rejected as unrealistic – the fighters would go around it.

The 'destroyer' or 'strategic fighter': e.g. the German *Kampfzerstörer* or Soviet *Krejser* (cruiser); a heavy twin-engined multi-seat and multi-rôle fighter, often with a bomb bay and defensive as well as fixed guns; to be sent in waves ahead of the bombers to fight a path through; various types were in service, notably the Messerschmitt Bf110, but not proven in this role or as an escort.

The single-seat, single-engine escort fighter: scarcely thought credible in 1939 because of the long range required; but the key to long range, the jettisonable auxiliary fuel tank had been suggested in the US in 1929, and had received some development in the USSR, Germany and Japan; the

Mitsubishi A6M *Zero-sen* already offered long range even on internal fuel.

The single-seat twin-engine escort fighter: half way to a 'destroyer', such a fighter offered longer range but less manoeuvrability than a 'single'; examples included the radical Lockheed P-38 Lightning, the first fighter to use exhaust turbosuperchargers for high performance at altitude; and, potentially, the four-cannon Westland Whirlwind.

The parasite fighter: almost uniquely, the Soviets had been experimenting with having a TB-3 bomber carry two or more small fighters which could be released in flight to provide protection to the bomber formation when necessary; this *Zveno* programme, under V.S. Vakhmistrov, was still under way, but a projected purpose-built parasite aircraft combination had already been cancelled.

The 'wing-tip convoy escort': newly advocated in Japan with a version of the Mitsubishi G4M twin-engine medium bomber; a heavily armed and armoured escort aircraft which, instead of breaking off to dog-fight with attackers, would maintain formation and use its flexibly-mounted guns to shoot down the attackers.

Bomber Armament

Defensive Guns; Gun Positions

Although a few light and medium bombers carried a fixed, forward-firing gun (e.g. LeO 451, Battle), bomber armament was mostly defensive. It ranged from fixed rearward and/or downward pointing installations (e.g. Bloch 174) to light, hand-operated machine guns on flexible mounts through to heavier or multiple guns in powered turrets. Rifle calibre guns were common, if barely adequate despite a high rate of fire. Examples included: the 0.303in Browning (USA, adopted as standard by the British); 7.5mm MAC 1934 (France); 7.62mm ShKAS (USSR); 7.7mm Breda-SAFAT (Italy); 7.7mm KM Wz.37 (Poland);

7.7mm Type 89 (Japan); and 7.92mm MG15 (Germany). Some air forces were introducing heavier calibre machine guns offering greater bullet energy and range, e.g. the 12.7mm BS (USSR) and 12.7mm Breda-SAFAT (Italy), while the USAAC had standardized on the Browning 0.5in gun. More lethal still because of their explosive shells, cannon were larger and less easy to mount flexibly on a bomber than, say, fixed on a fighter. Nevertheless, a few bombers carried them, e.g. the Mitsubishi G3M2 Model 22 (one 20mm Type 99) and the LeO 451 (one 20mm Hispano-Suiza 404).

Gun locations on bombers varied, with nose, mid-upper, tail and ventral positions common. Tail guns were important, and were most practical on larger bombers, although as yet the B-17 did not have them. While ventral positions were also difficult, many medium and heavy bomber designs included one, some (e.g. Whitley and LeO 451) being retractable. But the Wellington had only nose and tail turrets, the ventral guns having been replaced by beam guns. The Stirling introduced the RAF's standard heavy bomber armament of eight Browning 0.303in guns (two each in nose and dorsal turrets, and four in a tail turret); the lack of a ventral gun position was to cost Bomber Command crews dearly. The Soviet TB-7/Pe-8 was unusual in having manual gun positions in the rear of each inboard engine nacelle, reached by crawling through the wing structure. But it was never possible to provide a single bomber with as great a fire power in every direction as a fighter could have in just one direction; hence the argument for a tight group of bombers providing mutual protection.

Gun Turrets

In the 1930s, some bombers having open positions with manually handled guns were still in service. But increasing flight speeds made it more necessary to protect the gunner from windblast, and to help overcome the strong and turbulent air loads on the protruding guns. By the mid-1930s most new bombers had enclosed gun positions (albeit with gun/viewing apertures) but retained manual gun handling. The mid-upper gun on the CANT Z.1007bis was given an aerodynamic balance, an opposed aluminium tube geared to the gun and elevated with it to counter the air load on the gun itself. The dorsal turret on the Mitsubishi Ki-21 had manual rotation by the gunner, via bicycle pedals and a chain drive. Meanwhile the development of powered turrets was being pursued. In Britain, the Boulton Paul Overstrand nose turret had introduced (compressed air) power drive for azimuth only. In Germany, the DL131 turret for the Dornier Do217 introduced (electric) power drive for coarse positioning in elevation as well as azimuth. By the outbreak of war, fully powered turrets with electric, hydraulic or electro-hydraulic drives included examples from SAMM in France, Frazer Nash and Boulton Paul in Britain, and Bendix and Sperry in the USA. Most replaced hand-changed magazines with belt-fed ammunition, and they incorporated cam-operated cut-outs to suppress firing when the guns' line of fire traversed some part of the aircraft itself. The least favoured turrets were retractable ventral 'dustbins', since these gave high drag in use, just when the bomber needed its maximum performance to escape. But despite the widespread development on power turrets, in September 1939 Britain was the only country with its front line aircraft equipped with them, notably the Whitley and Wellington (nose and tail) and Blenheim (mid-upper); all used a fighter-type reflector gunsight for aiming. The French had power turrets on the LeO451 and Farman 223. Elsewhere, even in the USA for the B-17, reliance was still mainly on hand-swivelled guns with ring and bead sights.

Remotely-operated Gun Barbettes

Some designers were already looking further ahead. The powered, manned gun turret was bulky and heavy, and compromised the bomber's weight distribution and aerodynamics. The alternative was to have powered but unmanned gun barbettes, sighted and operated remotely from some central crew position(s). Such a system would be complex, but the individual barbettes would be much smaller and lighter than turrets. They could be sited with greater freedom, and on smaller aircraft, and they would remove gunners from the gun noise, vibration, muzzleflash and air blast exposure of the typical turret. The first such barbettes were under development: in Germany, by Dipl. Ing. W.

Blume of Arado, with Rheinmettal Borsig; in Italy, for the outboard engine nacelles of the new Piaggio P.108 four-engined bomber; and in the USSR, for use from the pressure cabin of the BOK-7 high-altitude reconnaissance aircraft.

Balloon Cable Cutters

To counter the defensive barrage balloon hazard for low flying bombers, by 1938 an explosive cable cutter for aircraft had been developed in Britain by the Martin Baker Co., and tested at Farnborough by deliberately flying aircraft into balloon cables. In use, the cable cutter was mounted outboard on the (reinforced) wing leading edge. If the wing struck a balloon cable, the cable would slide outwards along the leading edge to the cutter's anvil, triggering a cartridge-fired chisel to sever the cable. The cutters were being fitted to RAF bombers before the war started; during the war, 250,000 sets were to be made. By 1941, the Germans were fitting similar *Kuto-Nase* cutters to their bombers.

Bomb Equipment and Bombsights

Bomb Mounting, Bomb Bays; Clusters

Bombs were normally mounted to a bomb rack or carrier having a longitudinal beam with fore and aft pairs of bomb steadies, and one or two shackles or claw slip releases engaging lugs on the bomb case. Some larger bombs were held via fore and aft slings each with a release. A bomb distributor could offer a choice of single, grouped or sequenced 'stick' bombing, the sequence minimizing c.g. shift. To minimize drag, bombs were preferably carried internally, fuselage bomb bays being the norm, located to straddle the aircraft c.g. Bomb-bay doors were hand cranked or powered, sometimes held closed by bungees and forced open by the weight of the released bombs. Given the emphasis on small bombs, there were structure weight advantages in spreading the bomb weight across the wing, hence variations included bomb cells in the wings (Battle, Whitley), containers under the wings (Wellesley), and small bays in the engine nacelles (Pe-2). Fortuitously, the Halifax and Lancaster were to have long unobstructed bomb bays (from a requirement to stow two 18-inch torpedoes), enabling the carriage of very large bombs later in the war. The bomb bays of some German aircraft (Ju86, He111) were unusual in having eight vertical bomb chutes, each for a single bomb attached nose up; release gave a characteristic nose-up to nose-down bomb toppling motion, well shown in film sequences. Small bombs were held in containers which remained attached to the aircraft (e.g. the RAF's SBC) and which opened to shower them down; or for reduced spread they were grouped in a 'cluster' which was itself carried and dropped like a bomb, a fuse causing it to release the bombs at lower altitude. Types included a 'bundled cluster' with beams, end-plates, nose and tail, all held together by circumferential straps which came apart; and a 'nose ejection cluster', a cylinder having a burster charge behind a rear pressure plate to push the nose cap off (with rods) and the contents forward and out.

Bombsights

Horizontal flight bomb aiming in 1939 normally used a vector-type optical bombsight. The bomb-aimer or bombardier viewed the ground track through a reflector or sighting plate, the angle of which was adjusted to allow for the aircraft's speed and altitude, wind speed and direction, and the terminal velocity of the type of bomb used. The bomb aimer gave course instructions to the pilot, and triggered release of the bombs when the cross-hairs on the sighting plate appeared aligned with the target. Such bombsights included the British Mk.IX CSBS (Course Setting Bomb Sight), French Bronzavia, German Görz-Visier 219, and Italian Jozza G.3. The accuracy of these sights was compromised by aircraft angular movements when making course corrections, and by errors in estimated aircraft speed and drift. The former could be obviated by gyro-stabilizing the sight, to decouple it from aircraft movements. The latter could be overcome with the more complex tachymetric form of bombsight in which ground speed and drift were obtained by maintaining a telescope aligned with the target, to enable measurement of apparent target movement relative to the aircraft. A tachymetric sight gave electric signals as output, usable for automatic bomb release at the correct point. It was more accurate than a vector sight, but needed continuous target visibility during the bombing run.

In 1939, the British had a part-stabilized (roll only) vector sight, the Mk.XI; and a tachymetric sight, the unstabilized Automatic Bombsight Mk.I, in service on Hampdens. The USA had the Sperry and Norden stabilized tachymetric sights. Aside from automatic bomb release, the intention was to be able to couple the Norden sight to the aircraft's autopilot, so that during the bombing run, movements of the sight to maintain correct alignment with the target caused appropriate movement of the aircraft's controls. The US regarded the Norden sight as super secret, and refused details to the British until June 1940. But in October 1937, German espionage in the Norden plant provided drawings of the sight, which was later copied as the *Luftwaffenzielgerät EZ42*. [Farago, 1972:39] Meanwhile the Germans were developing the comparable Zeiss *Lotfe* sight.

Dive-bombing for angles less than vertical required a special type of bombsight, e.g. the Swedish AGA and German BZA-1 sights already in service; the improved BZA-2 was under development at high priority.

Aircraft Bombs

High-explosive Bombs

Large bombs had been developed in World War One, including a 3,300lb British bomb for the Handley Page V/1000. But, during the inter-war years, air forces mostly favoured the use of smaller bombs in 'stick bombing', releasing a salvo in a slightly staggered sequence so as to straddle the target. Given the difficulties of bomb aiming, a spread of small bombs would be more likely to cause damage to most targets than one large bomb. High-explosive (HE) bombs had altered little in design, having: a steel case filled with the burster charge; fins or a ring tail for stability; mounting points; a fuse; and an arming device. Bombs of slim, streamlined form gave improved dropping accuracy and greater penetration; short stubby bombs offered a higher charge-weight ratio (CWR) and easier stowage. Whereas the tails of German bombs were permanently fixed on, those of British (and US) bombs were attached prior to use, and were to give a much higher failure rate, the bombs striking flat, or rear first, due to the tail coming off. The bomb's explosive was usually either: TNT (trinitrotoluene); a mix of TNT and ammonium nitrate (e.g. 'amatol'); TNT and aluminium powder (e.g. 'tritonal' – US); or TNT, ammonium nitrate and aluminium powder (e.g. 'minol' – British). The fuse was of simple impact type, e.g. a mechanical pistol; or a time fuse for penetration or delayed-action in a low-level drop to enable the aircraft to get clear. Time fuses were mechanical or pyrotechnic type, or (for German bombs only) an electrically-operated device using a condenser charged from the aircraft's electrical supply.

Most of the HE bombs in use were 'general-purpose' (GP) or 'demolition' bombs. The other principal types were thick-walled fragmentation bombs, for use against vehicles and personnel; and slim, armour-piercing (AP) or semi armour-piercing (SAP) bombs, relying on a strong case and kinetic energy (high impact speed, from a high altitude drop) for penetration, primarily for anti-shipping use. The US had introduced small parachute fragmentation bombs for use in ground attack. The war was to see considerable use of thin-walled 'high capacity' bombs having a high CWR for maximum blast effect. In 1937, the British updated their range of bombs, while the Germans at that time were so short of bombs that Hitler apparently advocated the filling of compressed gas cylinders with explosive as a stopgap measure. [Faber, 1979:104] In 1939, the RAF's main and largest HE bombs were GPs of 250 and 500lb respectively, although a 2,000lb AP bomb was available, and 1,000lb and 2,000lb GP bombs were under development. For their part, the Germans were mainly equipped with 50 and 250kg GP bombs, but had a 500kg bomb as well, plus AP bombs in all three sizes. During the war, the British especially were to pursue much larger bombs.

Incendiary Bombs

Bombs intended to destroy buildings, stores, etc. by generating fire were commonly in service, although their limited use in World War One had given little indication of the destruction they would wreak in World War Two. Typically, they contained an incendiary compound or mixture, e.g. white phosphorus (lethal – being liable to burn flesh through to the bone – but accepted for smoke and for incendiaries) or thermite (aluminium and iron oxide) which would ignite the magnesium case. Mostly they were small, and dropped in cluster containers which released them at lower altitude to provide limited spread over the target area. The standard German incendiary was the 1kg B1El (*Brandbomb*, 1kg, *Elektron*) dating from the end of World War One. The B1ElZA version incorporated a delayed action explosive charge to deter firefighters. The BSK36 canister carried 36 of the bomblets, held by a tie rod between end plates, with mid-air release by a clockwork mechanism. The British had recently introduced an RAE-developed 4lb magnesium bomb, later copied for the US forces as the M50. It was hexagon-shaped, for ease of stacking, and for most of the war was to be carried in SBCs (Small Bomb Containers) which remained in the bomb bay, allowing the incendiaries to scatter too widely.

Guided and Glide-bombs

A glide-bomb, having wings for aerodynamic lift, offered increased aircraft safety by allowing launching further away from an AA-defended target; a guided bomb, having control surfaces able to alter the trajectory under remote or homing control, offered improved accuracy; a guided glide-bomb promised both. Such categories of bomb had received spasmodic development. Wire-guided gliders had been tested by the Siemens-Schuckert Werke in 1915. A stabilized glide-bomb devised by A.Crocco in Italy was flight tested in 1920-22 as the *Telebombe*, a miniature biplane with a simple autopilot and servo controls. Several radio-controlled experimental glide-bombs were built and tested by the Breguet company in France in 1938-39, the largest being the Breguet 910 with a 1,000kg warhead, launched from a Farman F.224 bomber. Finally, 1938 saw the first flight trials with experimental radio-guided free-fall bombs, developed under Dr Max Kramer of Ruhrstahl AG, at DVL in Germany. These used a 250kg SC250 bomb fitted with a new cruciform tail assembly incorporating the radio receiver and thickened aerofoil surfaces with built-in solenoid-operated yaw and pitch spoilers.

Chemical, Biological and Nuclear Warfare Developments

Chemical Weapons

During World War One, some 63 different chemicals were used against personnel, incapacitating or killing by toxicity rather than by explosive energy. After the war, the USA and Japan declined to sign the League of Nations 'Geneva Gas Protocol' prohibiting the use of such weapons, but France, Italy, Britain and the USSR all ratified it. All carried on with chemical weapons development in secret, and all acquired an aerial chemical warfare (CW) capability. In 1930, US Gen. W. Mitchell pointed out that it was now unnecessary to destroy enemy cities, e.g. to disrupt munitions production; the population could be driven out by dropping gas bombs.

Aside from the low-lethality 'tear gases' (White Cross gases), the chemicals usable as weapons in 1939 included: the 'choking gases' (Green Cross), e.g. chlorine and phosgene (carbonyl chloride); the 'nettle gases', lethal at the higher concentrations; the 'blood gases' (Blue Cross), principally hydrogen cyanide and cyanogen chloride; the 'vesicants' or 'blister gases' (Yellow Cross), in two classes; the 'arsenicals', notably lewisite (chlorovinyldichloroarsine), and mustard gas (dichlorethyl sulphide) and its derivatives; and finally, secret new 'nerve gases' or anticholinesterase agents. The first two of the latter, *tabun* (cyanodimethylaminethoxphosphine oxide) and *sarin* (fluoroisopro-poxymethylphosphine oxide) had been discovered under Dr G. Schrader at I.G. Farben in Germany, in 1937 and 1938 respectively, while researching insecticides. They were, respectively, some ten and twenty times more lethal than previous chemical weapons, and totally unknown elsewhere.

Chemical Bombs and Spraying

Since the chemicals used were liquids which would evaporate to form a heavy toxic vapour, chemical bombs were purpose-built with tight sealing for handling and storage, and usually had some means of ejection or dispersion (e.g. air burst, spray, ground burst, or tail ejection) by explosive charge or compressed gas. At the outbreak of war, Germany had stockpiled 50kg KC50 bombs containing Green Cross and Yellow Cross chemicals; Britain had 30lb, 50lb and 250lb LC mustard gas bombs; Japan had developed parachute-dropped mustard gas spray bombs; and the French had a 200kg phosgene bomb and small mustard gas grenades dropped in clusters of 50. The Italians had mustard, phosgene and lewisite bombs, and for visually assessing wind strength and direction for optimizing chemical drops, introduced a 5kg *Vento Marker* in two versions, giving smoke for day use and a flame for night.

Low-altitude spraying of chemicals from an aircraft in flight used a special sealed tank with dispensing pipes and nozzles, and compressed gas to force out the tank contents; some smoke-laying canisters, e.g. the British SCI (Smoke Curtain Installation) were also usable. The major nations had such an operational capability. The Germans seem to have been the exception, although gas spraying trials using low-flying Do17 bombers had been carried out at Neustadt; and He115 floatplanes could carry SN50 tanks and spraying equipment in their floats. In the USSR, the experimental KhB (*Khimicheskii Bojevik* = chemical warrior) derivative of the STAL-5 twin-engined airliner had been designed for gas attacks. Elsewhere, in collaboration with France, using the French proving ground in the Sahara, the British had developed a high-altitude (15,000ft) aerial spraying technique to reduce vulnerability to AA. It used 'HT', a derivative of the normal 'HS' mustard gas, with the necessary much lower freezing point.

Chemical Warfare Reappears

Operational CW reappeared in 1935 when the Italian *Regia Aeronautica* began using chemical weapons in Abyssinia; first mustard gas bombs, then in 1936, mustard gas sprayed from the air by formations of up to 18 aircraft; then 250kg aerial-burst mustard-gas spray bombs disintegrated by time fuse at some 60m above ground. In 1937, the Japanese began extensive use of poison gas against the Chinese, with aircraft bombs and artillery shells using phosgene, chlorine and (in 1938, in its first operational use) lewisite. As the Nations moved towards war in 1939, the stockpiling of chemical weapons had become so widespread that their use on a large scale in the coming conflict seemed almost certain. Mass production of gas masks for civilian populations as well as troops became an urgent priority, notably in Britain where 50 million 'respirators' had been made by the outbreak of war. Civil defence units were trained in anti-gas measures; and some armies acquired specialist chemical units, e.g. the German *Nebeltruppe*. That chemical warfare didn't happen, largely for fear of retaliation in kind, was one of the unexpected features of the Second World War.

Biological Warfare

Germ or Biological Warfare (BW) aimed to inflict damage or death on the enemy's personnel, crops or livestock by the spread of infection or disease using bacteria, viruses and spores as agents, often carried by living creatures to aid spreading. But despite an equally long history, in the late 1930s BW development was neither as advanced nor as widespread as that for CW. Compared with using chemicals, the spread of living organisms was much less predictable or controllable; plagues would not respect battle front lines or national frontiers. So, while some countries were actively working on BW defence, as at Britain's Porton Down Establishment, work on BW weapons seems to have been confined initially to the USSR. But, after reports of severe casualties to Japanese forces due to cholera and anthrax weapons used by Soviet saboteurs in China in 1935, the Japanese themselves set up a major BW plant, at Pingfan near Harbin, under Gen. Shiro Ishii. Developments there included work on aircraft delivery systems; more so than chemical weapons, biological weapons were primarily for use at long range, far beyond the front line.

The Beginning of Nuclear Weapons Development

The prospect of converting matter into energy to give an atomic bomb was foreseen in H.G.Wells' novel *The World Set Free* in 1913. Harold Nicholson's 1932 novel *Public Faces* warned: ' ...the experts had begun to whisper the words "atomic bomb", and that ... a single bomb could by the discharge of its electronic energy destroy New York'.

In 1934, the physicist Leo Szilard persuaded the British Admiralty to take out a secret patent on a nuclear chain reaction that would make an atomic explosion possible. But few people thought an A-bomb practical until, in January 1939, Prof. Otto Frisch and Dr Lise Meitner made the first public announcement of a laboratory demonstration of the fission of uranium 235U atoms by bombarding uranium with neutrons. It was Miss Meitner who first appreciated that fission was taking place, the 235U atoms being split into two smaller atoms with release of energy and more neutrons. Szilard (now in the USA), repeating the experiment in March 1939, saw that 'the World was heading for sorrow' [Kurzman, 1945:21]; a large enough mass (critical mass) of 235U could give a chain reaction, in which each neutron generated would cause further fission and more neutrons, so leading to an atomic explosion. Others noticed also. In France, a patent for a uranium bomb was filed. In the USSR, nuclear research received increased priority, under a committee set up to investigate the feasibility of an A-bomb. In Germany, physicists P. Harteck and W. Groth wrote to the German War Office on the possible use of nuclear energy as a military explosive, and the government quickly stopped the export of uranium ore from newly-occupied Czechoslovakia. Prompted by Szilard, in August 1939 the world's most respected scientist, Albert Einstein at Princeton, wrote to the US President F. D. Roosevelt urging intensive research towards developing a nuclear bomb before Nazi Germany did so.

Navigation, Blind-bombing Systems and Radar

Radio Systems for Navigation; Blind Landing; IFF
In the 1930s, aircraft crews still relied mostly on visual navigation plus dead reckoning and/or astronavigation in darkness or overcast conditions, or when over the sea. But radio aids included Direction Finding (D/F) services; and ground radio beacons at known locations, from two of which (or from a single beacon twice) the aircraft's crew could themselves obtain a triangulation position fix, using a rotatable D/F loop aerial on the aircraft. By 1939, the Germans had deployed a network of such beacons. In 1938, R.V. Jones in Britain proposed a long-range radio navigation aid using pulses from three transmitters – in essence the future 'Gee'. In 1939, the Telefunken company in Germany worked on a similar system, stopping because of other priorities. More radical still, the first exploration of airborne radar for aircraft navigation (the future 'H2S') was begun in Britain early in 1939. Ground-imaging radar using short enough wavelengths would show major differences in the terrain below (built-up areas, lakes, etc.) which would allow navigation at night or in overcast conditions, at any range.

For landing in poor visibility, the German Lorenz AG blind approach radio aid enabled an aircraft's crew to home in on an airfield and approach in line with the runway, by keeping to the centre of a composite (dots and dashes) audio radio beam. It was in use by civil aircraft and airports, and by the Luftwaffe and RAF. In Britain, a derivative, the STC Standard Beam Approach (SBA) system, was under development.

In the coming air war, fought at high speed and with increasing reliance on electronic aids, the need for controllers to be able to differentiate quickly between friendly and hostile aircraft would be vital. IFF Mk.I, the first operational 'Identification, Friend or Foe' system, giving an amplified coded response to pulses from a CH radar, entered RAF service in 1939. IFF Mk.II, usable on all CH frequencies, followed.

German Blind-bombing Radio Aids

Under wartime 'blackout' lighting conditions, targets would be difficult to find and identify at night, while in northern Europe especially, even in daylight, they were frequently obscured by overcast cloud. But it seems that only in Germany was there much interest in blind bombing radio aids to enable attacks in such conditions. The first, begun under Dr H.Plendl in 1933, was *X-Verfahren*, the airborne equipment being known as *X-Gerät*. It used directional radio beams intersecting over the target. Flight tests began in 1936, using Ju52/3m bombers. The developed system used five Lorenz-type composite radio beams transmitted from aerials mounted on steerable platforms; two were the 'Director' beams that the aircraft flew along (one being a reserve); and three were separate cross beams on the approach to the target. The 'Advance' cross beam provided a warning for the 'Fore' and 'Main' cross beams by which the crew started and stopped a mechanical clock device which computed the timing for automatic release of the bombs. In 1938, *Luftnachrichten-Abteilung 100*, the first specialist blind bombing unit was set up to develop use of the system. While *X-Verfahren* was being perfected, work was advancing on Germany's second and third blind bombing aids. *Knickebein*, was simpler than *X-Verfahren*, using just two Lorenz-type radio beams intersecting over the target. The bomber was to fly along the centre of the 'flight' beam and release its bombs when crossing the centre of the 'cross' or 'marker' beam. *Y-Verfahren* differed in using only a single but complex radio beam aligned with the target, plus a ranging signal. The aircraft was to fly directly along the beam while a transponder on board the aircraft received, amplified and retransmitted the ranging signal. The ground station continually measured the time taken for the ranging signal to travel to the aircraft and back again, and at the correct range sent a bomb release instruction to the aircraft's crew.

'Radiolocation' and Countermeasures

Detection and range-finding by 'radiolocation' (later termed radar) – by transmitting radio pulses and picking up any echoes – offered defence forces early warning of the incursion of hostile aircraft at night or through cloud, and at long range. Since the first successful detection of aircraft by radar in the USA in 1930, radar sets had also been developed in Germany, Britain, France, USSR, Italy and Japan. But radar had been pursued most intensively in Britain and Germany, under code names RDF (Radio Direction Finding) and *DT-Gerät* (*Dezimeter Telegraphie*) respectively. By September 1939, Germany had eight FuMG80 *Freya* sets operational, and Britain had its CH (Chain, Home) system of 19 'AMES Type 1' RDF stations on the East and Southern coasts of Britain, plus three similar CO (Chain, Overseas) stations at Malta, Aden and Alexandria. Whereas the British CH radars were mounted on tall masts, and looked only out to sea via fixed 'floodlight' beams, the *Freya* used shorter wavelength, allowing a smaller, steerable antenna. But the more defence-minded British had incorporated their radars into an integrated air defence system, declared operational in August 1939. That same month also, the RAF took delivery of the first six Blenheims equipped with the primitive AI Mk.I radar; at this time no other country was developing radar night fighters, the real answer to the night bomber.

In the coming war, a successful bombing offensive could need some neutralization of the enemy's radar defence system, via intelligence and some form of countermeasure. But the intelligence aspect was failing badly. In 1938, German *Feldmarschall* Erhard Milch mentioned the radio detection of aircraft while in Britain, and later showed French Air Force officers a German radar set. The Germans routed Lufthansa airliners over the masts of the British CH stations, and in the summer of 1939 used the rigid airship LZ130 *Graf Zeppelin II* to make two radio monitoring cruises off Britain's coast. But neither Britain nor Germany entered the war with any real appreciation that the other side might have operational radar. However, at least in Britain there were some who were looking at ways of countering radar. Dr R.V. Jones in 1937 noted that radar could be jammed by distributing foil strips or wires in the air as reflectors (the future 'Window'). And in 1938, RCM (Radio CounterMeasures) work under Dr E.C. Williams included the successful airborne noise jamming of CH radars using a hospital diathermy set installed in a Sunderland flying boat.

II   1939–40

Bomber Developments

New Bombers
The first 16 months of the war brought a flood of new
bombers. Those making their first flights in the last months
of 1939 included: the Handley Page Halifax (Britain, 24
September), the RAF's second four-engined heavy bomber,
without the span restriction of the Stirling and therefore
enjoying higher performance; the Mitsubishi G4M twin-
engined land-based naval medium bomber (Japan, 23
October), with high fuel capacity for exceptionally long
range, but vulnerable; the unorthodox Heinkel He177 V1
four-engined heavy bomber (Germany, 19 November); the
Piaggio P.108B (for *Bombardiere*) four-engined heavy
bomber (Italy, 21 November), with gun barbettes; the
Consolidated Vultee XB-24 four-engined heavy bomber
(USA, 29 December); the Nakajima G5N *Shinzan*
four-engined long-range land-based naval heavy bomber
(Japan, December), based on the US Douglas DC-4E and
built in prototype form only; and the Polikarpov SPB/D
twin-engined dive-bomber (USSR).

The new bombers of 1940 were twin engined, including:
the Arado Ar240 multi-rôle bomber (Germany, 10 May),
with advanced features including gun barbettes; the
Yermolaev Yer-2 long range night bomber (USSR, June),
some versions of which were to have ACh-30V diesel
engines; the North American B-25 Mitchell medium bomber
(USA, 19 August), which was ordered 'off the drawing
board', and was to become a very adaptable and successful
bomber; the Martin B-26 Marauder medium bomber (USA,
25 November), also ordered 'off the drawing board', with a
relatively high performance via a clean design and an
exceptionally high wing loading; and the De Havilland

DH98 Mosquito high-speed unarmed light bomber (Britain, 25 November). In Germany, the Blohm und Voss BV141 asymmetric reconnaissance aircraft was tested as a bomber; and for deception, the already cancelled twin-engined Messerschmitt Bf162 was promoted as Germany's new high-performance bomber.

Bombers entering service in 1940 included: in the USSR, the Petlyakov Pe-2 and Pe-8; in Japan, the Kawasaki Ki-48 ('Lily'); in Britain, the Avro Manchester, Short Stirling and Handley Page Halifax; in France, then Britain, the Douglas DB-7 Boston; in the USA, the North American B-25. But with any new bomber, technical problems and training requirements meant that there could be many months between first deliveries into service and the first operational use.

Among technology developments, the first remotely operated gun barbettes appeared in 1939–40: first, barbettes on the outer engine nacelles of the Italian P.108B; then the German Arado/DVL FA13 hydraulically-operated system on the Ar240, using a periscope sight. New bombsights also appeared: in Germany, in April 1940 the Zeiss Jena *Lotfe 7C* bombsight showed impressive accuracy; and in Italy, in August the new Borletti-Colnaghi bombsight was tested on a Fiat BR20. With some bombers too cramped to enable crew members to change places, the problem of the pilot being killed or injured by enemy action was treated on the Martin 167 Maryland and Douglas DB-7 Boston by providing a second simplified set of flying controls in another crew position. In Britain, the discovery of self-sealing linings in the fuel tanks of an He111H-2 bomber shot down on 28 October 1939 led to the rapid development and introduction of similar linings on RAF bombers. In 1940, a Manchester bomber was successfully launched from the RAE 'Frictionless Take-off' catapult, before the catapult programme was halted.

Heavy Bombers: Heinkel He177, Consolidated B-24

Powered by four P&W Twin Wasp radials, the B-24 was the first production heavy bomber with a tricycle u/c. Other features included the low-drag, high aspect ratio 'Davis Wing', conferring exceptional range and endurance which made the B-24 the war's most widely used four-engined aircraft; and 'roller-shutter' bomb doors which retracted upwards inside the fuselage, giving less drag than downward-opening hinged doors. But a longitudinal keel and catwalk allowed only relatively small bombs stowed either side.

The He177 was the most innovative heavy bomber of the time. Features included: a structure stressed for dive-bombing, if necessary; full-span Fowler flaps, combined with ailerons; a quadruple main u/c; and doubled DB605 engines reducing drag, roll inertia, and engine-out yawing moment, while giving the aircraft the appearance of being twin-engined. But the He177 was to become the most trouble-plagued bomber of the war. As a stopgap, bomber conversions of the Focke-Wulf Fw200 *Condor* entered service, but these could carry just four 250kg bombs under the wings; they took part in the night blitz on Britain, but were mostly used for anti-shipping duties.

With the Stirling and Halifax coming into service, each with eight guns in three power-turrets, the RAF believed it now had the best armed heavy bombers; the Pe-8 had two 20mm cannon and two machine guns, but all were manual.

High-speed Unarmed Bombers: De Havilland Mosquito

The DH98 Mosquito unarmed light bomber was effectively in a class of its own, becoming the fastest military aircraft in service anywhere. For much of the war, no other bomber could match its performance, and no service fighter could be relied upon to catch it and shoot it down. Powered by two RR Merlin liquid-cooled engines, the Mosquito was exceptionally clean. Its high performance, and the low radar signature given by its wooden structure (panels of balsa wood sandwiched between layers of birch), were to enable the Mosquito to roam virtually at will over German-occupied territory even in daylight, despite its lack of armament.

Elsewhere, there was little interest in such a bomber. The Japanese acquired a manufacturing licence for the German He119, and in May 1940, two prototypes to evaluate, but production plans did not materialize.

High-altitude Bombers

The year 1940 saw serious efforts to achieve stratospheric bombers. In Germany, the Junkers Ju86P-1 unarmed pressurized high-altitude bomber was to make a silent glide approach to the target from around 12,000m with the engines throttled back. After bombing from around 10,000m, it was to climb back to the cruise altitude for the return. Several entered service late in 1940 with occasional sorties over Britain. Meanwhile, work began on the Heinkel He274, a high-altitude derivative of the He177 with a pressure cabin, long-span wings, and four separate engines with turbosuperchargers. In Britain, high-altitude variants of the Wellington had a bulbous pressure cabin with a tiny viewing dome for the pilot. The Mk.V had turbosuperchargers, the Mk.VI two-stage gear superchargers and, later, an extended span wing. But as with other attempts elsewhere, severe development problems were encountered with the turbochargers and with icing and lubrication. Only one Mk.V was built, and 60 of the 67 Mk.VIs were scrapped.

New Long-range Heavy Bomber Projects

In January 1940 the US issued a requirement for a 'Hemisphere Defense Weapon', a superbomber to replace the B-17 and B-24, with performance far beyond either. It resulted in four competing designs: Boeing XB-29, Lockheed XB-30 (a bomber derivative of the Model 049 transport which became the Constellation airliner), Douglas XB-31 and Consolidated XB-32. The B-29 was chosen, with small numbers of the B-32 ordered as a back-up. While, in mid-1940 US and British military representatives discussed possible future US bombing against Germany from bases in Britain should the USA be drawn into the War, in Germany the possibility of striking at US cities from Europe was being considered. Initially, one-way raids were proposed, the bomber crew having to ditch at a pre-arranged spot in the Atlantic on the way back, for rescue by submarine. Later, submissions were invited for a bomber with an unrefuelled Europe–USA round-trip range. The project submissions offered were the Me264 and developments of the Fw300 and Ju290.

Bomber Rear Defence; Deterrent Weapons
In the absence of a rear turret on smaller bombers, fixed
rear-firing gun installations were tried: e.g. a 'stinger' tail
gun on the Heinkel He111H and Mitsubishi Ki-21-1b; twin
guns in the rear of each nacelle on the Douglas A-20A; and
on some Martin Baltimores, a ventral group of four guns
angled slightly down and out. Later, rear 'scare-guns' were
tried in the nacelles of a Mosquito, and the Ar234 was given
a rear-fuselage pair of 20mm cannon. Mostly, such guns
could be fired by the pilot sighting via a mirror/periscope and
manoeuvring the bomber until the fighter was directly to the
rear. Unfortunately this gave the fighter a simple
no-deflection shot, at a bigger target, and usually with far
greater fire power.

As an alternative to rear guns, the French had
experimented with catapulting time-fused grenades rearwards into the path of attacking fighters. Now, in 1940, some
German bombers carried SKAV launchers for this task, the
0.5kg grenade being dropped down a chute and ejected
rearwards by compressed air; a small parachute deployed to
slow the grenade, to open up a safe distance from the
bomber before detonating. Other rear defence /deterrent
devices tried by the Germans apparently included a towed
kite and a rear-firing flame thrower. 'Scarecrow' devices
used by Japanese crews early in the Pacific War included a
firecracker filled with flash-producing pellets and hand
thrown from the bomber; and an inert weight tied to a small
paper parachute, hand thrown in clusters into the path of the
fighter. Other ploys tried by bomber crews included firing
Very cartridges, dumping shredded paper from the flare
chute, and using an Aldis lamp to try to simulate gun flashes.
But such attempts rarely had much effect.

Weapon Developments

German Bomb 'Screamer Tubes', Retarder Rings and Nose Spikes; 'Land Mines'

In 1940, German bombs especially were acquiring new features, e.g. various fuses with delayed action and anti-tamper devices making an unexploded bomb a booby trap. On 21 June, bombs with 'screamer tubes' attached to the tail fins were first dropped over Britain. The metal or cardboard tubes had holes or cuts to generate a shrill whistle as the bomb descended through the air, to help unnerve the civilians being bombed. With delay-fused bombs released at low altitude tending to bounce beyond the target, some SC-series bombs were given a tail retarder ring (*Kopfring*) to increase drag and so increase the trajectory angle at impact. Others (*Stachelbomben*) were built with a large steel nose spike to dig in and reduce bouncing.

The Royal Navy's sweeping of German magnetic sea mines proved so effective that stocks of 500kg LM-A and 1,000kg LM-B mines were re-assigned as blast bombs for raids on Britain, with a first use on 16 September. They were variously fitted with time delay or impact fuzes, sometimes a long pistol probe for above-ground detonation, or a cluster of 36 1kg incendiaries to be scattered by the explosion to start fires. The 'land mines' were dropped on their normal parachutes, drifting with the wind as they descended; aiming being impractical, they were normally used against built-up urban areas. The parachute helped the defence: some caught in trees etc. in which case the mines did not explode; also, the slowly-dropping mines proved suitable targets for any nearby Bofors AA guns.

The British 'Wallis' Proposed Penetration Bomb

In Britain, the RAF ordered its first 1,000lb HE bombs; and a 2,000lb SAP bomb was first dropped by a Hampden in a raid on Kiel on 1 July. Germany was already using 1,000kg

(2,200lb) bombs. But Vickers' chief scientist, N. Barnes Wallis, noted that against structures of thick reinforced concrete, conventional bombs of even this size would be ineffective. He proposed a much larger (10 tons) special 'penetration' or 'earthquake' bomb, slender with a pointed nose and strengthened case, dropped from high altitude to achieve supersonic speed for deep penetration into the earth beside the target before detonation. The large explosion underground would cause a *camouflet* effect, the seismic shock wave shattering the foundations of the target building, splitting its base, and allowing parts of the structure to fall into the cavern created by the explosion. Wallis's proposal was judged impractical for the aircraft of 1940, but the idea was to be resurrected later, with the 'Tallboy' and 'Grand Slam'.

Penetration and Liquid Incendiary Bombs; Unorthodox British Incendiaries

The Germans began using incendiaries against Britain on 5 June. When hitting a house some bounced off, others crashed through the roof and ceiling to burst in an upstairs room. But already there was interest in heavier incendiary bombs, to penetrate strongly-built roofs. One such, *c*.June, was the first liquid incendiary, the 250kg C250GB 'Oil Bomb', filled with a heavy oil but with a central incendiary core. It was later replaced by the *Flam* C250C and 500kg C500, some versions of which were fused to ignite prior to impact, to help spread the contents. In Italy, the penetration problem resulted in a 20kg incendiary with an SAP nose; some were dropped on Britain by the *Regia Aeronautica* on 21 December.

At the RAE in Britain in 1940, there were various attempts at new incendiary bombs, largely intended to cause fires in the Black Forest to undermine morale and damage secret installations there. [Turnill and Reed, 1980:58] The 'eggshell bomb' was a four-inch diameter ball of phosphorus, with a coating of varnish intended to burst on impact to ignite the phosphorus. In practice, the coating was damaged when the bomb was ejected down the flare chute, and the bomb fell – it was said – 'like a flaming meteor'. The parachute-dropped 'sausage bomb' was intended to catch in trees to start forest fires. It consisted of three sacks (later, rigid tubes) tied together and containing wood shavings, wax and igniters. It proved difficult to eject, the slipstream holding it against the aircraft, and ineffective. The British also improvised a 250lb petrol bomb (containing petrol-soaked rags), and experimented with butane as a bomb filling.

'Incendiary Leaves' developed under Project 'Razzle', were to be dropped in large numbers to destroy German crops and forests. 'Deckers' were superseded by 'Wafers', consisting of a phosphorus-impregnated pad between squares of celluloid. Phosphorus being inert in water but igniting in air, the leaves were to be carried and dropped in wet condition, to dry out later. But they proved unable to ignite even dry wheat sprayed with paraffin. Operational drops from Wellington and Whitley bombers in September were a failure, some leaves blowing back up into the aircraft where they caused fires, even though the crews carried water and syringes for such an eventuality. A proposal to edible-wrap the wafers in the hope that rats might drag them into basements and start fires was not tried.

Chemical Weapons Developments; Spray Glide-bomb; Anti-crop Chemicals

In September 1939, the British and French agreed with the Germans, via Swiss mediation, to abide by the Geneva protocol and not use poison gas. But the Poles reported the dropping of mustard gas on Warsaw, and the Germans claimed the Poles used British-supplied chemical weapons against them. On 19 September, a speech by Hitler warned of 'fearsome new weapons', possibly the nerve gases, for which a secret new plant at Dyhernfurth was authorized in that same month. The Allies, who failed to develop such weapons throughout the war, assumed the speech was a bluff.

In 1940, Britain's Porton Down Establishment was developing a 'Flying Cow' unguided glide bomb, intended to dispense a swath of mustard gas drops during its descent [Harris and Paxman, 1982:52]. It seems the 400lb weapon was later stockpiled and supplied to the US 8th AF.

The principal new Allied chemical weapons of the war were anti-crop chemicals. In 1940, in Britain, aerial spray tests of herbicide types 1313 and 1414, developed by ICI, showed 1lb per acre could destroy most crops by arresting growth; stockpiling was begun. Proposals to contaminate (rather than to destroy) crops, by spreading toxic chemicals, e.g. arsenic, were also made. A 1941 plan to have Bomber Command saturate German food-growing areas with chemicals was shelved because of the large scale of operations needed, and because Britain was judged vulnerable to attacks in kind, whereas the Germans had wide access to crops in the occupied countries. [Harris and Paxman, 1982:98] Later in the war, the US Fort Detrick developed new anti-crop chemicals having a hormone-like effect on plants, causing them to grow rapidly and die. Two of these, dichlorophenoxyacetic acid and trichlorophenoxyacetic acid (later 2,4-D and 2,4,5-T) became the US Agent Orange air-sprayed defoliant used in the Vietnam War. [Hersh, 1968:99]

Japanese and British BW Developments: Anthrax and Plague Weapons

By 1940, the Japanese at Pingfan had tested BW aerial spraying devices, and nine different types of aircraft BW bomb. Two of the latter, the *Uji* and *Ha* fragmentation bombs both used anthrax spores. Reportedly, on 4 October 1940, a Japanese aircraft over Changteh in China dropped plague (*Bacillus pestis*) contaminated wheat and rice grains in what may have been the first operational BW drop. Sporadic Japanese BW air raids in China continued into 1942, mostly with devices incorporating plague bacteria. [Harris and Paxman, 1982:78,80] Reports of these raids spurred Allied BW development.

Britain's Porton Down had already been working on BW vaccines. In 1940, work began on BW weapons themselves, under Dr P.Fildes. The initial project was for a small, anthrax-impregnated cattle-cake, to be dropped by RAF bombers to infect the enemy's livestock. This was apparently the world's first mass-produced biological weapon, some five million eventually being made. They were not used operationally, and were incinerated after the war.

Bombing up: on a summer evening in 1941, a Short Stirling being prepared for a night raid, with bombs ready for loading, and a fuel bowser in attendance. The Stirling was the RAF's first four-engined heavy bomber of the War, but with a performance predictably compromised by a short span wing. Note the blackout curtains for night operations.

'*Sowing the wind*': the German night blitz on Britain was the first major bombing campaign against cities. Here, in Eastcheap, London Fire Brigade crews attempt to limit the damage from incendiary bomb attacks. The War's evolved firebombing technique used GP bombs to break water mains and create rubble and craters to hinder firetrucks, blast bombs to smash roofs and windows for air for the fires, then the incendiaries themselves.

Tri-motor bomber: Italy's fastest bomber, the Cant Z1007bis, used especially in high-level bombing by tight formations, including against Malta. The curious dorsal V-shaped feature is a manually handled gun with an aerodynamic balance – a metal tube raised at the opposite angle to counteract the air loads on the gun.

The unique Shturmovik: as important to the Red Army as bread, was Stalin's view of the Il–2 *Shturmovik*. Built in greater numbers than any other aircraft of the War, it was one of the most effective ground-attack aircraft on any front. The heavy armour plate gave the Il–2's crews the extra confidence to press home their attacks through a storm of AA fire.

Destruction incomplete: apparently severe bomb damage to factories could often be cleared and repaired quickly. This photo shows part of the devastation achieved in the RAF raid (of 3 March 1942) on the Renault factory near Paris, making trucks for the *Wehrmacht*. Under the debris, most machine tools survived or were repairable, and only two months' production was lost.

Fast and effective: Petlyakov Pe–2 bombers taxiing on a bleak, wintry Soviet airfield. The two-seat Pe–2 was one of the more successful and versatile light bombers of the War, with air brakes for dive-bombing and later used in that role. RAF Hurricane pilots flying escort for Pe–2s near Murmansk in autumn 1941 were surprised at the throttle level needed to keep pace with them.

Desert dust plumes: an unusual view of RAF Boston light bombers on a featureless North African desert airfield in 1942, starting engines in preparation for a raid. The pervasive and abrasive dust kicked up, e.g. by propeller slipstreams as shown here, or by moving vehicles or high winds, were a major menace to desert operations.

Blitzkrieg in action: a Junkers Ju87 *Stuka* dive-bomber releasing one 250-kg and four 50-kg bombs. With fighter cover, the Ju87 performed with devastating effect over the battlefield during 1939–41. Despite pleas from the British Army for similar support, the RAF refused to recognize the potential of the dive-bomber, and used the Hawker Henley for target towing.

Above: *A curiously peaceful scene*: Luftwaffe Dornier Do17Z light/medium bombers being serviced on a grass auxiliary airfield at Freux in German-occupied Belgium, summer 1940. The close dispersal and absence of AA weapons, sandbags, revetments, etc., suggest there was little fear of air attack.
Left: *The Eindhoven Raid*: on Sunday, 6 December 1942, 93 RAF light bombers made a low-level daylight raid on the buildings comprising the Phillips electronics works at Eindhoven in Holland. Here, late in the raid, two Bostons have approached above the smoke for a better view to find the best aiming point. The raid was a success but 15 aircraft were lost.

Heinkel over London: the distinctive bends of the River Thames enabled German crews to navigate over London even at night; attempts to disguise it by floating a non-reflecting layer of coal dust over the surface were unsuccessful. Here, a Heinkel He111 medium bomber, mainstay of the German bomber force, flies over London in daylight, summer 1940; the Isle of Dogs is on the right.

The U-boat pens at Lorient: the British had other priorities when they were incomplete, and the Americans were the first to attack them when they had their 4-m thick concrete roofs in place and were no longer vulnerable. Here the flat-roofed shelters are partly visible through the tail of one of a pair of 2,000-lb M34 GP bombs. The lack of prior craters confirms this as the start of the first 8th AF raid on Lorient, on 21 October 1942.

US Navy contribution: Lockheed PV-1 Ventura land-based bombers of the US Navy at a wet and windy base in the Aleutian islands, preparing for raids on Japanese bases at Paramushiru and Shimushu in the Kurile Islands, 1943. The four-man Ventura was faster than its portly figure might suggest, and served also with RAF, Commonwealth and USAAF (B-34) units.

The Dams Raid: one of the most famous aerial photographs of the War: the Möhne dam as seen by a recce Mosquito on the morning after the 617 Squadron 'Dambusters' raid on 16 May 1943. The print, signed by participating crewmen (Gibson across the breach), shows the twin towers used for sighting on the attack run, and the 200-ft-wide breach exactly half-way between.

Low-level night raid: the RAF's unarmed two-seat Mosquito flew low- and high-level missions, day and night, without escort. This striking view shows a precision attack by Mosquitos on the railway workshops at Namur in France, on the night of 3 April 1943. Taken from one aircraft, the photo shows a second lit by bombs bursting on rail lines in between workshop buildings.

Operation 'Robinson', Target 'Creusot': a rare daylight raid by RAF heavy bombers in 1942. The Lancasters are over Chatillon-sur-Loire in France, en route for a low-level attack on the Schneider works at Le Creusot, 17 October. Routing via the Bay of Biscay and shallow penetration at below radar height achieved surprise and birdstrikes became a greater hazard than enemy fighters.

The Potential of the Atomic Bomb; German Nuclear Acquisitions

In April 1940, Dr O.Frisch and Dr R. Peierls in Britain, prepared two secret memoranda on a 235U bomb. These advocated secret development work before the Germans, and for the first time: envisaged two hemispheres of 235U, brought together by springs to achieve the 'critical mass'; spelled out its potential ('... a 5kg bomb would be equivalent to several thousand tons of dynamite'); highlighted the lethality of the radiation: 'radioactive material will kill everybody within a strip estimated to be several miles long ...'; and noted that 'the only defence would be the deterrent effect of possessing such bombs oneself'.

With 'heavy water' (D_2O) usable to slow neutrons to aid 235U fission, the entire stock of the Norsk Hydro-Electric Company in Norway, the world's sole producer, was smuggled to France, then Britain. But the occupation of Norway and Belgium enabled the Germans to increase production of heavy water at the Norsk plant and to seize Belgium's stocks of uranium ore. In Germany itself, the Army allocated funding for atomic research, under Dr K. Diebner at Kummersdorf. For the Allies, the Norsk plant, especially, was to become a vital target. In the USA, in June 1940, a secret Advisory Committee on Uranium addressed the construction of an atomic pile, while US agents began quietly buying up what was left of the world's supply of uranium ore.

Navigation, Blind Bombing and Radar

Navigation Systems: Broadcast Transmitters; Beacons; 'G' (Gee) and 'H'

In accordance with the secret Nazi-Soviet agreement on Poland, on 1 September 1939 the Soviet radio broadcasting transmitter at Minsk near Poland's eastern border began operating for extended periods with frequent station identification, as a navigational aid to German bombers on deep penetration raids. [Bethel, 1976:303]. These included the first of 60 attacks on Warsaw itself, and one on the PZL aircraft factory near Warsaw. In Britain, to prevent enemy bomber crews from taking bearings on the BBC broadcasting transmitters, a contingency plan was implemented whereby stations at three different locations transmitted the same signal on the same frequency.

In May 1940, the Germans began installing radio beacons on the Channel coast to aid flights over Britain. But the first British GPO/Plessey 'Masking Beacon' or 'Meacon' countermeasure became operational in July. This could pick up a beacon's signal and retransmit it from a different location, the duplication preventing a true position fix. As the number of Meacons grew, the effect on German operations over Britain increased, despite continual changes of frequency and call sign.

In Britain, two new radio navigation aids were proposed at the Telecommunications Research Establishment (TRE) in 1940, the 'G' system (passive – transmitters on the ground), and the 'H' system (active – transmitter on board the aircraft). The 'G' system (later 'Gee') was adopted for development. Although it was less accurate, enemy fighters could not home onto aircraft using it, and it was usable by many aircraft at a time. The 'H' system would be resurrected later. Also developed in Britain in 1940 was the revolutionary 'resonant cavity magnetron' valve devised by J.R. Randall and H.R.H. Boot. This offered the prospect of airborne radar using much shorter (centimetric) wavelengths, giving higher resolution usable, e.g. for ground imaging.

German use of Blind-bombing Aids: X-Verfahren and Knickebein

The invasion of Poland enabled the Germans to try out *X-Verfahren*. The mobile transmitters had been moved to E.Germany beforehand, and on the first day of the invasion, He111s of *LnAbt-100* made the first ever operational blind bombing attack using a radio aid, against a munitions factory near Warsaw. Further such raids followed. In Germany itself, development of the other two blind bombing aids

Y-Verfahren and *Knickebein* was continuing. In preparation for future night bombing against Britain, in December *LnAbt-100*, now renamed *Kampfgruppe 100*, began flying experimental long range *X-Verfahren* sorties over London, without bombs. In February 1940, after a KGr100 He111 over Britain was shot down into the sea, *X-Gerät* equipment was removed from other aircraft to ensure that its secret was held until needed for a major offensive. But the Germans continued to risk limited operations over Britain using *Knickebein*, via three huge transmitters now operational in Germany, at Kleve, Stollberg and Lorrach. *Knickebein* was less accurate, but did not require special equipment or training like *X-Verfahren*, only an extra-sensitive but ordinary-looking Lorenz FuB11 Blind Landing receiver. Notes in a wrecked KG26 He111 in March alerted British Intelligence to *Knickebein*, and although crashed German bombers appeared to have no suitable receiver for it, a hidden microphone picked up a POW's remark that 'they'll never find it!'; a closer look revealed the real use of the Lorenz receiver. The British hurriedly set up a WI flight unit, with Avro Ansons fitted with VHF receivers. On the night of 21 June, one of them found the 30Mc/s *Knickebein* beams, intersecting over Derby. Improvised jamming of the beams (code-named 'Headache') began in August; purpose-built 'Aspirin' jammers became operational in September.

By September the Germans had built nine smaller *Knickebein* transmitters on the coast facing Britain. But with the jamming showing that the beams had been discovered, the fear arose that RAF night fighters would patrol along them. Accordingly, Luftwaffe crews took to flying well to one side of the beam, moving into it only near the target. Meanwhile, measures introduced to evade the jamming included: frequency switching; leaving the beams switched off until the bomber was close to the target; and having the beams intersect over a decoy target and turning them to the real target only when the bomber was close to it. A British system for 'bending' the beams (to intersect in the wrong place) was devised at TRE, but not developed; and attempts to generate a decoy cross beam ahead of the real one (to cause bomb release over open country) were abandoned. But a German myth grew up that the British were 'bending'

the beams to divert the bombers, even though the Luftwaffe
apparently flew intelligence missions along the beams to
investigate the British countermeasures. [R.V. Jones,
1978:179]

Radar Intelligence Failures

Knowledge of the enemy's early warning defence capability,
and implementing countermeasures against it, were important for bombing operations on any scale. But, for months,
neither the British nor the Germans had much appreciation
that the other had operational radar, and neither appeared
well able to assimilate intelligence on the subject. The
Germans ignored an agent's report on Britain's coastal chain
of RDF stations; dismissed as inferior a British mobile radar
set captured in May 1940; failed to probe French knowledge
of British radars; and in a Luftwaffe Intelligence paper on
the British defences on 16 July 1940, omitted any mention of
radar. During the Battle of Britain, German appreciation of
the conspicuous British CH stations remained limited until
early August. Thereafter, air strikes on them were made,
but not pursued. On the British side, the 'Oslo Report' on
German military developments – including radar – was
disregarded as a 'plant'; the Admiralty's discovery that the
pocket-battleship *Graf Spee* had radar was not passed to the
Air Ministry; and the latter were to debate the possibility
that the Germans had operational radar repeatedly into
1941, long after *Freya* had been discovered. [R.V. Jones,
1978:252] Critics were to argue later that the nightly sorties
over Germany by Whitley bombers could have been far
more productive if they had carried radio receivers instead
of (or as well as) propaganda leaflets. Detection of the
radars and radio beams mentioned in the Oslo Report would
have been very useful.

German First use of Radio and Radar Jamming

Despite pre-war British experiments with radio countermeasures, the Germans were apparently the first to make
offensive use of RCM to support bomber operations. For
Operation *Paula*, attacking targets around Paris on 3 June
1940, the Germans began jamming the Eiffel Tower
transmitter being used for directing French fighters. Early in

September, the German *Funkmessstörung* jamming service set up ground jamming transmitters near Cherbourg and Calais, and began operating them against the British CH radars. The British had learned to make some differentiation between a real trace and jamming interference, but despite the low power of the German jammers, the British radar performance was noticeably degraded.

German use of X-Verfahren and Y-Verfahren; Countermeasures

With *Knickebein* jammed, the Germans reintroduced *X-Verfahren*, with a first raid by KGr100 He111s on the night of 13 August 1940; eleven bombs hit the Nuffield Spitfire factory near Birmingham. Subsequent raids were less accurate. In nine raids on the Westland, Gloster and Rolls Royce factories, only two got within five miles of the target. The British detected the 70MHz *X-Verfahren* beams in September. By November, Ultra/Enigma decoding of German signals sometimes made known the target, and the time, height and line of approach for that night's raid. But Britain's night defences were too weak to gain much advantage from this information [R.V. Jones, 1978:192], while the early 'Bromide' jammers proved ineffective. On 6 November, the crew of a KGr100 He111 got so lost due to 'Meaconing' that they landed on the beach near Bridport. Examination of its equipment (albeit immersed by the tide) enabled the Bromide jammers to be improved, although too late to counter the Coventry raid on 14 November. By October, three transmitters for the third German blind bombing aid, *Y-Verfahren*, were operational in Northern France, and its use against Britain was begun by He111s of III/KG26. The British had learned of a new beam system in June, and in October noted that two aircraft bombed the Bovington army depot with high accuracy in range, but not in direction. The British picked up *Y-Verfahren* signals in November, and began development of a countermeasure.

British Attempts to Bomb the German Beam Transmitters

When KGr100 used *X-Verfahren* for their own small scale raids (instead of pathfinding in major attacks), the British noted a characteristic bomb pattern – the craters falling on lines which could be extrapolated back to a point at Cherbourg, evidently the transmitter. This led to the first British attempts at blind bombing, using the German radio beams as a means of attacking the transmitters themselves. This was done by flying back along the beam, timing the passage through the 'cone of silence' above the transmitter, and then making a further pass to bomb the mid point of the cone. After practising using an SBA transmitter, on 12 November 1940 WIDU Wellington bombers, equipped with suitable receivers, made the first such attack. The *X-Verfahren* transmitter at Cherbourg was disabled for two days [Saward, 1984:202], but subsequent attacks failed, the target being too small to hit consistently by this means.

Bomber Support

Escort Fighters: Drop Tanks; The Zero; Towing; Convoy Escorts
Fighter drop tanks could have aided the Germans in the Battle of Britain, by allowing daylight sweeps and escorted bombing well beyond the south-east corner of England. The Bf109E-7, equipped with the connectors, pipes, pumps and shackles to use them appeared in August. But the 250 litre moulded plywood/fabric tanks leaked badly, and were not used operationally; improved drop tanks did not appear until 1941. Far from the Battle of Britain, the IJN's new A6M *Zero-Sen* fighter featured lightweight construction, exceptional internal tankage, and a ventral jettisonable tank. In daylight raids, unescorted Mitsubishi G3M bombers had proved vulnerable to Chinese Air Force fighters. Now, on 19 August 1940, A6M2 fighters escorted G3Ms over an unprecedented 1,000 nautical miles round trip from Hangchow to near Chunking. But the performance of the *Zero* remained unknown to Western Intelligence. An alternative, achieving extended range escort with the bomber towing its own escort fighter, was tried by the

Messerschmitt company in mid-1940, with a Bf110C towing a Bf109E via a towline attaching to the fighter's airscrew spinner. The fighter would be powered for take-off, restarting when disengaging to attack enemy fighters. The concept was not adopted. In Japan, in 1940, 30 Mitsubishi G6M1 Navy Type 1 'Wing-tip Convoy Fighters' were the first bombers to be converted as wing-tip escorts for bombers, with extra armament, ammunition, armour and gunners in place of the bomb load. They were to remain in formation, defending the G3M2 bomber force using their four flexibly-mounted 20mm cannon. Although the Navy soon withdrew them as being too heavy and too slow, the Japanese Army returned to the concept repeatedly, with the experimental Nakajima Ki-58 (1940), Ki-69 (1942) and Ki-112 (1943).

Support Aircraft: Balloon Destroyers; Dedicated Raid Damage PR Aircraft
To counter British barrage balloons for low-level raids, the Germans devised Ju88A-6 and He111H-8 'balloon destroyer' conversions. Each had a full-span fender forward of the propellers, strut-supported from the aircraft nose and wings, with a cutter at each wing tip. The fender was swept back so that any cable encountered in flight would slide outboard to the cutter. A formation of balloon destroyers, carrying reduced bomb load, was to cut a path through the balloons for the main force following. But operational attempts in autumn 1940 brought little success, and showed the aircraft themselves to be vulnerable to fighters. Most were reconverted to conventional bombers. Strafing of the balloons by fighters was used as a simpler alternative, but not systematically. In the USSR, similar balloon destroyer conversions included Pe-2 and Tu-2 *Paravan* variants.

In view of doubts as to the accuracy of the British night bombing, in November 1940 RAF Bomber Command was given the first PR (Photo-Reconnaissance) unit, 3PRU, to be dedicated to raid damage assessment. Equipped with long-range Spitfire PR Mk.1C aircraft, the unit was required to overfly and photograph the target area in daylight, after the previous night's attack. For close detail, a long focal length lens was used. Two camera-equipped Wellingtons were also acquired and used for trials with night flare PR assessment of bomb damage.

German and British Air-sea Rescue Developments

With the increasing numbers of overwater raids, the provision of survival equipment to aircrew and the making of determined efforts to rescue aircrew from the sea, became recognized as essential for morale as well as for minimizing losses of trained personnel. Initially only the Germans had a dedicated ASR service, using search aircraft and pick-up launches, later moored 'life buoys'; in May 1940, the British started building one also.

German military aircraft carried life jackets, and a dinghy equipped with a radio transmitter, coloured flares, a Very pistol, and a container of fluorescine dye to stain the water green to aid searches. When ditching, Ju87 crews were the worst off; if they baled out the dinghy stayed with the aircraft, whereas if they remained on board they were unlikely to survive the nose down somersault and break up as the fixed undercarriage dug into the water. Built-in flotation bags, inflating automatically by pressure switch at water entry to keep the aircraft afloat, were introduced first on Do17 bombers; and automatic SOS radio beacons were fitted to dinghies. RAF bombers were fitted with a dinghy stowed in the wing, releasable by hand or automatically if the aircraft sank. The bombers also carried 'Mae West' life-jackets, and a pair of carrier pigeons which, in the event of radio failure when ditching, could be released with a note giving the location.

Ground-attack Operations

Blitzkrieg: the German Invasion of Poland

The first air offensive of the war began with Operation *Ostmarkflug*, the German invasion of Poland on 1 September 1939, with a 5 to 1 advantage in numbers of aircraft. Three Ju87s of III/StG1 made the first attack, using precision bombing to destroy detonation points for two vital bridges at Dirschau on the Vistula. Thereafter, support for the invading armies was provided by Luftwaffe units (mainly with Bf109 and Bf110 fighters, and He111, Do17, and Ju87 bombers) systematically bombing and strafing, in close support at the front and against key targets beyond, especially airfields. The bombing was largely short range, in daylight, with extensive fighter support, against relatively weak opposition. Variations included low-level cannon attacks by Bf110s against Polish transport, especially railway locomotives. As the land offensive continued apace, spearheaded by the Panzers, dive-bombing by the Ju87s proved extremely effective in support, exploiting the lack of air opposition. Luftwaffe liaison officers in radio vans called up close air strikes as necessary when resistance was encountered. While diving, the Ju87s could shift target, and even 'corkscrew' with the ailerons to deceive AA gunners. The psychological effect of such steep and fast diving attacks on the defending ground troops and their horses was marked, as apparently was the excruciating engine noise generated by the Henschel Hs123 biplane close support aircraft. Despite first-hand accounts from Poland, the British and French learned little of the new German method of warfare, and remained unprepared for it, in its much more developed form in May 1940.

The Polish Air Force Response

Most aircraft of the small *Polskie Lotnictwo Wojskowe* survived the initial German onslaught by prior dispersal to camouflaged airfields, but many of these were secondary sites without communications and this hampered any co-ordinated response. The P-23 *Karas* light bombers carried out their first raids on 2 September, including the first and only one on German territory, a single P-23 dropping eight 50kg bombs on rail installations at Neidenburg. Apparently as a result of Allied pressure to approve bombing attacks, it was not until 4 September that the P-37 medium bombers flew their first raids, 27 of them attacking Panzer columns.

The Poles failed to co-ordinate operations such that fighters provided air cover for the bombers; and fighters as well as bombers were soon diverted to a ground-attack rôle to try to halt the advancing German armies. Many were lost to AA fire as they attempted low-level attacks on the well-protected enemy armoured columns. With heavy losses of reconnaissance aircraft also, it became necessary to use surviving fighters and bombers for reconnaissance. As communications and supplies deteriorated, some of these missions were to look for fuel tankers which could be commandeered to provide the fuel for further missions.

Air Operations in the German Invasion of Norway

On 9 April 1940, the Germans began Operation *Weserübung*, the invasion of Denmark and Norway, the Danes capitulating immediately. The simultaneous sea and air invasion of Norway included attacks on the main Norwegian air bases at Sola (Stavanger) and Fornebu (Oslo) before their capture by parachute- and air-landed troops. By the 10th, bomber and fighter units had flown into these bases to support the German landings, aided by a shuttle service of Ju52/3ms flying in supplies. The 330 bombers quickly began flying bombing sorties against Norwegian forces and Allied warships, and later against the short-lived Allied landings intended to counter the German invasion. The bombing virtually destroyed the small ports of Namsos and Molde. With Norway too distant for fighter escort, the RAF response was limited. On the night of 11 April, six Wellingtons made the first British bombing attack on German-occupied inland territory, bombing Sola airfield. Further small attacks followed. With the Norwegian airfields in German hands, attempts were made to use frozen lakes, by variously using skis (Norwegian aircraft at Lake Vangsmjösa), trampling the snow (using 3,000 reindeer at Vaernes), or clearing it (using civilians, Lake Lesjaskog). RAF Gladiators flew onto Lesjaskog on 19 April, but German Ju88s and He111s quickly strafed them and made the ice unusable by bombing.

Air Operations in the German Western Offensive; Ju87 Close Air Support

Following the Polish campaign, the Germans refined the techniques of blitzkrieg, revolutionizing the role of airpower to support the ground forces. The *Sichelschnitt* plan for the invasion of the Low Countries and France included the biggest and most complex air support operations yet seen. On 10 May 1940, as the panzer divisions poured into Luxembourg and Holland, and waves of Ju52s carrying troops and paratroops crossed the Dutch frontier, all available German bombers were airborne. The *Stuka* dive-bombers supported the ground forces, the medium bombers headed to attack airfields in Holland, Belgium and France, and to hamper any Allied response by laying mines in the Channel and bombing road and rail targets deep in France. That day, much of the small Dutch and Belgian air forces were destroyed. Over the next several weeks, the Germans – well trained, well equipped and well co-ordinated – moved westwards at a speed which the Allies found impossible to counter. The ground offensive was aided by a ubiquitous fighter cover which enabled Luftwaffe reconnaissance aircraft to patrol freely, while overcoming any Allied reconnaissance missions. As the panzers sped forward, they were closely followed by signals unit vehicles which laid cables at up to 20mph to provide communication with newly captured airfields. Luftwaffe task forces made each airfield operational within hours, Ju52/3m transports then flying in bombs, ammunition, spares, groundcrews and fuel, enabling Luftwaffe units to leapfrog forward from base to base. Ju52/3m signals aircraft also flew into the forward airfields, to serve as advanced radio and D/F stations. This ground support kept the Ju87 *Stuka* dive-bombers close to the rapidly moving front, allowing six or seven sorties each per day. Military obstacles met by the ground forces were swiftly dealt with by Luftwaffe liaison officers calling down close support air strikes by the Ju87s when required. These proved very effective, the Allied troops mostly putting up so little resistance to dive-bombing attacks that the Germans themselves were surprised. [Horne, 1969:290-2] The enhanced psychological effect of sirens now fitted to the u/c legs of the *Stukas* and operated during the dive, contributed to this success. On 19 May, the vulnerability of tanks to skilled air strikes was confirmed, a French armoured counter-attack led by De Gaulle against Guderian's panzers being largely destroyed by *Stukas*.

Allied Bombing Attempts in Response to the German Blitzkrieg

The Allied air attempts to counter the German May offensive quickly showed how unfit the aircraft, techniques and training were, the response being severely hampered by lack of preparation, disrupted communications, liaison failures, and the general enemy superiority and speed. Initial daylight low-level raids were unescorted because of the confusion. In the first such attack, made on the first day against Guderian's panzer columns, which were well protected by light flak and fighter cover, 13 out of the 32 RAF Fairey Battles were shot down, the rest all damaged. Belgian *Aéronautique Militaire* Battles and RAF Blenheims also suffered heavy losses even when escorted; and on the 12th when the French finally managed to mount their first bombing raid, 8 out of 18 Breguet 693 bombers were shot down. This result virtually ended low-level daylight bombing by the Allies. On the 13th, the German crossing of the Meuse at Sedan, supported by some 1,500 aircraft, was unopposed by Allied air power. Thereafter, although improvised dive-bombing was attempted, mostly the Blenheims and the French bombed from higher altitude, the Battles at night. This reduced losses, but resulted in ineffective bombing against the (generally small) targets, especially for the night bombing Battles because the crews, unable to see their targets, dropped their tiny (50lb) bombs at the ETA (estimated time of arrival) over the target, despite orders to the contrary.

Dunkirk

When the remaining Allied forces were cut off on the Channel coast at Dunkirk late in May, the Panzers halted, Hitler acceding to Göring's proposal that the final blow be carried out by the Luftwaffe. Fog kept *Fliegerkorps VIII*'s dive-bombers grounded for three days. But on 27 May, German bombers dropped 2,000 tons of bombs on Dunkirk itself, destroying harbour installations and much of the town, and killing over 1,000 civilians. Many other raids were hampered by cloud, mist, haze – and the RAF. Although British troops being attacked by Ju87s and Bf109s bemoaned the apparent absence of the RAF, Blenheims (by day) and

Wellingtons (by night) bombed German positions, while RAF fighters intercepted German raids far from the beaches. Many raids got through, taking a toll of the ships evacuating the troops under Operation 'Dynamo' and forcing a change to night operations. But even by day the smaller boats proved difficult to hit, while bombs hitting the beaches dug deep into the sand which muffled the blast. By 4 June the fleet of boats had taken 338,000 troops off the beaches. Although huge amounts of *matériel* – including 75,000 vehicles – were left behind, this was the first real setback for the German bomber force.

Ground-attack Developments

The Rise of the Dive-bomber; British Idiosyncrasies
The evident German successes with the *Stuka*, brought increased appreciation of the value of ground attack, and especially of dive bombing. The Italian *Regia Aeronautica* received its first dive-bombers, the twin-engined Savoia SM85 in March 1940, followed by standard and tropicalized Ju87B *Stuka* dive-bombers supplied by Germany. Meanwhile the French had ordered US (Brewster Bermuda) dive-bombers, and in July, the USAAC ordered the A-24, a denavalized version of the SBD Dauntless carrier dive-bomber. In Germany, the new Arado Ar240 twin-engined *Kampfzerstörer* had a dive-bombing capability. In Britain, the German May offensive brought demands from the British Army to have the same kind of close dive-bombing support that worked with such phenomenal success for the Germans. But the Air Ministry and RAF remained strongly opposed to dedicated dive-bombing and resisted the procurement of dive-bombers. The existing 200 Henley dive-bombers remained assigned to target towing. With the fall of France, the British government took over the French order for US dive-bombers, and ordered further ones (Vultee Vengeance); but an unwilling Air Ministry maintained that it would not supply or train pilots for these

aircraft when they arrived. [Smith, 1981:91] But while remaining opposed to dedicated dive-bombers, the RAF had instead resorted to small scale use of a variety of obsolete and unsuitable aircraft (Battle; naval Swordfish; Lysander and Hector liaison aircraft) as improvised dive-bombers in France. Then in October, the RAF began dive-bombing experiments with Wellington and Hampden medium bombers, the bombs being released from a shallow angle and too high an altitude (3,000 – 8,000ft) for accuracy without a special dive-bombing sight. In December, the RAF decided to pursue dive-bombing with yet another unsuitable aircraft, the Fairey Albacore biplane.

The Germans Introduce the Fighter-bomber

With the dive-bomber at its peak, the Germans were looking at its successor, the fighter-bomber. A fighter with external weapon racks and release systems, and ideally additional armour-plate protection and heavy-calibre cannon, could be used for strafing and releasing bombs from a shallow pass. Its high speed and small size would make it less vulnerable to AA, so offering a very practical ground attack weapon. During the Battle of France, *Erprobungsgruppe 210* began evaluating such a fighter-bomber (*Jagdbomber* or '*Jabo*') using the Bf109E (carrying one bomb of up to 250kg below the fuselage) and the Bf110C (two 250kg bombs below the fuselage). The *Jabos* began operations against shipping in July, and in small low-level raids on Britain on 5 September. The small and fast Bf109 was so successful that every *Jagdgeschwader* soon acquired a Bf109 *Jabo Staffel*. Bombs were dropped in low-level passes or dives at up to 45 degrees, using the Revi gunsight for aiming. In December, the British began using Spitfires on low-level 'Rhubarb' sweeps over France, but these used strafing only.

British Preparation for Chemical Warfare

With the fall of France, the British prepared to initiate chemical warfare if necessary, Churchill being ready to go to 'all lengths' to repel the expected German invasion. In July, 16 squadrons of aircraft (2 Wellington, 5 Blenheim, 4 Battle, and 5 Lysander squadrons), at a dozen airfields, had been secretly equipped with gas bombs and/or spray tanks for mustard gas. Training for low altitude spraying used Battles with tanks filled with water, and special charts to allow for height, airspeed and wind direction. Experiments at Halton used Tiger Moth training biplanes to dispense an arsenic-based insecticide in liquid form from a tank in the front cockpit, and in powder form from canisters under the wings. Spraying attacks on the invasion beaches and landing craft could have been suicidal, given the German AA, but the invasion did not come. Britain continued CW training and the production of aircraft conversion kits. By December, the still-neutral USA was secretly supplying Britain with poison gas (mainly phosgene) to supplement the meagre British stocks. At the time Germany had twenty times as much, including tabun nerve gas. [Harris and Paxman, 1982:111]

British Developments for Close Support
British attempts at close support in France had been a failure. However, a useful concept had emerged, the use of a safety 'Bomb Line', ideally an easily identifiable feature (e.g. a road or river) which troops would approach at risk, and beyond which aircraft could attack at will. Since under- or overshoot were the commonest bombing errors, it was preferable to attack parallel to the bomb line, to minimize the risk to friendly troops.

British improvised adaptations of aircraft for ground attack in 1940 included a Westland Lysander tested with a dummy four-gun tail turret, another given belly-mounted twin 20mm cannon; and Tiger Moth biplane trainers given underwing racks for 20lb bombs, all to help repel the expected German invasion. They would have stood little chance against the German light AA. In August 1940, the British began experiments with close support, Col. J.D. Woodall devising a system for co-ordinating troops and aircraft, using a signals network with 'tentacles' – ACC (Army Cooperation Command) officers with the troops, radioing requirements for support to an Army/Air Force control centre. Woodall's system was to become one of the successes of the war, evolving into ASSUs (Air Support Signals Units) and FCPs (Forward Control Posts), with army ALOs (Air Liaison Officers) with the squadrons. Meanwhile in North Africa, loss of airfields as the British Army retreated led the RAF to provide maximum co-operation to help prevent further such occurrences. On the night of 8 December, obsolete Bombay bomber/transports were flown back and forth over the front line to drown the noise of British tanks positioning for Wavell's offensive. Gauntlet biplanes were tried unsuccessfully as dive-bombers, while inadvertent attacks by Hurricanes and Blenheims on British troops led to experiments with ground marker panels and Very pistols to aid recognition. This improvised Army/RAF co-operation in the desert helped Lt. Gen. R. O'Connor to one of Britain's biggest victories of the war, against Italian forces – a success which brought the Germans into North Africa.

Daylight Bombing Operations

The German Bombing of Warsaw; Soviet Bombing
The German Blitzkrieg in Poland succeeded by augmenting surprise and speed with *Schrecklichkeit* (frightfulness). When it became clear that civilians fleeing to the rear severely hampered the Polish forces, bombing of towns and villages at the Front to increase panic and confusion became an integral part of the German policy. Then on 15 September 1939, the Germans began Operation *Seebad*, the war's first large-scale bombing of a city, the encircled capital Warsaw, with 1,176 sorties on 25 September alone. The attacks included dive-bombing by Ju87s and, with most He111 units already withdrawn, the dropping of incendiary bombs by Ju52 transports. Reportedly, crateloads of incendiaries were simply pushed out of the side loading hatches over the burning city, without any attempt to aim. The Poles had withdrawn their surviving aircraft to airfields in eastern Poland. But on 17 September the USSR invaded Poland from the east. SB-2 bombers attacked these airfields as well as Polish troops retreating towards the frontiers of Rumania and Hungary. Polish resistance in the air ceased within days.

The 'Phoney War'; Proposed Allied Bombing of Soviet Oil

Although Britain and France declared war on 3 September 1939, hostilities with Germany settled into a muted 'phoney war' or *Sitzkrieg*, based on German hopes of an accommodation, British weakness, and French fears of German reprisals. In Britain, Bomber Command's front line strength shrank abruptly as 17 squadrons were assigned as advanced training units, beginning the build-up for a long war. With the British and the French agreeing not to bomb German territory, the British began occasional attacks on German shipping instead. These were made in daylight, at relatively long range and therefore without fighter escort. In effect they were a try-out for future British strategic bombing. They reflected Bomber Command's belief, albeit unverified in war exercises, that unescorted bombers could penetrate fighter defences in daylight.

Later, aware that the USSR was supplying much of Germany's oil needs, the Allies planned a bombing campaign against the USSR's 122 Caucasus oil refineries, mostly around Baku. The rather optimistic plan, using six French and three British bomber squadrons flying from Turkey and Iraq, was being considered when the Germans struck in Scandinavia, and never materialized.

British Attempts with Unescorted Daylight Bombing

The RAF attacks on German shipping off Brunsbüttel and Wilhelmshaven in 1939 were the first attempts at unescorted daylight bombing against an adversary equipped both with modern fighters and EW radar. The initial tactic was to fly at low altitude, below cloud. On 4 September, 7 of the 29 Blenheims and Wellingtons were lost; on 29 September, 5 out of 11 Hampdens; and on 14 December, 5 out of 12 Wellingtons. Bomber Command assumed most of the losses were due to light AA, but many were not. In the last action, German reports credited all five kills to fighters.

Reacting to the losses sustained at low altitude, the RAF ordered bomber crews to fly at above 10,000ft to reduce the risk from AA, and to maintain close formation to provide mutual protection against fighters. The inadequacy of this quickly became apparent. On 18 December 1939, German radar-directed fighters intercepted an RAF raid heading for German shipping off Wilhelmshaven. Caught in clear skies by Bf109 fighters, which far outpaced and outgunned them, 10 of the 22 Wellingtons were shot down and five others had to ditch or crash-land back in Britain. The German report spoke of the 'criminal folly' of the British crews in maintaining course and formation, even when attacked from the side, which was out of the field of fire of the Wellington's nose and tail guns. The RAF's report was critical of those crews who did break formation to take evasive action (three did, all had survived), and noted the desirability of armour-plating, self-sealing fuel tanks, and a mid-upper gun turret. But attention quickly turned to night bombing instead.

Bombing in the Soviet Invasion of Finland

The second major air offensive of the war was mounted by the USSR. After imposing the use of bases in Estonia, Latvia and Lithuania, the Soviets invaded Finland on 26 November 1939. In the air, some 900 Soviet aircraft (with mainly SB-2 bombers) were deployed against the 114 serviceable aircraft (including Blenheim and Fokker C.X light bombers) of the Finnish *Ilmavoimat*. On the first morning, Soviet aircraft flying from Estonia dropped leaflets calling for a workers' uprising. But shortly after noon, further waves of bombers began raining HE and incendiary bombs on the centre of Helsinki and other towns. Soviet radio claimed that the bombers were dropping bread to the starving people of Finland, Soviet incendiary containers thereafter being known to the Finns as 'Molotov's bread baskets' [Condon, 1972:21]. Despite limitations due to poor weather, and the four hours of northern daylight, Soviet bombing raids, largely unescorted, became a regular feature of the Winter War, some 7,500 tons of HE and incendiary bombs being dropped on towns, docks, railways (especially the vital Kemi-Tornio supply link to Sweden), villages, even individual farms. Fighter escort increased, and by 1940 some night raids were being flown. The Finns managed to mount a few small-scale raids themselves, attacking Murmansk, Leningrad, Kronstadt, and Paldiski, one innovation being the use of a DC-2 airliner with underwing bomb racks and a nose 20mm cannon. Overall, the Soviet forces suffered great casualties and losses, including 872 aircraft as against 61 for the Finns, but the more purposeful second-phase campaign using 2,500 aircraft in clear weather successfully wore down the Finns.

Bombing in the German Invasion of the Low Countries and France

The German western offensive which began on 10 May 1940, included many strikes by escorted medium bombers, against bases, troop concentrations, rail and road transport, airfields, and the French Maginot Line forts. The forts survived 500kg bombs dropped by Ju87s as well as bombardment by 28cm railway guns, but were bypassed by the German offensive. But there were other significant attacks: On 10 May, the crews of three He111s, believing they were over a French town, bombed the German town of Freiburg, killing 57 people. The shrapnel confirmed the bombs as German, but German propaganda claimed the raid to be a terror attack by French bombers, justifying subsequent German bombing of Allied towns. On 14 May, 57 He111s failed to receive radio and flare recall signals, and bombed the centre of Rotterdam while surrender negotiations were under way. The final death toll was 980, but the initial Dutch estimate of 30,000 forced the capitulation of Holland that evening, shocked World opinion, and – with Churchill now in power, and prepared to take a more offensive role – triggered the British night bombing of Germany. Despite these raids, strategic bombing by the Luftwaffe during the Western offensive remained limited. But on 3 June, Operation *Paula* brought attacks on French airfields and aircraft factories around Paris by three formations of 100 bombers each, plus fighter escort.

Meanwhile, almost unnoticed as the world's eyes were focused on Europe, on 29 April 1940 the Japanese began a major bombing offensive against Chungking, the capital of 'Free' China, using up to 100 Army and carrier-based aircraft per day. The campaign met little effective air opposition, and lasted until September.

Italy Enters the War

Mussolini took Italy into the conflict on 10 June 1940, with its armed forces ill prepared for major action. But limited escorted daylight bombing raids were begun: SM79s made two raids on Malta on the 11th, and attacked French bases in Tunisia on the 12th; on the 13th, BR20s with CR42 escorts attacked targets in the south of France, including airfields. Successes included 3 Lioré 70 flying boats destroyed by bombing, six Vought 156s by strafing CR42s. On 11 June, 12 RAF Wellingtons moved to Salon in southern France to bomb Italy, but for several days were prevented from taking off; the local population feared reprisals. On the night of 11 June, 36 RAF Whitley bombers staged via the Channel Islands to make bombing attempts against Turin and Genoa. The French themselves began small night bombing raids against Northern Italy, using LeO451s and F222s. But France surrendered on 22 June. In some estimates, the short Battle of France had cost the French 757 aircraft, the RAF 959, the Luftwaffe 1065. [Terraine, 1985:164]

The German Offensive Against Britain

With the fall of France, the Germans turned their attention to Britain. On 30 June 1940, attacks began on Channel shipping and ports, primarily to draw the British fighters into battle. The first major raid came on 10 July, some 70 German aircraft (Do17, Bf110, Bf109) attacking a convoy off Dover, the raid being picked up by the CH RDF system and countered by RAF fighters. For the British, this first major air engagement was counted as the start of the Battle of Britain. On 16 July, three German air fleets (*Luftflotten*) based across the Channel and North Sea, were assigned to a daylight offensive against Britain. This was the war's largest bombing campaign yet, and the first campaign intended to achieve victory by the use of air power alone. The objective was to destroy the British fighter force, to achieve air superiority over the Channel for Operation *Seelöwe*, the intended invasion of Britain. The RAF had been forced to give up daylight bombing in December 1939 because it was unable to provide long-range escort fighters. Now, the Luftwaffe began daylight bombing on a large scale, with escorted missions against south-east England from airfields in Northern France, limited by the short range of the Bf109 escorts.

The War of Attrition over Britain

On 12 August 1940, the Germans began their raids against RAF Fighter Command's airfields, control centres and installations in south-east England. The forward fighter airfields at Manston, Hawkinge and Lympne were seriously hit; a force of Ju87s penetrated the balloon barrage at the naval base at Portsmouth; and for the first time, the Luftwaffe attacked the British early warning radar system. Five CH stations were damaged, that at Ventnor being put out of action for 11 days. *Adlerangriff*, the all-out effort against Britain on 13 August, was disrupted by poor weather. The really big attack came on the 15th, with over 2,000 sorties and for the first and only time, daylight attacks on northern Britain from across the North Sea. But the latter, without Bf109 escorts because of the range, proved too costly, and the campaign thereafter continued against south-east England only.

The daily air battles gave serious losses to both sides, the Luftwaffe's bombers receiving a mauling despite the escorts. But after 15 August, the Germans believed that four more days of heavy air raids would finish the RAF's ability to fight. In reality, British fighter production and repair had increased sharply and the RAF's main problem, shortage of fighter pilots rather than fighters, was not yet acute. The war of attrition in the skies over Britain continued. The climax came on 15 September when Dowding, primed by 'Ultra' intercepts, judged that now was the right moment to use the RAF's fighters to the full. With Fighter Command allegedly a spent force, the effect on the German crews of encountering so many fighters was profound. Luftwaffe air superiority seemed as far away as ever. Within days the British had indications that the invasion was being postponed, although preparations continued until well into October.

In belated retaliation for the British bombing of Italy, the *Corpo Aereo Italiano*, with 40 Fiat BR20 bombers plus Fiat CR42 biplane escort fighters, moved to Belgium to aid the German air offensive against Britain, with a first (night) attack on Harwich on 25 October. Limited Italian raids against British east coast towns continued into January 1941, dropping 100kg HE bombs and incendiaries. But during October, major German daylight raids petered out, and the British came to accept 31 October as the effective end of the daylight Battle of Britain. It had already been superseded by the German night bombing of British cities. In recent estimates, during the Battle the Luftwaffe lost 1,882 aircraft, the RAF 1,255. [Terraine, 1985:219]

Strategy in the Battle of Britain
The Luftwaffe's failure to achieve its objectives made the Battle of Britain Germany's first serious setback in the war. The campaign had been an improvised short-term one, against the operational British fighters and bases within easy reach; without drop tanks, the Bf109 fighters had only a small radius of action as escorts, and the RAF could have withdrawn its fighters out of range if need be. But the Luftwaffe had given little priority to a longer-range night offensive against Britain's other airfields, the supply ports, or the factories which had been steadily increasing the supply of fighters to the RAF. It had relied on daylight raids, giving relatively high losses, and mainly on large fixed formations (apparently intended to intimidate) rather than many small raids that might have drawn more fighters and saturated the British defence system. In addition, the Germans had failed to increase the jamming or maintain the attacks on the CH radars.

The RAF's strategy had been to ensure the survival of an effective fighter force in being, to help counter the expected landings. A fighter pilot shortage had reinforced Dowding's caution, so the fighters had been used sparingly. But confining engagements to British airspace reduced the interception rate, increased the bomb damage incurred on the British airfields, and made the air battle one of attrition. Critics were to argue later that the RAF might have destroyed German aircraft more efficiently by using either Fighter Command (by day) or Bomber Command (by night) to attack them when they were most vulnerable, namely massed on the French airfields in between raids. Aside from raids on the Ruhr, Bomber Command had made repeated attacks on the invasion ports and barges, but few on the airfields further inland. An indication of what the fighters could have done came in 1941 when Sqdn.Ldr H.R.Allen led 66 Sqdn in an unauthorized strafing attack on Lannion airfield in Brittany, the 13 Spitfires destroying 12 Ju88 bombers without loss to themselves. [Allen, 1974:174]

The Mediterranean Air War; Vichy France and Greece
With Italy in the war, the Mediterranean and North/East Africa became a new theatre of conflict. The British struck first, nine Blenheims attacking the El Adem air base early on the first morning, 11 June, when the defences were unprepared. The Italians responded on 12 June, 12 RA (*Regia Aeronautica*) aircraft bombing Sollum. The SAAF's entry began with Ju86s bombing an Italian airfield in Ethiopia on 19 June. Italian raids on Malta became an almost daily occurrence, first at high altitude, then with escort, then at night. But mostly the air conflict settled into one of mainly small-scale tactical raids, by forces operating with difficulty, often with obsolescent aircraft and spread over a large theatre; losses were difficult to replace, so conservation became the rule. In Africa, the RA had a 4:1 numerical superiority, and a bomber (the SM79) which could outpace the RAF's Gladiator biplane fighters. Escorted formations of SM79s made daylight raids on British bases, especially Alexandria, and on 16 October a single SM79 with strafing fighters destroyed 10 RAF aircraft at Gedaref. SM81s made a few night raids. But although the RA's supply route was easier, its maintenance and repair organization was inferior to that of the RAF, and Italian raid effectiveness reduced as aircraft serviceability declined. The RA itself made little effort to knock out the RAF's repair depot at Aboukir. British attacks on Italian targets in Libya were made by Blenheims by day, and by Bombays and (later) Wellingtons by night. Wellesleys from Aden bombed the Italian air base at Addis Ababa. Blenheim reconnaissance aircraft carried two 250lb bombs, dropped 'at the pilot's own initiative'.

On 24 and 25 September, Vichy French LeO45 and Martin 167 bombers from Algeria and Morocco made escorted daylight raids on the British base at Gibraltar. The

second, by 83 bombers, was larger than any raid mounted by
the *Armée de l'Air* against a German target. On 28 October,
Italy invaded Greece, bombing with escorted SM79s and
BR20s. The Royal Hellenic Air Force responded with its
handful of Blenheims, Battles and Potez 63s, using them
mostly in close support. RAF Blenheims were sent to aid the
Greeks, attacking ports and airfields, while Wellingtons
began long-range night raids on Italy from Egypt and Malta.

Daylight Bombing Tactics and Techniques

German Attacks on Aircraft on the Ground

Although in a long campaign, an enemy could replace
aircraft more easily than trained crews, in the short term the
destruction of the aircraft alone could be decisive. During
1940, the Germans showed repeatedly that enemy aircraft
could be destroyed efficiently by catching them on the
ground; stationary targets were easier to hit. On 9 April,
Bf110 heavy fighters used surprise strafing attacks to destroy
the small Norwegian *Haerens Flyvapen* at its main bases at
Fornebu and Sola. Then, during the German Western
offensive, many more attacks were made on airfields.
Normally, these used an approach at low level for surprise,
the raids being led by strafing Bf110s. The following
bombers released time-delay bombs enabling all aircraft to
get clear. On 11 May, Do17s destroyed a squadron of
Blenheims lined up at Conde-Vraux. On 19 May, 12 He111
bombers wrecked 40 of the 50 LeO451 bombers at
Persan-Beaumont. Successes during the Battle of Britain
included: on 13 August at Detling, 22 aircraft destroyed by
Ju87s; on 15 August at Driffield, 10 Whitleys destroyed by
Ju88s; on 16 August at Brize Norton, 46 aircraft destroyed
by just two Ju88s. Such results, and Britain's need to stave
off imminent invasion, make the RAF's policy of attacking
targets in the Ruhr, rather than the German aircraft massed
on the airfields of Northern France, a surprising one.

The Vulnerability of Bombers in Daylight; the Ju87 Stuka

The air battles of 1940 confirmed that in daylight, most bombers were vulnerable even with an escort. Allied light bombers suffered crippling losses in France, and even the modern medium bombers of the Luftwaffe, flown by practised crews and mostly with strong fighter cover, experienced major losses. In the Battle of Britain, on 15 August, 7 of 50 Ju88s of KG30 making the long North Sea crossing in daylight without escort were shot down by RAF fighters; the Luftwaffe flew no more such raids. On the British side, despite all Bomber Command's previous experience, Blenheims were sent on unescorted daylight bombing attacks on German-held airfields, e.g. 9 July (Stavanger in Norway, 7 out of 12 shot down) and 13 August (Aalborg in Denmark, all 11 shot down); neither airfield was playing a major role in the Battle of Britain. Seemingly, these German and British experiences with unescorted daylight bombing had little effect on USAAC planning.

For the Ju87 dive-bomber especially, prior local air superiority was proving essential. On 12 May, French Curtiss Hawk fighters shot down all 12 Ju87s in one unescorted group and several in another. Even with escorts, the Ju87s still had to peel from formation for a strike, and could be pounced on while unprotected, climbing to reassemble; with no dive-brakes, the escort fighters were unable to stay with them during the dive. With major losses over Britain, after 18 August the Ju87s were withdrawn, the intention being to reintroduce them for close support in the invasion itself. Meanwhile, in May, French land-based naval Vought V-156 dive-bombers had also suffered heavy losses.

German Bomber Formations

During the Battle of Britain, the Luftwaffe mounted many raids by large groups of bombers. Normally they flew in a tight formation in Vee's of three aircraft, taking off as a Vee in the case of a grass field, otherwise taking off singly and forming up once airborne. A tight formation enabled mutual defence against fighters, and reduced the number of rounds that could be fired at the bombers by any given AA site. But it took time and fuel to build up, and as the USAAF was to find later, it had its own risks: inadvertent bomb hits from aircraft above, if the formation got distorted; inadvertent gun hits from adjacent bombers when under attack; and collisions from other bombers, especially if one was hit and out of control. Typically, the German bombers took off in pre-set sequence, then would rendezvous and circle at low altitude, gradually assembling into the required formation, and then climb on course for the target. The short-range fighters took off last, from the airfields closest to the coast, and climbed to join the bombers as they crossed the French coast at the chosen raid altitude. Over the target, the bombers maintained formation if enemy fighters were present, otherwise bombed at leisure, including from low altitude if AA fire was light. Individual bombing was the norm, but pattern bombing by a formation was used at times, via radio direction from the formation commander.

German Bomber Tactics: Decoys and Co-ordinated Attacks

Heavy losses by the Luftwaffe over Britain on 15 August 1940 led Göring to issue a directive banning German bomber crews from having more than one commissioned officer per crew. Meanwhile, new tactics were being tried against the British defences. During August, the Luftwaffe assigned 7/KG3 as the *Lock-Vogel* (decoy bird) *Staffel*. The unit's task was to fly its Do17 bombers, without bombs in order to improve performance, in a tight formation over Britain, to entice the RAF's fighters to attack. Bf109 units flew high above the decoy force, ready to pounce. [Townsend, 1970:350] On 18 August, the Luftwaffe attempted co-ordinated high and low level raids on the Fighter Command sector station at Kenley. Escorted high-level bombers (He111, Do17 and Ju88) were intended to draw the AA fire and fighters while nine Do17s, flying near line-abreast to avoid each other's slipstream, sneaked in for a surprise low-level attack. But the high-level bombers were delayed, the Do17s took the undivided defence action and only two survived. Even so, three of Kenley's four hangars were destroyed, along with eleven RAF aircraft. On 24 August, the Luftwaffe began varied patrols and feints over the Channel, the formations concealing the build-up for genuine attacks.

German Escort Fighter Tactics: the Failure of the Bf110
Although faster than a Hurricane and having a formidable forward-firing armament, the Messerschmitt Bf110 heavy fighter could not match the manoeuvrability and acceleration of a single-engine interceptor. Encountering such fighters on sweeps over France in May, Bf110 pilots resorted to forming a 'Lufbery' defensive circle. Introduced against Britain in an escort role, which required attempts at dogfighting to keep enemy fighters away from the bombers, the Bf110 proved a disappointment. On 15 August, 21 Bf110D fighters flew escort for He111 bombers from Stavanger; intercepted by RAF fighters, some Bf110s were shot down, others abandoned the bombers – some forming a Lufbery, others turning for home. After subsequent losses, the Germans attempted an inefficient concept in which the Bf110 escort fighters were themselves escorted by Bf109 single-seat fighters. Clearly the heavy escort fighter was not viable, and the Bf110 was withdrawn from the role, the Luftwaffe relying thereafter on the single-engine fighters only, despite their poor range without drop tanks.

Meanwhile, continuing bomber losses brought a Göring directive requiring escort fighters to remain close to the bombers, thereby handing the air fighting initiative to the RAF. Although a high escort was flown, most Bf109s flew at either side, above and below the bombers. Tied in this way, the German fighters lost the speed, height and freedom of action needed to counter the British attacks. Although limited fighter sweeps were implemented ahead of the bombers, the escort fighters were now prevented from chasing and destroying the British fighters, even though this was the Luftwaffe's stated primary objective.

German Introduction of Strategic Fighter-bombers
Luftwaffe Bf109E and Bf110C *Jagdbomber* fighter-bombers had already carried out low-level bombing attacks against shipping and against the British CH radar stations. But in September 1940, they were introduced for high-level strategic bombing, Göring apparently reasoning that as the fighters had failed to provide adequate escort protection for the bombers, the fighters should carry the bombs themselves. Seven fighter wings each began conversion of

one squadron into fighter-bombers, the Bf109 to carry one 250kg bomb, the Bf110 two 250kg bombs and four 50kg bombs. The first operational use came on 24 September, in a raid on the Supermarine factory at Southampton. Early raids were made at around 18,000ft, with fighters escorting a central group of fighter-bombers, but British fighter pilots soon made the inner group the primary target. In response, raid altitudes were increased, and the fighter-bombers spread through the whole formation.

The experiment was no great success. Bomb loads were small (nuisance only), bomb aiming was rudimentary, and the pilots were eager to release their bombs as early as possible in order to revert to their 'real' role, as fighter pilots. [Galland, 1959:50-1] Nevertheless, the British found these escorted fighter-bombers difficult to counter when they began to fly at altitudes of 30,000ft or more.

Night Bombing

The First Leaflet Raids of the War; Leaflet Balloons
On Britain's first night of war on 3 September 1939, ten RAF Whitley bombers dropped 13 tons of propaganda leaflets over Hamburg, Bremen and the Ruhr, in the first of many such raids under Operation 'Nickel'. Leaflet drops were also soon implemented by the French in Germany, by the Germans in Poland (apparently along with bank notes to depreciate the currency) and by the Soviets in Finland. But a sceptical Air Ministry saw the RAF's leaflet raids as 'special reconnaissance missions', providing practice in night navigation and target finding over blacked-out enemy territory. Later in the war, RAF Operational Training Units were to drop leaflets into German-occupied countries, while main force bombers carried leaflets along with their bomb loads on raids into Germany itself. The British leaflets ('Nickels') eventually saw a variety of forms: single sheets, booklets, newspapers, forged ration cards, etc. Britain's No.1 (and only) Balloon Unit began launches of

leaflet-carrying balloons from France on 30 September 1939, the balloons drifting eastwards over Germany. The hydrogen-filled balloons carried bundles of leaflets tied on by string. A slow-burning wick burned through the string pieces, releasing bundles periodically.

The British Adopt Night Strategic Bombing; the Target Visibility Problem

For the RAF, the main conclusion from the disastrous daylight raid on 18 December 1939 was inescapable: the loss rate was ten times the level Bomber Command had estimated it could afford. But the alternative was already clear. For three months, Whitley bombers had been roaming at will across Germany at night, dropping leaflets; and the Germans were making little effort to improve their AA and night fighter defences to stop them, even though these leaflet raids were clearly giving useful experience for night strategic bombing. But the visibility of landmarks and targets from the air at night was questionable. A Bomber Command report in October had noted that under moonlit but ground blackout conditions it would be impossible to see separate buildings, let alone features like tall chimneys or towers, from normal bombing heights. So, in February 1940 five Whitleys were sent over Germany to investigate the ability to see and identify rivers, cooling towers, marshalling yards, etc. from different altitudes. One crew got lost, others reported some success in three-quarter moon conditions for altitudes up to 8,000ft. But searchlight dazzle made visibility much worse; if British night bombing caused the Germans to deploy more searchlights, the prospects for accurate bombing would deteriorate unless new aids could be provided.

Hörnum; British and German use of Parachute Flares

The first RAF night bombing raid, by 50 Whitley and Hampden bombers on the German seaplane base at Hörnum, Isle of Sylt, on 19 March 1940, was in retaliation for a Luftwaffe attack on Scapa Flow on 16 March. Using flares for illumination, 41 crews claimed to have bombed the target, but subsequent PR coverage showed little evidence of damage. In trying to use flares for ground identification, the RAF found that the dropping aircraft moved too far ahead of the illumination given by a standard 4.5-inch parachute flare. Various solutions were considered: use of several aircraft at intervals; use of flash bombs having much greater brightness, albeit of short duration; and use of an electrically ignited flare towed behind the aircraft rather than being dropped. Eventually a 5.5-inch parachute flare was developed, to give brighter, longer duration burning, but dropping at intervals by a series of aircraft was still needed.

The Germans with their blind-bombing radio aids had less need of flares than the British. Nevertheless, the Luftwaffe introduced LC50 parachute flares for night raids on Britain. Probable first uses were: for position fixing, 5 June 1940 over Norwich; for target identification and illumination, 5 August over the Isle of Sheppey; and as route markers, 15 September over the North Sea. It became Luftwaffe practice to use red, green or yellow flares for route marking; and white flares for ground illumination, dropped singly or in packs of four. The British public called these brilliant white and coloured flares 'chandelier flares'. With the British success in jamming the *Knickebein* system, by October the Luftwaffe's II/KG55 was at times resorting to using flares for target illumination during night attacks on Britain.

Diversion of Bombers: Minelaying; the Clandestine War

On the night of 20 November 1939, German He115 floatplanes had begun the first ever air minelaying campaign, dropping LM-A and LM-B magnetic mines off the British coast. On 2 April 1940, the minelaying effort was increased by the first use of bombers in this role, He111s being diverted for the task. On 13 April, RAF Hampdens were used to drop mines ('vegetables') in the first British use of bombers for minelaying ('gardening').

While leaflet raids and minelaying continued, small scale diversion of bombers to the clandestine war was under way. In August 1940, German He111 bombers dropped supplies and empty parachutes into Britain to instil fear of an active Fifth Column; then an unmarked black He111 from Chartres parachuted the first two German agents into Britain, near Salisbury. This was the start of considerable secret traffic, carried out by all of the combatants, much of it using bombers at night. As resistance groups began to form in occupied territory, the dropping – and picking up – of agents was accompanied by much larger drops of weapons and other supplies. On the Allied side, the major missions were flown by RAF and US bombers on behalf of the SOE and OSS respectively.

Routing and Attack Techniques; Time-and-bearing; the Bassingbourn Error

For the early British night raids, most sorties were individual ones; the tight bomber stream awaited the coming of 'Gee'. The pre-flight briefing gave no prescribed route, time of attack, or bombing altitude. Each crew made its own way, and bombed as convenient. Some crews desynchronized engines to foil sound locators (as did many German crews). Some preferred to bomb from as high as possible to reduce AA accuracy. Others adopted a glide approach with the engines throttled back, to counter sound locators and cause the radar (if any) to give a misleading altitude setting for the flak. To try to improve night bombing in the absence of radio aids, in January 1940 Bomber Command began exercises employing timed directional runs from a recognizable landmark near the target, and then bombing blind. The technique was first used in June, with Rotterdam as the landmark for an attack on a troop concentration 35 miles away. But even for short timed runs, blind bombing by such methods gave poor accuracy. 'Bombing on ETA' (Estimated Time of Arrival over the target) became discredited as a policy, although still used by individual crews. But the difficulty of inflicting real damage by bombing was also becoming more evident. On the night of 27 May, a magnetic storm upset the compass of a Whitley sent to attack an airfield in Holland. The crew, lost, mistook the Thames estuary for the Rhine and bombed RAF Bassingbourn instead. This mistake gave Bomber Command an opportunity to make a direct assessment of its bomb damage in a realistic case, but the ordnance experts were discouraged to find the damage so slight. One result was increased interest in bigger bombs.

Civilians Become the Main Target: The Switch to Attacking Cities

On the world scene, bombing of cities (by the Japanese, Germans, Soviets, and British) had been escalating steadily. In the bombing war between Britain and Germany, the British were the first to attack a mainland population centre [Rumpf, 1963:24], 36 Whitley and Hampden bombers attacking the rail centre of Mönchen Gladbach on the night of 10 May 1940, killing just one person – an Englishwoman. Then, on the night of 15 May, the RAF carried out its first major night bombing raid, all 99 serviceable bombers being sent to attack oil and rail targets in the Ruhr. For the RAF, as for the Luftwaffe, the bombing at this period was still largely confined to military/strategic targets. In June, RAF crews received instructions to bring their bombs home if they could not clearly identify the chosen target. Meanwhile, on the night of 7 June, a solitary French Navy Farman 223.4 made the first token Allied bombing raid on Berlin. During the Battle of Britain, Bomber Command's own priority remained the strategic bombing of Germany. For the Germans, heavy raids on 24 August resulted in the airfield at Manston being abandoned by the RAF, while other vital fighter airfields also sustained severe damage. The strikes on the Fighter Command airfields and sector communications were beginning to succeed. But that night, He111s sent to attack oil installations at Thameshaven, dropped bombs in 16 different places in east and south-west London, [Ramsey, 1987:247], reportedly by mistake. That mistake altered the course of the Battle. In retaliation, on the following night 80 RAF Wellington, Hampden and Whitley bombers were despatched to Berlin. Some 21 crews claimed to have bombed the city, although apparently only two Berliners were slightly injured, most bombs falling in open country. But Hitler reacted by ordering an intensive bombing campaign against British cities. Now, for the first time in the war, the aim was widespread systematic destruction by bombing, to crush civilian morale. London was to receive day and night raids, cities too far away for fighter escort would receive only night raids.

The First Night Bombing Campaign: the German 'Blitz'
on Britain
Small-scale night raids on Britain had served to train
German crews, but also accustomed the British to air attacks
and helped to get their civil and AA defence system
operating smoothly, although the AA capability remained
small. Now, the first major night bombing campaign of the
war began on 28 August, when Liverpool was attacked by
around 160 bombers on four successive nights. Meanwhile,
RAF raids against Berlin followed on 28, 30 and 31 August,
and 1, 4 and 6 September. But with much shorter ranges to
travel, and many more aircraft, the German bombing
capability against Britain greatly exceeded the British
bombing capability against Germany; and those raids on
Berlin provoked the onslaught on London. On the
afternoon of 7 September, 300 bombers carried out the first
heavy raid on London, the fires serving to guide a further
250 bombers that night. The night raid brought, in the
Surrey Docks area, the first man-made 'firestorm' – albeit on
a smaller scale than those later wrought on Germany. The
change of policy reduced Luftwaffe losses, more aircraft
being lost at night from navigation errors and accidents than
from British defence action, but it relieved the pressure on
the RAF's airfields. By 13 November, London had been
bombed on 67 consecutive nights except one, by an average
of 160 aircraft. It seems that some Spanish Air Force
personnel took part in the night bombing. The German raids
resulted in widespread damage, casualties, lost sleep, and
much disruption, with unexploded bombs (UXBs, malfunc-
tioning or delay fused) adding considerably to the difficulties
of civil defence. The introduction of 'land mines', especially,
signalled that the Germans had adopted 'area bombing'
against civilians, and this increased calls for retaliation in
kind, with the development of similar weapons in Britain.

German Bombing versus British Defences
By mid-1940, the Luftwaffe was exploiting Britain's
inadequate searchlight coverage. Many raids were routed up
a central unlit corridor which ensured their concealment;
searchlights and AA defences themselves denoted important
targets; their locations became known, the searchlights

acting as 'landmarks' for the German crews, helping them to steer around the AA defences and towards the required target. Meanwhile, in June, German night raiders began attacking the searchlights, flying down the beams and firing their machine guns before pulling out. Realizing that their AA defences were aiding the enemy aircraft while being ineffective at shooting them down, the British implemented new measures: at times keeping the ground defences inactive; firing AA guns by GL radar alone, the searchlights remaining switched off; operating searchlights in certain areas of the country only, varying these from night to night; and finally, keeping searchlights switched off, except when trying to pick up and track specific aircraft overhead. These measures gave the Luftwaffe increased difficulty.

On the night of 22 July, a Do17 of II/KG3 fell to an FIU Blenheim equipped with AI Mk.III radar; this was the first occasion when a bomber was shot down by a radar night fighter, but further instances were to remain rare for some time. The Germans had themselves introduced decoy lighting to help lead British bombers astray, now the British also introduced decoy factories (including night ones: QL-type with lights, and QF-type with dummy fires if the site was attacked); dummy airfields (K-type for day, and Q-type for night); then large decoy fire sites (SF-type, or 'Starfish') for cities. The early Starfish were unrealistic, but the Luftwaffe dropped 66 bombs on a Starfish near Bristol on 2 December 1940. Some Q-type airfields were bombed even when the same site had been recognized as a K-type dummy. For London itself, lacking resources for a full AA defence, the British had relied on a 'Fixed Azimuth System' with available guns, searchlights and sound locators concentrated along both sides of the Thames estuary, the expected approach route for enemy bombers. But fires still burning from the previous night's raid, and the use of radio beams for navigation, enabled the German crews to bomb London from the south instead. In addition, the bombers flew with desynchronized engines and were often too high to be picked up by the sound locators.

Luftwaffe Innovations: Fire-lighter Groups; Larger Bombs; Crocodiles

In an attack on Sheffield on the night of 15 September 1940,

He111 bombers of KGr100 used *X-Verfahren* to drop incendiary bombs instead of mainly HE bombs. The result was an intense *Brandbombfeld* (fire bomb field), in which the brilliant white light given by the B1E1 magnesium incendiaries was visible even through overcast cloud. With this experience, in October KGr100 became the first *Beleuchtergruppe* (fire-lighter group) – effectively a pathfinder unit, although the Germans did not use that term *Pfadfinder*) until after the RAF adopted it. KGr100 used *X-Verfahren* to blind-bomb the target with incendiaries, to mark it visually for the main bomber force following. To minimize diffusion of bombing and the effect of decoy fires, some of KGr100's aircraft followed at intervals in the main force to re-mark the centre of the target area. This technique was first used for the Coventry raid on 14 November. The Luftwaffe set up two further fire-lighting groups in November: III/KG26 using *Y-Verfahren*; and II/KG55 having no radio aids, relying instead on experienced crews using conventional navigation.

In November, III/KG26 and II/KG55 began using later model He111 bombers having wing racks able to carry 500kg bombs. It became Luftwaffe practice to drop these larger bombs early in a raid, to fracture gas and water mains and thereby promote fires and hamper firefighting. The idea was subsequently copied by the British. On typical night raids during the early period of the Blitz, the Luftwaffe spaced its bombers at around 12-mile intervals in long, often indirectly routed *Krocodil* streams, with up to seven miles spread either side of the track, and considerable altitude dispersion. A large raid continued right through the long hours of the winter night. He111s carrying 32 BSK36 incendiary containers could drop them at 50m intervals, giving a 1.5km-long path of fire. For maximum harassment on smaller raids, crews were at times instructed to loiter over the target, dropping say one bomb every five minutes; there was little risk from fighters or from the limited, and rather inaccurate, flak.

The Coventry and Mannheim Raids

Claims [Winterbottom, 1974:82] that the British had prior warning of the German *Mondscheinserenade/Korn* raid, but chose not to act on it in order to preserve the secrecy of

Ultra, have been disputed [R.V. Jones, 1978:200]. The raid on Coventry on the night of 14 November 1940, was the war's most destructive yet, with 469 bombers in three streams dropping over 500 tons of bombs. Factories were the main targets, but 20,000 houses were destroyed and 554 people killed. KGr100 provided the target marking, using the *X-Verfahren* transmitters at Cherbourg and Calais. Later crews had little need of guidance, the burning city being visible on the horizon while the bombers were still over northern France. Britain's night defences were still minimal and the Germans lost only one bomber. The raid shocked the world, but within five days virtually all of the city's factories were back in production. Coventry's casualties and destruction were small compared with those to be meted out on German cities later in the war.

Ordered by Churchill as a reprisal for the Coventry bombing, Operation 'Abigail-Rachel', an attack by 134 bombers on Mannheim on 16 December 1940, was the first RAF raid to have a city itself as the target, rather than factories or marshalling yards within the city. For the first time also, the RAF used the pathfinder concept, long before the Pathfinder Force was set up. Crews were instructed to aim at incendiaries dropped by Wellingtons spearheading the raid. But, although the weather was clear, many incendiaries went wide and little damage was achieved.

Despite all the experimenting, as the year ended the RAF night bomber crews' inability to find and bomb the correct target was still prevalent and still not fully appreciated. At this time Bomber Command was still assigned primarily to attacking small oil targets, which were far from easy to find. In December, after supposed heavy attacks on two oil plants at Gelsenkirchen, PR photos showed little damage to either. In mid-December, the Swiss protested at British bombs dropped on Zurich. [Piekalkiewicz, 1985:100]

III 1941

Bomber Developments

New Bombers

New bombers making their first flights in 1941 included: the four-engined Avro 683 Lancaster heavy bomber (Britain, 9 January); the twin-engined Junkers Ju288 (Germany, January), a bulbous-nosed further development of the Ju88, with an armament using remotely controlled barbettes; the twin-engined Samolet-103/KB-103/ANT-58 precursor of the very successful Tupolev Tu-2 medium and dive-bomber (USSR, 29 January); the twin-engined Martin Baltimore (USA, 14 June), designed to British requirements as a replacement for the Maryland; the massive, four-engined Douglas XB-19 (USA, 27 June); the twin-engined Lockheed Ventura (USA, 31 July), a militarized version of the civil Lockheed Model 18, to British requirements for the RAF; the Breda 201 single-seat single-engine dive-bomber (Italy); and the DAR-10F two-seat single-engine dive-bomber (Bulgaria), inspired by the Polish PZL P-23.

The largest bomber of its day, but built in prototype form only, the 212ft span XB-19 carried a combat crew of 16, two additional flight mechanics and a relief crew of six; it had a galley for hot meals, and a relief crew compartment with eight seats and six bunks. Powered by four Merlin engines, the Lancaster was developed from the coupled-engined Manchester. Although similar to the Stirling and Halifax, it had better performance and achieved a lower loss rate. It became the RAF's principal heavy bomber, rated by Harris as 'without exception the finest bomber of the war'.

New bombers reaching service in 1941 included: the Consolidated B-24 (initially for transport and maritime use); Mitsubishi G4M ('Betty'); Mitsubishi Ki-46 ('Dinah'); Nakajima Ki-49 *Donryu* ('Helen'); Avro Lancaster; Martin

B-26 Marauder; Dornier Do217; and Sukhoi Su-2.

Diesel-type aero engines promised improved fuel consumption with a less flammable fuel, but were heavy and only the Germans and Soviets had major development programmes for them. The Soviets introduced the war's only diesel-engined heavy bombers, some Pe-8s being re-engined with M-40 (later redesignated ACh-40) diesel engines; but the engines had received insufficient development to be reliable. In Germany, manned turret development lagged well behind British and US achievements, but a bigger advance, the remotely-controlled gun barbette entered service in 1941, on the Me210. This FDL131 (*Fernbetätigte Drehlafette*) system used a control handle to cause gears and linkages to clutch in two electrically driven friction drums, to move the gun in azimuth and elevation respectively. The improved FDSL system followed.

Bomber Projects; the British Glider-bomber; Bombers as Missiles

In November 1941, the US Army ordered prototypes of the Northrop XB-35 flying wing bomber, and the six-engined Consolidated XB-36 – a huge strategic bomber intended to be able to bomb targets in Europe from bases in the USA in the event of a German occupation of Britain. Both eventually flew in 1946. Some of the interesting bomber projects of 1941 did not materialize. Among them was the first British project for a turbojet-powered bomber; designed by the Gloster Aircraft Co., it featured four Rover W2B engines buried in pairs in the wings. Another was the Hawker P.1005, with twin Power Jets engines. In Germany, the Hs130B bomber version of the Henschel Hs130A twin-engined high-altitude reconnaissance aircraft was not built. But work began on the BV238-Land (later BV250), a land-based derivative of the very large six-engined BV238 flying boat, to be usable as a long range strategic bomber or transport aircraft; because of the high wing, the undercarriage included tall wing outriggers as well as fuselage bogies.

In Britain in 1941, the Airspeed Horsa Mk.I transport glider was adapted as a single-seat glider-bomber, the cargo hold being modified as a bomb bay to carry up to 8,250lb of bombs. This bomb-carrying glider was to be towed behind a bomber as a means of augmenting the total bomb load, the glider pilot releasing his bombs on command from the bomber. The glider carried 200lb of armour for the pilot, and a dinghy. The Horsa bomber was selected in preference to a design from Miles-Hooper, and reportedly, a prototype was built before development was curtailed. Clearly, the performance of the bomber, and its ability for evasive action, would have been severely compromised by having a glider in tow.

In 1941, the Soviets were the first to use a radio-controlled explosive-filled bomber as an improvised large cruise missile. The crew of one or two baled out after setting it on course and arming the warload. Thereafter the 'drone' was controlled from an accompanying 'mother' plane, and dived to impact on the target. This Soviet use of a TB-3 bomber as a missile was followed by similar use of an SM79 (Italy, 1942), and B-17s and B-24s (USAAF 'Aphrodite' and Navy 'Anvil' programmes, 1944). The German *Beethoven/Mistel* programme of 1944 used an unmanned Ju88 bomber as the missile, controlled by a Bf109 or Fw190 fighter mounted pick-a-back atop the fuselage and separating during the dive to the target.

Weapon Developments

GP, Blast and AP Bombs

Aware that their GP (General Purpose) bombs were deficient compared with German equivalents (which had a higher Charge-Weight Ratio – 50 per cent compared with 27 per cent), in 1941 the British began two new series of HE bombs, the MC/HE (Medium Capacity) and the larger HC/HE (High Capacity), with CWRs of over 40 per cent and around 80 per cent respectively. The 1,000lb MC later became one of the RAF's most used bombs. The HC bombs were intended for maximum blast effect, and since the thin, light cases ruptured on impact, delayed action fuses were impractical for such bombs. But the first, the 2,000lb HC was dropped on a parachute like the German 'land mine' on which it was based.

A German 1,700kg SD1700 heavy fragmentation bomb, carried externally by an He111, was dropped on Cambridge on 7 January, at which time it was the heaviest bomb in operational use. The slightly larger British 4,000lb HC/HE 'Cookie' blast bomb, first dropped by a Wellington on the night of 30 March, was of much simpler design – a cylindrical canister with no nose fairing or tail unit, and (initially) dropped on a parachute.

Early in the Pacific War, Japanese and US forces used armour-piercing (AP) bombs improvised from existing large AP shells, adding mounting points and a tail. Examples included the Japanese 800kg Type 99 bomb used at Pearl Harbor, and the US 1,000lb M52. They were unsatisfactory, due to having too low an explosive content (down to 5 per cent), the case having been designed to withstand the shock of gun firing. The first US purpose-built AP bomb, the Navy's 1,600lb AP Mark 1 appeared in May 1942.

Anti-personnel and Fragmentation Bombs

As the war progressed, the combatant forces made increasing use of a variety of anti-personnel and fragmentation bombs, of individual and small clustered type, for use against 'soft' targets, breaking at detonation to produce flying pieces of shrapnel. Variations included:

Concrete bombs: The German 50kg and 250kg SBe50 and 250, and the small Italian 2kg and 3kg *Mitroglia* had walls of concrete with embedded steel fragments to increase lethality.

Wire-wound bombs: The Italian 2kg and 12kg Type 'F' bombs and various US fragmentation bombs (e.g. 23lb M40, 260lb M81) were encased in separate rings or wound coils of thick square-section steel, to break and form shrapnel; some had V-cuts to aid breaking.

Butterfly bombs: The German 2kg SD-2 *Splitterbombe* anti-personnel bombs were dropped in containers and released during the descent. To aid scatter, each bomb's cylindrical casing opened out to form two 'wings' which caused it to drift downwards spinning like a sycamore seed. Some were dropped over Ipswich on 27 October 1940. Casualties were promoted by a variety of delayed action and anti-tamper fuses, and each use required a major ground search. The SD-2 was copied in the USA as the 4lb M83.

Parafrag bombs: Some fragmentation bomb types, e.g. the British 20lb 'F' (Parachute) bomb, were given parachutes which deployed automatically to retard them rapidly after release in low-level drops, to prevent bouncing and to enable the aircraft to get well clear before detonation. The later US 120lb M86 Parafrag also incorporated a short time fuse to give detonation in mid-air.

Rodded bombs: in 1941, the Germans improvised rodded 50kg bombs (later manufactured as *Dinortstäbe*) for Ju87 attacks on Crete's airfields. The nose rod, with an 8cm diameter disc on the tip to prevent the rod embedding itself, caused the bomb to detonate some 30cm above ground level, the extra height improving the dispersal of the shrapnel. Later, on 5 September 1942, RAF Halifaxes raiding the airfield at Heraklion, Crete, dropped 250lb rodded bombs.

Hand Grenades: These were at times dropped by hand in improvised small attacks; release had to be at very low altitude to be effective.

Chemical Warfare Developments; Plague/Flea Bombs and Sprays

In 1941, the Canadian NRC set up a major new experimental CW station at Suffield, Alberta; for the British it replaced the French station in Algeria, lost after the fall of France. Other major CBW establishments followed in the USA, in 1942 (Pine Bluff and Dugway) and 1943 (Fort Detrick). The principal Allied CW development of 1941 was the discovery of DFP (di-isopropyl phosphorofluoridate), but it did not offer a great advance in toxicity. In the USSR, hydrogen cyanide was successfully compounded into a form for airborne spraying. After *Barbarossa*, the Germans were able to build up their CW capability by fitting their aircraft with copies of captured Soviet airborne chemical tanks and spraying equipment. German chemical bombs now available included the KC10, KC50 and KC250. The Germans also developed *Gasbrisanzbomben*, HE bombs incorporating a poison gas charge to incapacitate fire/rescue workers. Meanwhile, the Japanese were still using chemical weapons operationally, and reportedly had done so on a total of 876 occasions in the war against China up to June 1941. [Harris and Paxman, 1982:117]

Among BW developments in 1941, the Japanese carried out trials with plague-infested live fleas, dropping them in small aircraft bombs having a frangible case made of porcelain. Later, such fleas were successfully dispensed in mid-air by spraying from high-altitude aircraft. [Harris and Paxman, 1982:78] Elsewhere, August 1941 saw the US entry into the field of BW, the Edgwood Arsenal beginning BW development in co-operation with Britain.

Nuclear Weapon Developments: Plutonium

In July 1941, the Maud Committee in Britain made the first official recommendation to develop an atomic bomb, in a report to the British Government. In October, the British set up a small secret unit (cover-named 'Directorate of Tube Alloys') to begin work on such a bomb. The Maud Report was provided to the USA and it strongly influenced the US Government to escalate nuclear research. Meanwhile, a new possibility had emerged. In June 1940, physicists in Vienna and in the USA had independently discovered that the non-fissionable uranium 238 could absorb neutrons, transforming into a new element, later named plutonium, that ought itself to be fissionable. Now, in March 1941, physicists led by Prof. E. Lawrence, using the Berkeley cyclotron, obtained the first minute quantities of plutonium 239, and found that it could indeed be used as an alternative, and more readily obtainable, bomb material. The Americans had now adopted the more practical graphite as a nuclear pile 'moderator'; the Germans had concluded (wrongly) that it was unsuitable, and remained committed to using heavy water.

Navigation, Blind Bombing and Radar

Radar Jamming by Air-dropped Foil Strips: 'Window' and 'Düppel'

The first improvised dropping of foil strips (later 'chaff') to jam enemy radars was made by RAF Wellingtons during a raid on Benghazi in September 1941, with no obvious effect; the AA guns were in fact controlled using sound locators, not radar. Later, TRE began systematic trials with reflector strips, under the code-name 'Window', some in the form of metallized propaganda sheets, optimistically advocated as a means of disguising its true purpose. [Cruickshank, 1977:88] The strips needed to be of length equal to half the wavelength of the radar to be countered. When illuminated by the radar, each strip acted as a half-wave dipole resonating and re-radiating the signal. Released from aircraft, dispersing and drifting down in large numbers, the strips would give a huge multiple echo, swamping the radar screen. But when Window was ready, in April 1942, its use was banned to prevent the Germans discovering the secret and using it against British defence radars. In 1942 the Germans themselves tested *Düppel* foil strip reflectors (on the Düppel estate near Berlin). The effect on the German radars was so severe that Hitler banned its use, and Göring ordered the destruction of all copies of reports on it. Thus both sides held the secret, neither daring to use it, for over a year, for fear that the other side would use it against them.

British Air Navigation Developments; 'Gee'; 'Jay'
In Britain, the Butt Report stimulated work on new navigational aids for bombers. Cherwell advocated work on 'apparatus by which a bomber could follow along the German high tension grid' by receiving the very low mains frequency signals given by the power lines. [Webster and Frankland, Vol.I, 1961:248] Then the first flight experiments with ground-imaging radar were achieved on 1 November, using a Blenheim with a 9cm AI Mk.VII nose radar tilted 10 degrees downwards. Although extremely crude, the imaging demonstrated the potential for navigation and blind bombing at any range, independent of ground stations. The concept was duly pursued as 'BN' (for Blind Navigation), later as 'H2S'. Meanwhile, 'Gee' had reached pre-operational status. Gee used a master transmitter sending out regular radio pulses, and two (later three) further slave transmitters at different locations sending out further pulses at fixed time intervals after receiving the pulses from the

master. Installed on the east coast of Britain, Gee provided a grid of pulses fanning out over Western Europe. An aircraft's crew could determine its position using a receiver able to measure the time intervals between received pulses, and special charts having an overlay of hyperbolic curves. Gee was the first pulsed radio navigation aid, and the first to give area coverage usable by many aircraft travelling to different destinations at the same time. Surprisingly, Bomber Command risked trials with Gee over enemy territory and on 13 August, a Gee-equipped Wellington was lost over Germany. Hoping that the Germans had not, in fact, recovered the receiver, the British quickly implemented deception measures, including disguising the receiver as an ordinary radio TR (transmitter/receiver); camouflaging the transmitters; desynchronizing the pulses, and altering them to look like radar pulses. Finally, at the instigation of R.V.Jones, a spoof 'J' or 'Jay' beam system, copied from *Knickebein*, was set up and information leaked to German Intelligence. The spoof worked, Jay being jammed while the real Gee remained unjammed. When Jay was eventually discovered to be a hoax, jamming of it ceased, and it remained in use as a homing device for Allied aircraft right to the end of the war.

Blind Bombing: Y-Verfahren; British Tries at Radar Ranging

The 'Domino' countermeasure to the *Y-Verfahren* blind bombing system picked up the ranging signal, to amplify and relay it via the BBC TV transmitter at Alexandra Palace, the more powerful delayed signal overriding the normal return and causing the Germans to command bomb release short of the target. *Y-Verfahren* was first disrupted in February 1941. Then in May, examination of the equipment in crashed KG26 He111s enabled the British to devise 'Benjamin', a simpler jammer.

Meanwhile, TRE adapted a CHL early warning radar for ranging in blind bombing, used with an IFF set carried by the bomber as a pulse repeater. In April, this ranging system was first used in further attacks on the German radio beam station near Cherbourg. The Wellington bomber homed along the German beam towards its source, maintaining course and releasing its bombs on radio command from the CHL station. Such attempts remained unsuccessful. For providing a bearing to more general targets, the first approach was TRE's 'Howler Chaser', giving an audio signal which increased in pitch as the bomber deviated either side, as judged by the split beam of the CHL radar aligned with the target. A second approach was the 'Bailie beam', the aircraft flying along a composite (dot-dash) *Knickebein*-type radio beam devised by G.Bailie at RAE. In October, under 'Operation Trinity', the CHL ranging system and the Bailie beam were used in night raids by Stirling bombers on the battleships *Scharnhorst* and *Gneisenau* in Brest harbour.

Bomber Support

Identification Developments: IFF/FuG25/Rebecca;
Lights, Colours of the Day
In 1941, the British introduced a 'universal' IFF Mk.III using a dedicated transmitter and receiver at GCI (Ground Control of Interception) stations. It was later adopted as standard for all the Allies, including the USSR. A 'distress' setting was incorporated. The first airborne IFF interrogation device, the British 'Rebecca' was fitted to RAF night fighters in 1941, for identifying returning friendly bombers. An alternative approach, dim recognition lights in the bombers' wing tips and shielded so as to be visible only from close astern, was used for a while but judged dangerous. The first IFF-type set on the Axis side, the FuG25a *Erstling* entered Luftwaffe service in August 1941, used with *Würzburg* ground radars. FuG25 remained the German standard, the replacement FuG226 *Neuling* only entering production late in the war.

As the war progressed, both the British and the Germans were usually able to learn the others' 'colours of the day' recognition signals. Crews on both sides carried Very pistols, and in an emergency at low level at night, could fire a signal which would often silence the enemy's AA fire.

Support Aircraft: Command Bomber; Twin-engined Escort Fighters

In Japan, the Army explored the use of a heavily armed and armoured bomber conversion, to carry a bomber formation commander in relative security during a bombing raid. One such conversion, of the twin-engined Nakajima Ki-49, was made under the designation Ki-80 in October 1941, but only two were built. Later, the idea was to be revived with the Kawasaki Ki-81 conversion of the Ki-48 bomber, but the prototype did not reach completion.

With twin-engined fighters now largely discredited as long range escorts for bombers (the turbocharged US P-38 being potentially the main exception, thanks to its high altitude performance), the Soviets nevertheless re-evaluated them. Those tested in 1941 included Pe-3 fighter conversions of Pe-2 bombers, and the experimental two-seat Polikarpov TIS(A) and single-seat MiG-5 (DIS). Further experiments were to come in 1944 (Pe-2I) and 1945 (ANT-63P or Tu-1 version of the Tu-2 bomber).

Bombing Casualty Survey in Britain

In Britain in autumn 1940, the decision had been made to record every enemy bomb dropped on the country, and the damage and casualties caused. In 1941, a team led by Dr S.Zuckerman carried out the first detailed casualty survey, classifying the types of injury sustained, and relating them to the cause (blast, fire, shrapnel, debris) and to proximity to the explosion; whereas blast bombs mostly left corpses intact, GP and especially fragmentation bombs often severed heads and limbs. The work was supported by experiments to observe the effects of explosions on live animals, causing some public concern when this became known. Later, in 1942, further work looked at the different casualty rates caused by six different types of German HE bomb, identifiable from shrapnel fragments and especially the tail fins. The conclusion was that, ton for ton, the smaller bombs (50kg) caused the most casualties in urban areas, by giving a greater spread of explosions. The RAF's trend remained towards heavier bombs, able to damage plant and equipment. [Zuckerman, 1978:134-7]

A detailed study by Zuckerman and Dr J.Bernal, on the

effect of bombing on two typical cities (Hull and Birmingham) found no real evidence of civilian panic or loss of morale; but the report's conclusions were misread by Cherwell and later used to justify British area bombing of German cities. [Zuckerman, 1978:143]

Ground-attack Developments and Operations

Dive-bomber Developments

In Germany, the new BZA-2 dive-bombing sight entered service on Ju88s. It incorporated an electro-mechanical calculator which used flight data to determine automatically the required release point for any dive angle and speed. Consistently accurate results were claimed. [Stahl, 1984:111] The Germans were still trying to adapt the Do217 as a dive-bomber, with wing-mounted slotted plates as an alternative to the original four-petal tail dive brake. But by autumn, the dive-bomber version had been abandoned. In the USSR, the Tu-2, designed by the Tupolev design bureau incarcerated in TsKB-29 Special Prison, was to operate as a dive-bomber as well as a conventional medium bomber. Like the Pe-2, it had underwing dive-brakes and a prone ventral gunner; armament included two fixed forward-firing cannon in the wing roots. In June, the US Army began receiving its first dive-bomber, the Douglas A-24 version of the Navy's SBD. But it was to be little used, its performance and armament being judged inadequate. The conclusion that a single seater might have better speed and manoeuvrability for close support was to lead to the Brewster XA-32. Noting continuing German success with dive-bombing, in October the Japanese began development of their first purpose-designed twin-engined dive-bomber, the Kawasaki Ki-66.

German Intruder Operations over Britain

Since July 1940, German night fighters had performed intruder sorties over Britain, catching RAF bombers returning from a raid and preparing to land. By 1941, these night operations included attacks on the bases themselves, all-black Do17Zs and Ju88Cs of NJG2 strafing and bombing the airfields, attacking buildings and aircraft. The bombs used were incendiaries and 50kg HE. Once an intruder had observed a British aircraft firing the 'colours of the day' on an approach, this was radioed to other intruders, enabling them to use the recognition signal both to silence any AA and to get an airfield's lights put on for a dummy approach, ending with an attack. But intruder operations were halted in October for over two years. Hitler wanted the RAF's *Terror Flieger* bombers destroyed over Germany where the people could see the wreckage.

Air Operations in the Mediterranean; British Identification Problems

With Italian forces failing, the Germans had moved the He111, Ju87 and Ju88 bombers of *Fliegerkorps X* to Sicily, attacking British convoys and Malta. In February 1941, part was relocated in North Africa in support of Rommel's new *Deutsches Afrika Korps*, helping to push British forces back towards Egypt. In April, the SAAF set up a pioneering Close Support Flight of Gladiators and Hartbees, providing air support 'on tap'. But that same month, the Germans transformed the military situation in the Mediterranean, with a blitzkrieg assault through Yugoslavia and Greece, including savage bombing of Belgrade, with 17,000 killed on the first day. Heavy air attacks on the airfields destroyed most of the Yugoslav and Hellenic aircraft, plus RAF aircraft in Greece, as the British withdrew to Crete. A week of air strikes preceded the German airborne invasion of Crete itself on 20 May. Elsewhere in May, at the RAF Flying Training School at Habbaniyah in Iraq, 70 Audax and Oxford training aircraft were hurriedly adapted to carry bombs and used to relieve a siege by Iraqi forces. In May and June, RAF and Vichy French aircraft clashed in the skies over Syria, the French bombing British airfields and vice versa. In June *Fliegerkorps X* moved to the Aegean and began attacks on Alexandria, Cairo and the Suez Canal. In July, RAF aircraft made attacks on German forces west of Benghazi from a secret 'landing ground "X" ' behind enemy lines. In August as British and Soviet forces invaded Persia, RAF air strikes on the Ahwaz airbase wiped out the 50 aircraft of the Persian air force. In September, the Germans announced that there would be no bombing of Egypt during the Festival of Ramadan.

The British 'Crusader' offensive in North Africa in November was supported by bombing by Blenheim, Maryland and Wellington bombers, and the new Hurricane fighter-bombers. Initially, the ground-attack operations worked well. But as the Germans counter-attacked, the RAF and SAAF at times either failed to attack or attacked Allied forces. In the mobile land war, the general difficulty of determining 'whether any particular cloud of dust was friend or foe' [Richards and Saunders, Vol.2, 1975:176] was compounded by an insufficiency of identification flags and by German use of captured British vehicles. In December, superior Allied airpower was held unused for three days because of the identification problem.

Desert Conditions; Airfields

It was often difficult to hide from air attack in the open terrain of North Africa, but air operations were themselves affected by the local conditions: searing heat by day, reducing take-off performance, distorting perspex and making airframe repairs difficult due to expansion; cold at night; sandstorms; sometimes a quagmire of mud. For the crews, the problems included the lack of water, and at times dysentery and malaria. For equipment serviceability, the major problem was sand and dust, blown by vehicles, propellers and the wind; its abrasion of perspex transparencies, and damage to engines, u/c and propeller mechanisms could exceed the attrition rate from enemy action. Maintenance and repair became a major activity, and included mobile units able to salvage aircraft crash-landed in remote areas, sometimes towing them back. New desert airfields were set up close to the front by marking out a large flat area beside a road, clearing areas of stones, erecting a windsock, and introducing tents, caravans, stores and aircraft in dispersed positions and with camouflage nets to reduce vulnerability to air attack. Dummy airfields were similarly marked out and tented, and given unserviceable and dummy aircraft, and dummy guns. Dummy airfields were bombed at times, and had 'friendly' aircraft land on them by mistake. To enable operations in the wet Algerian winter especially, some Allied airfields were given Sommerfeld tracking or (later) the US PSP (Pierced Steel Plate), the latter being much heavier and bulkier to transport but less prone to sink into the mud. When they were able eventually to advance, the RAF usually found it easier to create new airfields than to clear the ploughed, mined and booby-trapped old ones.

German Blitzkrieg in Operation 'Barbarossa'

June 1941 brought 'the most devastating pre-emptive attack ever visited by one air force upon another' [Boyd, 1977:108]. Ignoring evidence from PR sorties, intelligence reports, and foreign governments, Stalin had refused to believe that a German invasion of the USSR was imminent. VVS units were denied permission to pull back from vulnerable front-line airfields, or to disperse, camouflage and protect their aircraft. Early on 22 June, 30 He111, Ju88 and Do17 bombers began Operation 'Barbarossa', crossing the frontier at maximum altitude to avoid detection, then descending in groups of three to hit ten key Soviet airfields just as the German ground forces began rolling. At sunrise, 1,250 Luftwaffe bombers, dive-bombers and fighters began continuous attacks on 66 airfields carrying almost 70 per cent of the Soviet operational combat aircraft. The Soviets had only a few RUS-1 and -2 radars for early warning, and were unprepared anyway. Some 1,200 Soviet aircraft had been destroyed by noon, mostly on the ground; the total reached 1,800 (for 35 German aircraft lost) by the end of the first day, over 4,000 in the first week. In Berlin, Göring refused to believe the figures; in Moscow, Gen. P. Rychagov the C. in C. of the Baltic VVS, was executed.

As in previous German Blitzkrieg operations, 'Barbarossa' made widespread use of close air support, now with Luftwaffe tank liaison officers (*Panzer Vebindungs Offizier*) in UHF-equipped forward tanks, in contact with the air units. Innovations included widespread air attacks on the landline system used for communications by Soviet forces; special 15kg bombs dropped from very low level at points on the overland wire system caused great disruption. [Erickson, 1975:73]

The Soviet bomber and fighter units reacted to the onslaught as best they could, sometimes with improvisation and expediency. Then as the German front advanced and widened, the Luftwaffe's bombers were operating on more makeshift airfields, and were frequently moved laterally to where they were most needed. As their supply lines lengthened and Soviet resistance gradually stiffened, the Germans became bogged down, first by rain and mud, then from mid-November onwards, by the ice and snow of the formidable Russian winter. In desperately trying to unstall the offensive against Moscow, Bf110, He111 and Ju88 aircraft were switched to ground strafing of Soviet troop positions. But this brought severe losses from Soviet AA fire, while the reduction in raids against Moscow itself released Soviet fighter units to step up ground-attack operations against the German forces.

Eastern Front Winter Hazards

For the Germans the winter brought unexpected results with HE bombs. Those impacting on hard frozen ground were apt to shatter without detonating. Those falling into deep snow often did not detonate either, but remained as a live booby trap for personnel and vehicles, a discovery which led the Germans to strew large numbers of SD-2 bombs in key areas to hamper Soviet movements. But when a bomb did explode in deep snow, it was much less effective than normal, the snow muffling the blast. More fundamentally, the Germans found themselves struggling with starting and operating problems, including freezing glycol; and with narrow-track u/cs unsuited to snow-covered grass and earthstrips. Ski-landing gears seemed unsatisfactory, except on the light Fi156 *Storch*. When possible, trimotor Ju52/3ms were used for snow clearing, the slipstream from the three propellers blowing it away as the aircraft was taxied up and down. Generally, the Germans were ill prepared for maintenance work and the severe icing on aircraft left in the open: canvas covers froze stiff and became unmanageable; greasing of surfaces to de-ice or prevent icing was often not possible; fingers froze to bare metal; gas masks had to be worn to prevent facial frostbite; engines had to be run up at 30-minute intervals to prevent a freeze-up; rubber tyres became brittle and deteriorated; tools needed to be heated before use. Efforts were made to step up the supply of aircraft equipped with de-icing systems (hot air or pulsating boot type). Warming stoves with ducts were improvised, and later the *Zwerg* petrol-fired hot-air engine heater was introduced to alleviate cold starting problems.

By contrast, the Soviets were accustomed to the severe winter and were better prepared, with suitable clothing, equipment, airfields with facilities, and logistics. Their 'obsolete' aircraft were more manageable, using the 'Hucks' starter, air-cooled radial engines, and wide-track large-tyred u/cs. The Soviets also used insulated engine covers, each with a duct through which a 'hot air lorry' could provide a flow of heated air to warm the engine. In addition they rolled the airstrip snow to compress it, aiding take-offs and suppressing snow clouds. By December, the Soviets were flying four times as many sorties as the Germans.

Daylight Bombing

British Daylight Raids: 'Circus' and 'Cloud Cover'; use of B-17 Fortress

After 'Rhubarb' fighter sweeps had failed to draw significant Luftwaffe opposition, on 14 June the RAF began 'Circus' operations: short range escorted daylight missions into Northern France, with 2 Group Blenheim light bombers attacking airfields and industrial targets. Later, 'long range' Spitfires with increased internal tankage allowed greater radius of action. But the raids were largely ineffective with substantial losses, and failed in the objective of drawing Luftwaffe squadrons from the Eastern Front. In December, the RAF began occasional small 'cloud cover' daylight raids ('Moling' for specific targets, 'Scuttle' for targets of opportunity), in weather which would allow the bombers to remain in cloud for most of the flight, emerging below or into gaps in the cloud to find and bomb the target. But of 190 Moling sorties by mid-1942, over half were abandoned due to inadequate cloud cover; only five crews bombed their targets.

To help develop the strategic bombing capability of the (officially still neutral) USA, a secret liaison with the British was implemented. USAAF personnel in civilian clothes were assigned to Bomber Command bases, observing and attending briefings. In 1941 Britain received twenty B-17C bombers, which by US theory would allow unescorted daylight bombing at high altitude. No.90 Squadron RAF, with the Fortress I bombers, was formed in May. The high-flying Fortresses being unpressurized and unheated, crewmen aged under 25 were specially selected after fitness and oxygen tests to ensure they could withstand the 30,000ft altitude and ambient air temperature of -50 degrees C. Raids began on 8 July, with three aircraft over Germany. US advisors trained the British crews and in some cases flew on operational missions. But without a tail turret especially, the B-17C's armament proved inadequate, while the weather over northern Europe gave severe icing problems and poor visibility which compromised effectiveness, including of the Sperry Mk 0-1 bomb sight. Several broke up in mid air after Clear Air Turbulence caused a violent spiralling dive. With eight aircraft lost after only 39 sorties, the British assigned surviving Fortresses to the Middle East and Coastal Command. The Americans claimed the Fortresses had been misused by not operating them in formation, but put in train major modifications to the B-17, notably for improved armament.

German and Soviet Daylight Bombing on the Eastern Front

With the German invasion of the USSR, daylight attacks on the Soviet airfields and communications system were interspersed with raids on Moscow itself, using Ju88 and He111 bombers. On the first three days of the campaign, Moscow was attacked by 127, 115, and 100 bombers respectively. The range allowed fighter escort, although the Soviets were unable to provide much effective fighter opposition. Later, in August, the Germans made heavy fire-bombing attacks against Leningrad. But subsequently, the Luftwaffe's bombers were largely withdrawn from strategic operations, and assigned instead to tactical support for the ground forces. While this helped to speed the German offensive eastwards, by December 1941 it had also allowed the Soviets to uproot and transport some 1.5 million freight railcar loads of vital factory plant and equipment much further east, where it was now out of reach of the bombers.

As the first morning of the German invasion progressed, Soviet bomber units began to react in a manner variously characterized as 'spontaneous', 'uncoordinated', 'purposeless' and 'reckless'. [Hardesty, 1982:12] Waves of SB-2 and DB-3F bombers, often without fighter escort, were committed in raids mostly against the Luftwaffe bases in Poland. Flying in groups in clear skies, unprotected, and without taking evasive action, the bombers were easy targets for the Bf109s, and the loss rate was high. On the second day, the bombers were again committed heavily, again often without escort, but now for short-range attacks against German troop positions. Ordered to reduce bombing altitude to 1,000m to improve accuracy, and again flying straight and level as per their pre-war training exercises, they were shot down in large numbers by German flak. On 26 June, Capt.N.F.Gastello of the 207th Long Range Bomber Regiment dived his burning Il-4 bomber onto a German motorized column, in the first of 70 recorded instances of suicide ground attacks by Soviet pilots. Later, VVS bomber units adopted a 'wedge' formation of up to 12 aircraft echeloned in altitude, in a tight formation for mutual defence. But even with escorts, losses in daylight remained high. Also, it seems only lead crews had maps and mission details, so German fighter pilots learned to attack the lead bomber; with this destroyed, other crews were apt to turn back. In September 1941, two RAF Hurricane squadrons sent to Murmansk began flying escort missions for Pe-2 bombers.

Bombing in Finland's 'Continuation War'

After the German invasion of the USSR, the Soviets again attacked Finland, in a 'Continuation War' that was initially much less one-sided than the Winter War. The VVS bombed 15 Finnish towns on 25 June, but heavy engagements against the Germans prevented a sustained offensive. This enabled the Finns to release fighters from home defence, and move them forward for strafing attacks on Soviet troops, and for bomber escort, as their forces commenced recapturing territory ceded to the USSR. On 30 July, the RAF bombed Liinahamari. The Finnish bomber force of mainly Blenheims was soon supplemented by captured Soviet SB-2 and DB-3 bombers passed on by the Germans, but it remained small. It was used primarily in support of ground forces, with attacks at or close beyond the Front Line. By November, the Finnish advance brought cannon-armed Morane 406 fighters within range to support Blenheim bombers in attacking the Soviet Murmansk railway now bringing in Lend-Lease supplies.

Soviet Long-range Parasite Dive-bombers

An original concept in air warfare, the parasite dive-bomber, made a brief appearance in the USSR. After his arrest and internment, Vakhmistrov's work on parasite fighters was adapted as a means of achieving a long-range dive-bomber force. Under a *Zveno II* programme, a special unit of the 92nd Fighter Regiment was equipped with six modified TB-3 carrier aircraft and 12 I-16SPB dive-bombers (SPB for *Skorostnyi Pikriruyushchii Bombardirovshchik* – fast dive-bomber). Each carrier was to transport two SPBs (each with two 250kg FAB bombs) mounted under the wings, and release them in flight. Carrying the SPBs close to the target before release and allowing them to return to base under their own power gave a 1,200km radius of action. After the German invasion, the unit stationed in the Crimea reportedly made 30 operational sorties before being disbanded. On 10 August 1941, two TB-3s each released two SPBs in a night attack on a Danube crossing point being used by German forces, the rail bridge at Cernavada; all six aircraft returned safely.

Later (*c*.1942) the Germans were themselves to consider the use of parasite dive-bombers, apparently for anti-shipping use; in one scheme, the dive-bombers were to have been able to re-attach to the carrier aircraft for the return flight. [Baumbach, 1986:110]

Japan Strikes: the Start of the Pacific War

On 7/8 December 1941, Japanese forces began co-ordinated surprise attacks and landings, spearheaded by carrier-based air power, over a 6,000 miles spread of ocean between Hawaii and Singapore. The first and most vital attack, on the US naval base at Pearl Harbor, used 353 carrier-based aircraft: escort fighters; Nakajima B5N-2 attack bombers for high-level and torpedo bombing; and Aichi D3A1 dive-bombers. Two separate strikes were mounted, but a third was cancelled as the Japanese overestimated their success. The raid damaged much of the US Pacific Fleet and destroyed most fighters and bombers on the bases at Wheeler and Hickam, at a cost of 29 Japanese aircraft; but the four US aircraft carriers had not been present, only the battleship USS *Arizona* was permanently sunk, and the vital oil installations and workshops remained intact. The Pearl Harbor attack precipitated the US entry into the war, so effectively deciding its outcome; and in one view of the attack's implications for naval/air warfare, 'the Americans learned vital lessons at negligible cost' [Hough, 1986:79]. The air raid on Singapore was achieved before dawn; despite 30 minutes radar warning, the 17 Japanese bombers from Indo-China found the city fully illuminated, with the night fighters grounded to give the AA guns a free hand. On that same day, the Japanese struck also at Malaya, Guam, Wake, Hong Kong and, crucially, US air bases in the Philippines. The Japanese had practised overwater flights of up to 12 hours duration with the A6M-2 *Zero-sen* fighter, and this enabled them to raid the Philippines from land bases in Formosa, so freeing aircraft carriers for other operations. These raids were delayed by bad weather, during which a traumatized Gen.D.MacArthur refused to sanction either a raid by B-17s in the Philippines on the Japanese bases on Formosa, or to disperse the aircraft to greater safety [Costello, 1985:152]. Some 26 G3M and 81 G4M bombers, escorted by 89 A6M fighters, struck at the US bases, destroying 14 out of 35 B-17s, 30 out of 40 P-35 and P-40 fighters, and the sole operational EW radar in the Philippines, an SCR270 at Iba. The US managed to mount its first bombing raid on 10 December, six B-17C bombers attacking the Japanese invasion fleet off Luzon.

To support the invasion of Malaya, Japanese aircraft systematically bombed and strafed the airfields in the north, the poorly equipped British quickly withdrawing south, at times leaving stores and runways intact. By the 9th, when six Blenheim bombers made the first of the limited British counterstrikes, the Japanese had flown in 150 combat aircraft to bases in Siam. Many soon moved forward to the captured airfields in Malaya and began 'using British fuel and British bombs to attack British troops'.

Night Bombing

German Bomber 'Streaming' against Britain; Deception for 'Barbarossa'

By early 1941 the Germans were anticipating enhanced British night defences, and replaced the long *Krokodil* bomber streams (attacking over 10 hours or so) by a single tight stream, bombing for less than one hour. This took all bombers through a given area in as short a time as possible to saturate the defences. After turning, the stream might break up, some crews descending for a fast exit at well below British night fighter patrol height. Another change resulted from the British jamming of the German blind-bombing aids: the Luftwaffe shifted away from inland targets and towards coastal targets which were easier to find visually. The German bombers also now performed frequent small course shifts, which AI radar operators had difficulty in following. But despite all the changes, the loss rate to RAF night fighters was now climbing steadily.

In May 1941, the Germans needed to withdraw a large part of the Luftwaffe bomber force away from the Western Front, for use in the invasion of the USSR. To keep the withdrawal secret, the reducing night raids on Britain were accompanied by spoof radio traffic to simulate the use of larger forces. Further, on the night of 10 May, double and triple sorties were implemented from airfields in France and Belgium to achieve a total of 550 sorties for the heaviest raid on London for the whole of the Blitz. The tactic was repeated at almost the same strength on 13 May.

Overall, the German night blitz on Britain had been a comparative failure in terms of military results achieved. For the Germans, it confirmed a preference for using tactical bombing on the Eastern Front.

Night Bombing Raid Photography

The RAF had begun its night bombing with no night raid photographic capability. Efforts to overcome this had begun in 1940: initial trials with a manually opened and closed shutter on the F24 camera, and an 8-inch Photoflash Bomb dropped from under the wing; further trials with the shutter opened manually but closed by a photocell sensing the flash itself; then modification of the 4.5-inch reconnaissance flare to give the 4.5-inch Photoflash Mk.1 which could be dropped via the normal flare chute. On 5 February 1941, a Wellington successfully bombed and photographed Brest in an operational night trial. By June around 1 in 10 RAF bombers carried an F24 in the rear fuselage, and flew at the rear of the main force, for a raid accuracy assessment. The photos supplied evidence for the Butt Report, which showed the poor accuracy of the RAF's night bombing.

By the start of the German blitz on Britain, the Germans had themselves introduced night raid photography, using the BLC50 flash bomb and relying on a manually opened and closed shutter.

Initial Eastern Front German and Soviet Night Bombing

On 21 July 1941, four waves of German bombers attacked Moscow for the first time at night, with HE and incendiary bombs. The Soviets lit decoy fires, but also flew Pe-2 and SB-2 bombers as 'decoy pathfinders' dropping incendiaries to try to divert the German bombers. As the raiders turned and headed back to base after the attack, some Soviet bombers followed in an attempt to bomb the German bases as the aircraft landed. Since early July, the Soviets had themselves resorted to night bombing to reduce losses, some attacks being made with obsolete TB-3 heavy bombers. On 8 August, the Soviets began limited night strategic bombing, with the first of a series of small raids against Berlin. This first raid was made by thirteen DB-3F land-based naval bombers of the Baltic Fleet, flying from the island of Saaremaa. On the night of 11 August, Pe-8 four-engined bombers of the DA were used for the first time against Berlin, 6 of the 11 used being shot down (one by Soviet AA, by mistake).

On 1 October, the Germans began their Operation 'Typhoon' offensive against Moscow, but their air operations flown mainly from grass strips quickly became bogged down by rain and mud. The Soviets, operating from home bases with concrete runways, were better able to mount raids, using Yer-2, Pe-3 and Pe-8 bombers at night against the Luftwaffe airfields, with some escorted day raids against German forces. Having previously lost so many aircraft on the ground to German attacks, the Soviets were left with more crews than aircraft. These were now put to use, with the same aircraft making repeated sorties with alternating crews. But the daylight raids gave high losses from flak, the crews being ordered to bomb from 1,000–1,500m altitude. In October, the Soviets began a major campaign of dropping propaganda leaflets into areas of the USSR now occupied by the Germans.

British Heavy Bombers Operational; Night Formation Bombing; 'Gee'

Britain's first two four-engined heavy bomber types made their combat debuts in night raids in 1941: the Stirling on 10 February, bombing oil tanks at Rotterdam; the Halifax on 10 March, bombing Le Havre. The Stirling was disappointing, while unexplained crashes of Halifaxes were resolved by correcting the rudder overbalance which could lock the rudders hard over and cause a spiral dive. But the British now had a powerful new weapon; although use of four-engined bombers had been rare in the war, for the British (and soon for the Americans) it was to become the norm for major raids. However, in March and April, some RAF bomber crews found themselves assigned to dropping packets of tea to the people of occupied Holland. Others performed 1,161 sorties aiming 1,655 tons of bombs at the battle-cruisers *Scharnhorst* and *Gneisenau* in Brest harbour, achieving just four hits.

Around July 1941, the RAF experimented briefly with night formation flying and bombing, using small groups of Hampdens. The attempts were made on clear, moonlit nights, the aircraft being fitted with dim blue lights to aid visibility. The technique proved possible, but showed no great advantage.

On 11 August, two RAF Wellingtons made the first operational use of the 'Gee' navigation system, in a raid on Mönchen Gladbach. Gee offered more precise routing and tighter streaming of bombers to and from the target, it could be used by an unlimited number of aircraft at a time, and it did not give any transmission from the aircraft that would reveal its presence or location. Blind bombing with Gee was code-named 'Sampson', but Gee's poor accuracy at long range (around 5 miles at 400 miles from the transmitters), made it better used for general navigation and for dropping flares in the expected target area to try to obtain a visual fix on the actual target.

Night Bombing Inaccuracy; the Butt Report and Consequences

Bomber Command's performance in the first two years of the war had been poor, thanks to its small size, inability to find and bomb targets with any consistency, and the continual changing of target priorities; no single target was bombed heavily or often enough to put it out of action. But thanks to a lack of raid photography by RAF bombers, plus inadequate daylight post-raid PR coverage until mid-1941, the RAF had scarcely recognized the inaccuracy of its night bombing. Nor, it seems, did the British draw any lessons from their knowledge of German night bombing inaccuracy: of 54,000 tons of bombs dropped on Britain in two years of night bombing, 40,000 tons fell in open country; in June 1941, Dublin was bombed in mistake for Liverpool. However, the poor results from night bombing were having other influences. First, the RAF's performance encouraged German complacency with regard to the need for better night defences and dispersal of industry. Second, intelligence from US personnel in Germany regarding the ineffectiveness of the British night bombing confirmed the USAAC in its advocacy of daylight bombing, to achieve greater accuracy. But an assessment by the US military attaché in London that the serious damage caused to Britain by the German bombing had been 'really surprisingly small' [Hastings, 1979:110] caused increased scepticism in the USA as to the efficacy of strategic bombing generally.

In recognition of the accuracy problem, in July Bomber Command was directed to attack Germany's nine largest rail centres when they were visible in moonlight, and its industrial towns on other nights. But the problem was now quantified by the Butt Report on 18 August, prepared by D.M. Butt of the Cabinet Secretariat. The report's statistics showed that although on average 67 per cent of the bomber crews despatched claimed to have attacked the target, only about 20 per cent dropped their bombs within a 5-mile radius of the target. For the Ruhr with its strong defences and industrial haze, only 7 per cent of bomber crews achieved this. [Webster and Frankland, Vol.1, 1961:247] Further, although night bombing was most accurate in moonlight conditions, it was becoming less safe to operate near full moon because of the increasing losses to night fighters. In response, Cherwell proposed to Churchill the use of expert navigators, or aircraft with special navigation aids, to fly ahead of the main force, to find and mark the target; this led eventually to the RAF's Pathfinder Force. In September, the Air Staff in Britain advocated a force of 4,000 heavy bombers; Churchill was not receptive, contrasting the already high cost of the bomber offensive with the meagre results achieved.

The Soviet Night Harassment Light Bombers; Women Pilots

In September 1941, Polikarpov R-5 and U-2 (later Po-2) biplanes were pressed into VVS service as light bombers for low-level harassment raids, especially at night. After heavy losses with daylight bombing, in October the Soviets adopted mainly night bombing, with special regiments, mostly equipped with the Po-2 'LNB' (*Legkii Nochnoi Bombardirovshchik* = light night bomber) having a black finish and exhaust damper/silencers. They flew in all weathers but especially on moonlit and starlit nights. Initially they flew singly at 5 to 15 minute intervals, harassing with their constant presence over the enemy troops, forcing precautions and lost sleep. Often they cut their engines and glided down over the target area for surprise. Weapons dropped by the Po-2s included small bombs and grenades, and even – when nothing more lethal was available – bags of combustible material ignited and thrown overboard. [Boyd, 1977:131]

Uniquely, the Soviets now assigned women crews to combat missions. Many (the 'Night Witches') flew night Po-2s, others Pe-2 bombers, and fighters.

British Work on Target Marker Bombs

Although the British had improvised one in the 1920s [Saward, 1984:39], no purpose-designed target markers for night bombing had been introduced. The Luftwaffe (and later, the USAAF in the Pacific) relied on flares and conventional incendiary bombs for night target marking. But in Britain, spurred by the Butt Report, development of a purpose-built marker began late in 1941. A radio marker bomb containing a homing transmitter was abandoned due to problems of impact survival (or wind drift, if parachuted down); vulnerability to jamming; and the detection resolution needed for accurate bombing. A special pyrotechnic marker had the advantage over a simple incendiary in that distinctive colours could be used. But it proved difficult as well; one falling fast enough for accurate marking would bury itself in the ground unless it could be made to burst and ignite in mid-air prior to impact.

IV   1942

Bomber Developments

New Bombers
New bombers making their first flights in 1942 included: the twin-engined Douglas XA-26 Invader (USA, 10 January), a more powerful successor to the A-20; the twin-engined North American XB-28 (USA, April), an experimental pressurized high-altitude derivative of the B-25, with turbosupercharged engines and remotely-operated dorsal and ventral gun barbettes (the Martin XB-27, a similar high-altitude derivative of the B-26, was cancelled); the twin-engined Junkers Ju188 (Germany, spring), a development of the Ju88; the twin-engined SAAB-18 (Sweden, 19 June), a light bomber and dive-bomber for the *Flygvapnet*; the twin-engined Arado Ar440 (Germany, summer), an experimental heavy fighter-bomber; the four-engined Consolidated XB-32 heavy bomber (USA, 7 September), ordered as the back-up to the B-29, but in much smaller numbers; the four-engined Boeing XB-29 (USA, 21 September); the single-engined Curtiss A-25 dive-bomber (USA, 29 September), a land-based version of the SB2C Helldiver; the twin-engined Messerschmitt Me410 (Germany, autumn), a developed version of the unsuccessful Me210, to replace the Bf110; the Mitsubishi Ki-67 *Hiryu* (Japan, 27 December), designed for performance and ease of production, and Japan's most important bomber in the latter part of the war; the four-engined Messerschmitt Me264A (Germany, December), the *Amerika-Bomber*, flown in prototype form only; the twin-engined Focke Wulf Fw191 *Bomber-B* (Germany), with innovations which included all-electrical systems, engine nacelle gun barbettes, and novel *Multhopp-Klappe* combined wing trailing edge flaps and dive brakes; the single-engine Kocherigin OPB

(USSR), a single-seat dive-bomber.

Bombers newly entering service in 1942 included the US Martin Baltimore and Lockheed Ventura, both with the RAF; the bomber version of the De Havilland Mosquito; in Germany, the He177A heavy bomber, although it was to suffer continuing structural and engine fire problems; in Italy, the Piaggio P.108B heavy bomber. New ground-attack aircraft in service included the German Focke Wulf Fw190A-4 *Jabo* version and the twin-engined Henschel Hs129B, the latter with a variety of *Rüstsätze* conversion sets for ventral armaments and equipment; the US Vultee Vengeance dive-bomber, initially with the RAF, later as the A-31/A-35 with the USAAF; and the A-36 dive-bomber version of the North American P-51 Mustang fighter, having dive brakes although these proved to be unsatisfactory.

Bomber Technology; Bomber Projects

The Boeing B-17E introduced the war's only fully successful ventral turret, the Sperry hydraulic 'ball' turret, using a gunner on his back in a near-foetal position, firing between his legs. For safety, the turret was not manned during take-off and landing; on the B-24, it was made retractable to reduce drag when not in use; and in an emergency it could be unbolted and dropped. Another Sperry turret, the mid-upper introduced a refined firing safety cut-out which treated the two guns individually; when only one gun would hit a part of the airframe, its neighbour could keep firing. In Britain the Mk.XIV gyro-stabilized semi-automatic 'Area Sight', the most advanced vector bombsight of the war, was introduced first with the PFF late in 1942, replacing the CSBS; a US T-1 version followed in 1943. In Germany, the Fw190A-4 *Jabo* introduced a cockpit selector panel, enabling the pilot to set the bomb fuses electrically prior to the attack, with settings for dive or horizontal bombing, and with or without time delay. Supercharging via an additional engine mounted in the fuselage (the *HZ-Anlage* system) appeared on the Dornier Do217P high-altitude reconnaiss-

Bridges were not the easiest of targets: here (facing) RAF Baltimore light bombers are attacking a rail bridge over a river identified as the Bamano, at Antimo, in Italy. The area is peppered with bomb bursts, and craters from previous raids. The adjacent road bridge has two cuts in it.

Above: *Fighter-bombers en route*: aiding the British 8th Army's advance in Italy in November 1943, cannon-armed SAAF Spitfires over the swollen River Sangro, heading to attack enemy gun positions and other targets; each carries a single 250-lb bomb. These are 'tropicalized' Spitfire Vcs, the deep chin housing a Vokes engine air intake filter for a desert/dust environment.

Left: *The Japanese Army's standard bomber*: the 7-man Mitsubishi Ki-21 ('Sally') was rated by the Japanese as a heavy bomber, although its bomb load scarcely exceeded that of the three-man Boston. It was used throughout the Pacific war. This particular one was photographed by the crew of a US 5th AF B-25, moments before they shot it down into the dense Pacific island jungle.

Right: *Daylight precision pattern bombing – the War's classic example*: the Focke Wulf plant, at Marienburg, after the raid by US 8th AF B-17s, on 9 October 1943. The photo shows 500-lb bomb craters among the complex of buildings, but few in the area outside. The Germans had not been expecting an attack so far east, hence accuracy was greatly aided by the absence of flak, enabling bombing from an unusually low altitude – 11,000 to 14,000 ft.

elow: *Monte Cassino*: at the quest of Allied ground forces, on February 1944, US B-17, B-25 d B-26 bombers dropped 427 tons 500- and 1,000-lb GP bombs on e mountain-top monastery of onte Cassino in Italy. The emolition was thorough. The dead cluded over 300 women and ildren who had sought refuge in e monastery, but German troops d not been present. Since the War, e monastery has been instakingly rebuilt.

Above: *Occupational hazard*: two photos taken seconds apart during a raid by 8th AF B-17 Fortress bombers. The bombers are out of position, and in the left photo bombs are heading down towards the B-17 below, one of them about to strike the port side tailplane near the root. In the right photo, the bomb has hit; it had not fallen far enough to be armed, so did not explode, but the impact has broken the tail off, leaving it dangling. The damaged aircraft successfully bombed and returned to base. Right: *Daylight strike*: RAF crews converting from Blenheims found the Boston light bomber was 80 mph faster, with twice the bomb load and a big improvement in comfort and reliability. Here, a gaggle of RAF Bostons are bombing individually amid a few black flak bursts, during an attack on a naval stores depot at Rennes, in France, on 8 August 1943.

Overlord Operations: the 5-man B-25 Mitchell medium bomber served with US, RA and Commonwealth units, a over 800 were supplied to th USSR. Here, AEAF Mitchells, in D-Day invasio markings, are pattern bombing a target in Normar in June 1944, dropping 500-bombs. The formation is impressively tight.

Limitations on daylight precision bombing: 15th AF B-17s raid the Wiener Neustadt Bf109 factory, near Vienna. Some bomb bursts appear to be in open country, but the photo also illustrates a serious limitation for daylight bombing: the target quickly became obscured by smoke and dust, preventing accurate aiming by later formations. Paradoxically, on RAF night raids the pyrotechnic markers often remained visible, even through considerable smoke.

'Reaping the whirlwind': Göbbels ordered the evacuation of a million people from Berlin, but the 49,400 tons of bombs dropped by the RAF on Germany's capital still took a considerable toll. Here, some of the dead from an RAF raid in December 1943 are laid out for identification in a Berlin gymnasium, which had previously been decorated with Christmas trees.

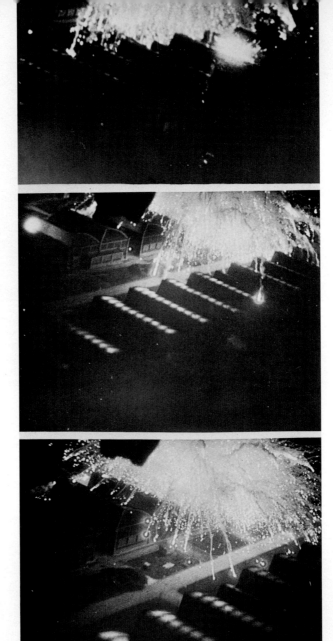

Precision low-level night marking: the RAF's raid on the undefended Gnome-Rhône aero-engine factory at Limoges, on the night of 8 February 1944, began with dummy bombing runs to enable the workforce to reach the shelters. Then, as shown by these cine stills taken from 'Master Bomber' Cheshire's Lancaster, marker incendiaries were dropped from 200 ft to cascade over the roofs of the factory, for the bomber crews to aim at.

US 9th Air Force en route: despite a high initial accident rate, largely due to an exceptionally high wing loading, the Martin B-26 Marauder medium bomber became a 9th AF success. Here, B-26s of the 9th AF head out for a major daylight raid on the German E-boat pens at Ijmuiden, Holland, on 26 March 1944.

FIDO in action: fog was a major operational problem in northern Europe. Here a Lancaster takes off, at RAF Graveley, using FIDO, dispersing fog by the heat from burning petrol from pipelines either side of the runway. FIDO's flames were often visible through the fog layer from some considerable distance, and attracted the crews of other aircraft in the neighbourhood.

Ground-attack sorties: the abrasive limestone dust on the temporary Allied airstrips in Normandy was an unexpected threat, eventually treated by spraying the airstrips with oil or sea-water. Here, 2TAF rocket- and cannon-armed Typhoons have dust plumes as they take off for a close-support operation, summer 1944; less than 30 minutes later they were back.

Mustang pilot's 'day out': cine stills taken from an RAF Mustang flown by Canadian F/O Duncan Grant during a single ground-attack sortie over northern France, when he shot up seven trains and four parked aircraft in 37 minutes. Picture numbers 1 to 7, and 12 show attacks on trains; numbers 8 to 11 show attacks on Fw190s on one airfield. Bf109s on another.

ance bomber. In September, Göring admitted that demanding a dive-bombing capability from the He177 had been 'asinine'; and with the Me210 also rendered 'useless' by compromising it for dive-bombing, a post-war German view was that pursuing the dive-bomber concept generally had 'brought ultimate ruin to the Luftwaffe' [Faber, 1979:152].

The bomber projects of 1942 which did not materialize included some advanced ones. In the USA, the Martin XB-33A Super Marauder was cancelled with two prototypes nearing completion. In Britain, proposals were made for a giant long-range bomber, similar to the US B-36; the Bristol design, adapted for the post-war 'Brabazon' airliner, featured a 'V' tail plus eight radial engines buried in the wings and geared in pairs to drive four pusher propellers. German projects included one for a fast precision bomber version of the Me155 fighter. A Dornier projected high-speed unarmed intruder bomber of novel twin-engined (fore and aft) push-pull layout became the Do335. A revised requirement for an aircraft able to bomb New York from bases in Europe brought competing proposals from Junkers (Ju390), Focke Wulf (Ta400) and Messerschmitt (Me264B, a six-engined derivative of the Me264A). Projected turbojet-powered bombers included the British Armstrong Whitworth AW50, a four-jet laminar-flow flying wing design.

The Boeing B-29 Superfortress

By far the most important new bomber, the four-engined B-29 Superfortress was the only true second generation heavy bomber to see major service during the war. It was larger and heavier, more powerful (turbosupercharged 2,200hp Wright R-3350 Cyclone radials) more advanced and more complex than previous production bombers, with all-round greater performance. It was the first heavy bomber to have pressurized crew compartments, for the cockpit, amidships and tail, with connecting crawl-tunnels; to avoid explosive decompression when hit, the compartments were to be depressurized when hostile action was expected, the crews reverting to the use of oxygen. Except for the (hydraulic) wheel brakes, its systems were electrical, as wiring was thought less susceptible to battle damage than hydraulic pipework, and easier to repair. Since Sperry periscope-sighted individually controlled gun barbettes gave inadequate fields of view, General Electric developed a computerized central fire control barbette system, with all except the tail guns operated from remote stations with viewing blisters; any gunner except the tail gunner could operate more than one barbette at a time. The computer made automatic corrections for speed, range, temperature, altitude, wind, deflection lead and bullet drop.

Weapon Developments

HE and Incendiary Bombs; Rocket-assisted Bombs

The war's largest bomb yet, the British 8,000lb HC/HE bomb (essentially two 4,000lb HC canisters in tandem) was first used in a night raid on Essen on 10 April 1942. The Halifax carrying it could only reach 11,000ft, where it was exposed to medium as well as heavy flak and was severely damaged. The crew had instructions not to drop the bomb if cloud would prevent observation of the explosion, but it was seen to explode with a 'tremendous orange flame'. [Renaut, 1982:75] Despite the difficulties, the British heavy bombers' ability to carry such large bombs gave the RAF extra effectiveness and flexibility. Among fragmentation bombs, the British 8lb 'F' airfield denial bomb was intended to be strewn across enemy airfields, and was fitted with anti-tamper and delayed action fuses. The Japanese introduced multiple scattering 'baby bombs', dropped in clusters or released in sequence from auxiliary bomb racks, to destroy parked aircraft. The US made limited use of the air-to-air Mk.34 5lb anti-aircraft bomb against ground targets. In 1942, the Germans introduced the 50kg *Sprengbrand* C-50 (the 'Firepot'), a weapon combining HE and incendiary elements, and the *Phosphorbrandbombe* derivatives of the C-50, namely the *Brand* C-50A and C-50B phosphorus/oil incendiary bombs. The British tried a 250lb LC with an incendiary filling, but it tended to break up on impact and was soon withdrawn. The small Braddock II incendiary was an SOE 'do-it-yourself' sabotage device with instructions in eleven languages; a Lancaster could drop 10,000 of them into enemy-occupied territory.

AP bombs boosted by solid propellant rockets could be dropped from lower altitude and still achieve high impact speed for penetration. By 1942, the Germans had developed versions of their 500, 1,000 and 1,800kg AP bombs, filled with 'desensitized' TNT, boosted by a tail group of 19 rockets, and intended to be released in steep dive attacks. But with use at dive angles of 30 degrees or less (causing failure to penetrate), 'their development was in vain' [Faber, 1979:152]. These weapons were primarily for anti-shipping use, but a number of the 1,000kg PC1000RS version were used on the night of 20 March 1942 by Ju88 bombers attacking Takali airfield, Malta, to destroy a supposed underground hangar. Further rocket bombs appeared in 1943: the US 1,250lb Mk.50, for use by US Navy dive-bombers; the Japanese 315kg Type 3 No.25; and the British 'Conkernut' for use against concrete defences. It seems these received even less use.

Bomb Containers
For carrying small bombs, the Germans developed the 500kg-sized *Abwurf Behalter Brandbomben* ABB500, one of a number of different types of expendable container, designated by the equivalent size of bomb. Some 140 B1El incendiaries could be carried in the ABB500, used with a barometric release pre-set to open at a low altitude, the resulting high concentration of incendiaries in a small area giving intense fires. Introduced in the 'Baedeker raids', ABB500 containers were also variously used to carry and drop 'crowsfeet', fragmentation bombs and parachute flares. Other, mostly later, German containers ranged from the 50kg-sized BdC10 (able to carry five SC10 anti-personnel bombs) to the 1,000kg-sized AB1000 (for up to 610 1kg incendiaries). The non-expendable BSB700 was especially complex, compartmentalized with an automatic distributor to spread the incendiaries. The containers were mostly cylindrical with tail fins, the larger ones being carried and dropped from external bomb racks. Similar containers were developed and introduced in other air forces.

New HE Techniques: 'RDX' Explosive; Hollow-charge Bombs
Discovered in 1899, 'cyclonite' (cyclomethylene trinitra-

mine) was a powerful explosive, but too expensive and sensitive for normal use. After the British found a wax additive which made it stable, Canada devised a manufacturing method and put the new 'RDX' (Research Department Explosives) into production in July 1942 for British and US HE bombs. Adopted in preference to 'pentalite', RDX had 30 per cent more power than TNT, and was to be the only significant new chemical explosive of the war. A mix of RDX, TNT and aluminium known as 'torpex' was developed primarily for underwater use. The Germans also used cyclonite (as 'hexagen'), in a mix of explosives.

Devised by Mohaupt in Switzerland, shaped- or hollow-charge (h/c) munitions used the 'Monroe effect' in which a concave front to the explosive charge directed the energy of the explosion forwards, e.g. to punch through armour plate. Use of the technique came in demolition charges (Germany, 1940), and field weapons (Bazooka, PIAT, etc.), then in 1942, aircraft bomblets for use against tanks; unlike AP bombs they did not need high impact speed for penetration and so could be dropped from low altitude. On the Eastern Front, Henschel Hs129s began dropping the 4kg SD4 h/c bomb, able to penetrate the armour of the new Soviet tanks. Later, the Soviets introduced the 2.5kg PTAB, 200 of which could be dispensed from DAG-10 containers under the wings of an Il-2 *Shturmovik*, to shower down onto a group of tanks. The Italians used a 3.5kg h/c bomb, and later the Japanese introduced the 100mm Ta-105 h/c bomb against landing craft and tanks; a container housed 21. Larger German examples included the open-nosed 250HL, 500HL and 800HL; and an unusual SD250 version with an added h/c nose attachment to punch a hole in thick armour large enough for the delay-fused main bomb to pass through before exploding. The British and US seem not to have used h/c aircraft bombs.

The British Bouncing Bombs: Golf Mine, Upkeep

The rolling/bouncing bomb/mine was devised in Britain by N. Barnes Wallis, as a means of breaching a massive concrete dam by placing a heavy explosive load right up against the base of the dam wall. A spherical bomb dropped from very low altitude would bounce and skip across the surface of the reservoir, so evading any defensive torpedo nets. If dropped at the right distance, it would slow down to hit the dam wall with little force and then sink down to explode at the base. After feasibility tests with children's marbles, then with golf balls catapulted along a ship test tank, the concept evolved into a spherical or cylindrical bomb, with back spin to enable dropping from slightly higher altitude to achieve a longer range trajectory. Use of an unwinding rope to achieve spin like a yo-yo was changed to a mechanical drive for spin up before release.

The proposed bomb became a family of weapons with the group code-name 'Golf Mine'. 'Upkeep' was the intended Dams bomb, now cylindrical in shape; the smaller 'Highball', proposed in light and heavy versions, was a spherical weapon for use against surface shipping; and 'Baseball' was a naval 'spherical torpedo' to be mortar-fired against enemy shipping. A half-scale dummy Upkeep bomb was first successfully test dropped on 12 December 1942, from a Wellington – with Wallis himself on board – off Chesil Beach, skipping half-a-mile over the surface of the sea.

Remote Bombing: Towed Bomb-gliders; Balloon Bombing

The US Army and Navy both developed experimental towed missiles in 1942. These guided bomb-gliders, or glider-bombs were explosive-filled unpowered unmanned aeroplanes, air-towed by a bomber and released to dive to impact under 'Dog' (visual tracking) or 'Fox' (TV-aided) radio control from the bomber. The USAAF 'BG' (bomb-glider) missiles were the Fletcher XBG-1 and XBG-2, and the canard configuration Cornelius XBG-3. The US Navy's 'GLOMB' (GLider bOMB) missiles were converted Army training gliders: Taylorcraft LNT, Piper LNP and Aeronca LNR – all lightplanes with the engine removed and faired over; the Waco LRW (ex CG-4A troop glider); and the largest towed glider-bomb of the War, the 110ft span Naval Aircraft Factory XLRN-4 glider of 1944. In Germany, the Gotha P-57 glider-bomb was cancelled.

The balloon-borne bomb made unsung appearances. In

1942 the British began limited offensive use of their leaflet balloons. With favourable winds, they were launched towards enemy-occupied territory carrying incendiaries and devices to jam radio communications and to snag overhead cables. [Kinsey, 1977:165] Later, balloon bombing systems were developed under Maj. S. Kondo of the Japanese Army in 1944. The little-used Manchuria version controlled altitude via barometric gas release, and dropped the three 10kg bombs by timer. The larger (10.7m diameter) trans-Pacific *Fu-Go* balloon used sand ballast and gas release; the load (two incendiaries and a 35kg HE bomb) was dropped after the last sandbag. Of 9,300 launched, at least 150 reached the USA and Canada. But a US news blackout (to prevent a 'germ warfare' panic) about the balloons caused the Japanese to assume that there had been no success at all, and the campaign was abandoned.

Unorthodox Approaches: the US Live Bat Programme; Trail Weapons

In February 1942, Roosevelt authorized US work on a proposal to use bombers to drop large numbers of live bats over Japan, based on an erroneous report that the Japanese people were inordinately afraid of the creatures. Later, experiments began, under Dr L. Feiser of Harvard, on the use of live bats, each carrying a tiny incendiary device surgically attached to its chest by string. The bats were to be air-dropped over Japanese cities, it being hoped that they would roost in buildings. Irritated by its load, each bat would gnaw through the string to release the bomb, which would self-ignite. Research included ground trials in which some bats escaped, damaging an aircraft hangar and a general's car; and air-drop trials in which some bats failed to leave their crates and were killed on impact. The programme was eventually abandoned in 1944.

Despite the importance of overhead power and telephone lines, use of airborne trail weapons against them seems to have been sporadic at best. In Germany, a purpose-built trail weapon was tested from a Ju88 in 1942. Evolved from an anti-aircraft cable bomb, this SBO 53 *Sagebombe* (saw bomb) consisted of a spherical weight on the end of a 400m-long steel cable deployed from a reel inside the aircraft to catch, and rip out, any overhead lines below. The device worked, but required considerable skill by the pilot, and it received little or no use. Soviet reports indicate that at times VVS Po-2 biplanes, trailing a grappling iron on a rope, made low-level sweeps over German rear areas to rip away telephone wires. Later, on 4 March 1944, RAF Mustang fighters trailing meat hooks on cables were used to sever telephone wires behind Japanese lines in Burma.

CBW Developments: German Nerve Gases; the British Anthrax Bomb

With a new 500lb LC phosgene bomb being tested, early in 1942 Churchill promised Stalin that Britain's 'immense stock of gas bombs for discharge from aircraft' would be used against Germany if the Germans began gas attacks on the Eastern Front. [Overy, 1981:56] But while the combatant countries all stockpiled conventional war chemicals, the principal CW development of the period came in Germany, where after further research, 'tabun' nerve gas was put into large-scale production in April 1942. Research on the second nerve gas 'sarin' continued. Sarin was twice as potent as tabun, and had the advantage of being non-persistent. But it was difficult to manufacture, corrosion problems requiring the use of silver-lined apparatus.

During 1942, the Porton Down team in Britain developed a 25lb Biological Warfare bomb containing an HE charge and a slurry of anthrax (*Bacillus anthracis*) spores. When the bomb exploded the spores would disperse as an invisible cloud, to settle on and infect anything in the downwind area. Field trials took place on the uninhabited Scottish island of Gruinard, first with static explosions among tethered sheep, then later in 1943 with a low-level drop from a Wellington bomber. Gruinard remained prohibited until a 10-year decontamination programme was completed in 1990.

The US 'Manhattan' Programme; the Beginnings of the Hydrogen Bomb

In May 1942, the US began work on facilities for separating out fissionable 235U from uranium, by different techniques and on a huge scale. In August, Roosevelt authorized the 'Manhattan Engineer District' programme for the development of an atomic bomb, under Brig. Gen. L.R. Groves and Dr J. Robert Oppenheimer. Given the possibility of A-bomb development by the Axis Powers, the Manhattan Project received top priority, with enormous funding and a Top-Secret rating. Centred on Los Alamos, it was to result in two types of A-bomb, using uranium 235 and plutonium respectively. On 2 December, Dr Enrico Fermi achieved start-up with the world's first critical atomic pile, at the University of Columbia in Chicago. This paved the way for large scale production of plutonium.

The first known statement on a possible thermonuclear or hydrogen bomb was made in May 1941 by Japanese physicist T.Hagiwara. In the USA in July 1942, Dr Edward Teller presented the first calculations showing how the million degree temperatures attained by an A-bomb could generate a fusion reaction. The bomb could utilize deuterium ('heavy hydrogen') in heavy water surrounding an A-bomb, the deuterium (2H) forming tritium (3H) then fusing to form helium, with accompanying release of enormous quantities of energy, giving a 'Super' A-bomb (or 'H' bomb) of almost unlimited power. Teller went on to lead the US H-bomb development which came to fruition after the war.

German, Japanese and Soviet Nuclear Weapon Developments

The Axis Powers were indeed working towards an atomic bomb, but at low priority. In Germany, nuclear physicists were now working under Prof. W. Heisenberg, at Hechingen. In March, Goebbels noted that: 'Research in the realm of atomic destruction has now proceeded to the point where its results may possibly be used in the present war.' The bomb bay of an He177 was enlarged to support A-bomb ballistic tests [Smith and Kay, 1972:287], but A-bomb development did not meet Hitler's requirements for rapid results, and in June, Speer approved preliminary nuclear work only. The prototype atomic piles at Kummersdorf and Haigersloch were still subcritical at the end of the war. The expectation that the Germans were more likely than the Japanese to achieve an A-bomb influenced the US adoption of a 'Germany first' war policy. But eleven days after Roosevelt authorized the Manhattan Project, the Japanese

Government approved their 'Project A' programme for an A-bomb. Initially, the work was for the Navy, later for the Army under Dr Y. Nishina. In December, a report noted that the programme would probably take 10 years; theoretical work continued at a low level right to the end of the war. Already authorized by Stalin in April 1942, the Soviet A-bomb programme, led by Dr I. Kurchatov, was to receive considerable help via espionage in the USA, notably by Klaus Fuchs at Los Alamos. Surprisingly, in 1943 the Soviets were to request (and apparently receive) from the USA under Lend-Lease the materials, including uranium oxide and heavy water, to enable a duplication of the Fermi atomic pile experiment. [Kilmarx, 1962:213]

Navigation, Blind Bombing and Radar

Navigation Aids: 'Gee', 'Loran', 'H2S'
On 8 March, the British made the first major use of the 'Gee' radio system, in a night raid on Essen. The Germans soon concluded that RAF bombers could find their way over Germany with or without the aid of German broadcast transmitters, but requests to restart evening broadcasting to the German public were rejected. The first Gee set reached German hands on 29 March, from a Wellington shot down off Wilhelmshaven; water immersion prevented ignition of the Gee set's self-destruct charge. But, thanks to the spoof 'J' beams, jamming of Gee did not begin until 4 August. In the USA, the LRN, later AN/APN-4 'Loran' (Long Range Navigation) system was developed using the same hyperbolic grid principle as Gee, and with the receivers made interchangeable. It used lower frequency (2Mc/s) for longer range over the sea, and would aid bombing missions over the Pacific. Unlike Gee, it used only two stations, giving position on a line; switching to a second pair was needed to achieve a position fix. In Britain, production 'H2S' ground-imaging radar sets were delivered late in 1942. H2S used a paraboloidal scanner in a ventral perspex housing,

and a PPI display. US work on a similar system was – temporarily – abandoned as being unnecessary for daylight bombing. [Hartcup, 1970:144]

The British 'Oboe' Blind-bombing System; 'Taub'

The British TRE 'Oboe' was rated as the most precise blind-bombing aid of the war [R.V. Jones, 1978:353]. It used radar-ranging from two ground stations, the 'Cat' or flight path station, and 'Mouse' or bomb release station. A radar repeater on the aircraft provided a strong return signal to both stations. With audio radio signals warning of deviations, the pilot flew along a precise arc of a circle centred on the Cat station and passing over the target. The Mouse station monitored the aircraft's progress, and provided the release signal when the aircraft had reached the exact range from Mouse which ensured that it was at the drop point. The aircraft had to fly at a precise speed and altitude so that the bomb release point accurately allowed for the descent trajectory of the bomb. Flight trials began in April. Due to the Earth's curvature, the Oboe aircraft had to fly high to be able to receive the radar signals at any significant range, hence it was proposed to use it with the pressurized Wellington Mk.VI for bombing. But interest shifted to using Oboe primarily for marking targets, to enable larger forces of aircraft to bomb, so development continued with the smaller and faster Mosquito. The 1.5m Oboe Mk.I was first used operationally for bombing on 20 December, and for target marking on 31 December. Navigation to the Cat curve used Gee or a Bailie beam.

Meanwhile, on the night of 23 April, KG100 pathfinders over Britain made the first use of the *Taub* version of *X-Verfahren* using modulation at supersonic frequencies. But British jamming was soon implemented.

German and British Airborne Radar Repeaters; the 'Boozer' Radar Detector

With a growing need for countermeasures against ground radars to aid bomber penetration, the Germans and the British both devised airborne repeaters for deception. Picking up a radar signal, amplifying and retransmitting it, could give a return signal far stronger than a normal radar echo, enabling one aircraft to give the impression of a large formation. The first such use came in February. To aid the escape of the German battle-cruisers *Scharnhorst* and *Gneisenau* through the English Channel, two RCM He111s flew parallel to the coast, each carrying repeaters simulating a formation of 25 aircraft. But this countermeasure was to receive little use in supporting German bombing against Britain. The British TRE 'Moonshine' radar repeater, installed in Defiant fighters, was first used on 6 August; eight Defiants simulated a bomber force assembling for a raid, causing 30 German fighters to attempt interception. But a separate set was needed for each *Freya* frequency; it could only be used to simulate a daylight tight formation; and it could only be used for a short distance, so as to remain out of visual range of the German defences. Moonshine was withdrawn late in 1942.

The first airborne radar warning receiver (RWR), the TRE 'Boozer', was fitted to bombers to give crews warning of radar activity, and hence of likely attack. The device registered illumination of the bomber on frequencies used by German radars, via warning lights in the cockpit (red for *Lichtenstein*, orange for *Würzburg*). Being passive, Boozer would not betray the presence of the aircraft carrying it. But it could not detect a night-fighter operating visually or homing passively onto some transmission from the bomber. Boozer was first used by PFF bombers on 13 November.

Airborne Jammers; the IFF 'J-Switch' and 'Shiver'; 'Mandrel'; 'Tinsel'

In Britain, Dr R.V.Jones had warned Bomber Command in September 1941 that the Germans could develop a means of triggering the IFF sets on RAF bombers, if the sets were left switched 'on', and so use the received signal to track or home onto the bombers. Little notice was taken. Worse, during 1942, RAF bomber crews began believing that pulses from their IFF sets helped to jam German searchlight control radars, and therefore afforded a measure of protection. The belief was erroneous, but was encouraged by Bomber Command on the grounds that it aided crew morale at a time when life expectancy was very low. [R.V. Jones, 1978:492] In June, IFF sets on RAF bombers were fitted with a 'J' (for jamming) switch enabling them to transmit continuously. In December 'Shiver' – a modified IFF Mk.II set incorporating a true jammer – replaced the IFF/'J' switch. But it was soon withdrawn from main force use, as ineffective.

The TRE 'Mandrel' airborne radar noise jammer countered German *Freya* radars by radiating signals in the same frequency range as the radar, to swamp the normal return echo and so obliterate formation size and range information. It was installed first in Defiant aircraft, and used to blind the coastal *Freya* chain by providing a 200-mile long 'Mandrel screen'. The screen was first used, along with 'Tinsel', during a raid on Mannheim on 3 December. Other Mandrel sets were fitted to heavy bombers and used on the raids themselves, to counter the inland *Freya* sets supporting the Kammhuber night-fighter system. 'Ground Mandrel', in giant constructions employing six transmitters at each of four sites in south-east England, also became operational in December. Elsewhere in 1942, a ground jammer to neutralize the British 'CO' early warning radar on Malta was developed in Italy.

'Gaston' and its successor 'Tinsel' provided airborne jamming of enemy defence R/T, disrupting voice communications between ground control stations and night-fighter crews. Fitted to RAF bombers, Tinsel employed a microphone mounted in an engine nacelle and linked to a radio transmitter. A German-speaking crewman used the aircraft's normal radio receiver to search for fighter control R/T, then tuned the transmitter to broadcast the engine noise on the same frequency.

Ground-attack Developments

Aircraft: Il-2 and Light Shturmovik; AVIA LM.02 Dive-bombing Glider

The key feature of the two-seat Ilyushin Il-2 *Shturmovik* was its armour plate, typically 7mm thick and now increased to 950kg, forming a fuselage keel, and protection for the cockpit floor, bulkheads, fuel tanks, coolant and oil radiators, and the underside of the engine. This, plus the bullet-proof windscreen gave the Il-2 exceptional protection against light AA fire, and coupled with its defensive gun, greatly reduced losses to fighters. By late 1942, Il-2s were being fitted with heavier (37mm) cannon; ordnance included small bombs in the wing bays or under the wings, and RS-82 and RS-132 rocket projectiles. Built in large numbers, the Il-2 was to prove highly successful in its role. Meanwhile, the success of the Po-2 harassment bomber led the Soviets to introduce the U-2VOM-1 or LSh (*Legkii Shturmovik*) close support version for use where low speed and manoeuvrability conferred advantages, e.g. for attacking trenches or camouflaged positions among trees. The LSh carried four RS-82 rockets, 120kg of bombs and a flexible gun for the observer, and served until the end of the war. The *Pegas* twin-engined light wooden *Shturmovik*, purpose-designed under D.L. Tomasevich while in 'Special Prison', was not adopted. In Italy, the unique AVIA LM.02 dive-bombing glider could be air-towed over the front line and released to turn and make a dive-bombing pass, pulling out and using its momentum to make a short glide to friendly territory. Having no engine or fuel tanks, the all-wood LM.02 was cheaper and less vulnerable than a powered dive-bomber. But it was not adopted for service.

Rocket Projectiles

Most RPs were fin-stabilized, usually with fixed fins and fired from launching rails; launching tubes needed 'flick-out' fins. The shorter spin-stabilized type RPs had no fins, and were also tube-launched, using tangential rocket efflux to give spin-up. By 1942, the potential of the RP as a ground-attack weapon was becoming recognized: the forward speed of an aircraft gave launch stability to a finned RP, which helped accuracy; and since rockets were recoilless, any aircraft could carry a high level of installed fire power by using them. The British adopted short launching rails, but later US work showed fore and aft mounting posts to be sufficient, giving reduced weight and drag.

RAF Mk.IIC Hurricanes carried eight 3-inch UP rocket projectiles on rails under the wings, fired in pairs or in salvo.

Steel plates protected the wings from efflux/blast. Warheads were interchangeable 25lb AP or SAP, or 60lb HE. A salvo with HE warheads was ranked with a broadside from a light cruiser. The solid head AP version was tested against tanks, but it was to become far more successful as an anti-submarine weapon. Also during 1942, the British tested the much larger 10-inch 'Uncle Tom' RP. In the USA on 6 July, the M8 4.5-inch RP was test fired in flight from a Curtiss P-40 fighter. The M8 was subsequently used with 10ft-long triple-tube launchers mounted under the wing; the RP's six 'flick-out' fins deployed on leaving the tube. In Germany, a Junkers Ju88C-4 was tested with a *Nebelwerfer* revolving six-barrelled recoilless projectile launcher for ground-attack use; it fired WGr21 or WGr28 projectiles. A Messerschmitt Bf110 was tested with a ventral battery of 12 tubes for RZ65 73mm rocket shells as a ground-attack weapon. Neither concept was adopted.

Anti-tank Aircraft/Gun Developments

On the Eastern Front, the Germans had found that the heavy Soviet tanks were less susceptible to near misses by *Stuka* dive-bombing than had been the case with most British and French tanks. This had led to increased use of anti-tank cannon instead. But the new Soviet T-34 and KV-1 heavy battle tanks had frontal armour which could withstand the Hs129's 30mm MK101 shells. This led the Germans to evaluate higher powered weapons including the 30mm MK103, 37mm BK3.7 and 50mm BK5. Also, a Ju88A-4 was tested with a ventrally-mounted 75mm KwK39 cannon against captured T-34 tanks. Then, late in 1942, the Germans introduced the Ju87G anti-tank version of the *Stuka*, with two underwing 37mm Flak 18 cannon. Being slow and precise, the Ju87G made a good gun platform and proved very successful in the role, but vulnerable to fighters. While tanks were the main problem, by 1942 the Germans had developed various types of aircraft bolt-on weapons pack (*Waffenbehälter*). One such, the WB81 'watering can' was used on Ju87s (one under each wing) against infantry, its 6 or 8 fixed, splayed MG81 machine guns spraying bullets fore and aft as it passed overhead.

In Britain, after 18 months of war, a report by AVM Sir

John Slessor in May 1941 had reaffirmed the Air Staff's view that, 'It is *not* the job of the Air Force to destroy tanks'. But in June 1942, the RAF introduced the 'tin opener' Mk.IID Hurricane. With the two 40mm Vickers cannon mounted low (underwing), the recoil pitched the aircraft nose down when fired, so to allow correction, the gun installation was made self-loading but not automatic firing. Having no other armament, the IID Hurricanes were themselves vulnerable to enemy fighters, but were used with success in North Africa and in Burma. After the Battle of Alam Halfa, a sick Rommel flew home, taking a sample of the US-made AP shells that the Hurricanes had been firing at German tanks; HQ staff, including Göring, would not take the news seriously. [Tute, 1976:158] In September, SAAF Hurricanes began dropping magnetic 'sticky bombs' in low-level attacks on German tanks.

Ground-attack Operations

Pacific/CBI Theatre Ground Attack
In the rapid Japanese advance in the Far East, attacks on the Allied airfields used fragmentation bombs, wiping out personnel, vehicles and aircraft, but leaving runways intact for future Japanese use. Staging into forward airfields, AAF and Navy units also flew widespread support operations against Allied troops, the Japanese air superiority enabling the *Zero* escort fighters to supplement the bombing and dive-bombing with strafing attacks. But the Japanese did not have the ground-to-air communications for rapid response against designated targets, most attacks being made at will. In Malaya, the British noted poor Japanese use of close support, but the air strikes added casualties and confusion among the retreating Allied forces. The Allied response was limited, the British still having obsolete or unsuitable aircraft, and losing many of these on the ground. With the Japanese approaching through Burma, the tiny Indian Air Force (*Bharatiya Vayu Sena*) adapted its Lysanders as

bombers. Elsewhere, hurried fighter-bomber conversions included US P-40, RAAF Wirraway and Dutch East Indies Brewster Buffalo fighters. A vital success was achieved on 6 May when eight P-40Es of Chennault's 'Flying Tigers' AVG attacked a Japanese armoured column invading south-east China via the Salween gorge. Dive-bombing of the gorge face at 70 degrees with Soviet 250kg bombs brought landslides down trapping the column, which over the next four days was attacked with fragmentation bombs and strafing; Chinese SB-3 and Curtiss Hawk biplanes added to the later attacks.

Eastern Front Day Ground Attack

In 1942, the Germans stepped up attacks on the Soviet rail system – bombing trains as well as stations, yards and bridges – and on river traffic, especially on the Volga. In February, a Ju87B unit, I./St.G5 based in Norway, was assigned to operations against the Soviet Murmansk railway transporting supplies delivered by the Allied convoys. Other railway squadrons followed in 1943. The Soviets reacted with fighters patrolling the lines, and with armoured, AA-defended trains. On rivers and lakes, the provision of armoured, AA-equipped gunboats was increased. Meanwhile, with the spring, the Soviets built new airstrips 15 to 30km from the Front (with main supply dumps at a safer 250km), set up observation posts, introduced mobile service/repair units, and began a more offensive approach. Il-2s flew short-range sorties from bases close to the Front, in groups of 4 up to 12 aircraft. Typically, the Soviet pilots flew over the front line to one side of the target, then turned and attacked while heading back towards their own lines. Whereas the Germans used precision dive attacks, the Soviets mostly relied on dispersed coverage of fragmentation bombs and strafing over the target area. [Piekalkiewicz, 1985:223]

Gradually, the Luftwaffe operations in the USSR became more and more orientated to close support of the Army, increasingly in trouble against Soviet ground forces. He111 and Ju88 bombers were committed in low-level attacks, with predictable results; the medium bombers were more prone to accidents when operating from the small temporary strips on the Eastern Front, and they were easier targets for the increasing Soviet light flak. In addition, those lost represented a greater drain in *matériel* and crews. The German ability to mount long-range bomber operations was declining.

German and Soviet Night Ground-attack Developments

By 1942, German close support air operations against the Red Army included the night dropping of flares to illuminate Soviet positions, so aiding nearby German Army units to bombard them using mortars and artillery. Later, the success of the Soviet night harassment units led the Germans to set up *Störkampfstaffeln* in a similar role. Aircraft used were obsolete and training aircraft, including the Heinkel He45 two-seat biplane and the Henschel Hs126, with machine guns and small bombs (10kg HE, incendiary and fragmentation). On the Soviet side, a directive in October ordered each ground attack and fighter regiment to begin training five crews for night operations. Il-2s went on to make over 400 night sorties in the defence of Stalingrad. By this time, Soviet use of ground radio direction of fighter operations had been extended to cover ground-attack operations as well.

Elsewhere, Britain's SOE Lysander 'special duties' aircraft were at times used in small night bombing attacks on rail and power targets in France, using machine guns and small bombs attached to stub wings on the u/c fairings. In June, RAF Bostons and Mosquitos began night intruder operations, bombing and strafing German airfields.

North Africa Innovations: Mine Clearing; Night Attacks on Tanks

Ground attack in North Africa saw several innovations in 1942. Among the improvisations: a Bf109 fighter dangling a bomb on a rope, its pilot trying to hit British tanks with it as he flew across the battlefield; and a US Navy floatplane pilot destroying three German tanks by dropping depth charges on them. In June, opening the Afrika Korps' drive against Tobruk, Rommel used Ju87 dive-bombers to clear pathways through the British minefields, each bomb explosion detonating a number of mines around it.

After the Afrika Korps' failure in the Battle of Alam Halfa on 31 August, through the following night the RAF mounted attacks on the German tanks and vehicles, relays of Albacore biplanes dropping flares to provide illumination for bomb and cannon strikes by other, low-flying aircraft. For the first time in the war, tanks were attacked from the air by night and day. [Bidwell and Graham, 1982:269] Later, flares and even truck headlights were used for US P-40s to take-off in darkness for surprise dawn strikes on German airfields. The Germans themselves improvised night bombing, but it seems with little success, due to crew inexperience with flares and markers. After Alamein, under Operation 'Chocolate' the British operated two Hurricane squadrons from an abandoned airfield far behind enemy lines, supplying them by air. Until Luftwaffe attention made the operation untenable, these made attacks on Rommel's forces who were far in the rear and thought themselves out of range of the RAF.

For rapid movement from one newly created airfield to another as ground forces advanced, the British (and later the Americans) adopted a 'two-party system'. Ground support was split into A and B parties. The aircraft operated from the current base under A party, while B party moved forward to prepare at the new airfield. The aircraft then flew to the new base while A party prepared to leapfrog to the next site. [Rust, 1970:20]

Paris; Dieppe – Failed Implementation of Close Support; Smokescreens

In a salute to occupied Paris, on 12 June 1942 F/L A.K.Gatward flew an RAF Beaufighter at very low level up the Champs-Elysées, dropping *tricolore* flags at the Arc de Triomphe and shooting up the *Kriegsmarine* HQ.

On 19 August, the RAF mounted its largest tactical air operation to date, for the extraordinary Operation 'Jubilee' amphibious landings at Dieppe, which ended in withdrawal after heavy casualties to Canadian troops. To help protect the landings, withdrawals and air support operations from the German defences, the RAF's 2 Group bombers provided smokescreens by two methods. Beauforts with SCI canisters flew in line astern along the beaches laying smoke curtains; evasive action was not practical and a number of these aircraft were lost. Other Beauforts and Blenheims dropped 100lb rectangular-can phosphorus smoke bombs in front of known AA and coastal defence gun positions, to provide more persistent local screening; the smoke bombs contained a phosphorus compound which generated smoke on exposure to air. Fighter cover was impressive (56 squadrons), but there was no prior naval bombardment or heavy bombing of the coastal and AA defences, only small scale – and quite inadequate – air strikes, some by cannon Hurricanes which flew low-level attacks over the beaches, making maximum use of the screening. Also, no attempt was made to try out the Army/Air Support organization and techniques built up over two years. No ALOs operated with 2 Group to help co-ordinate the smoke-laying and air attacks; no ASSUs with radio links were landed with the troops to call up air strikes; and although Army Cooperation Mustangs flew low-level reconnaissance missions over the beaches, they too had no radio links to the troops. [Carrington, 1987:104] Instead, direction of air support operations relied on an RAF observer/controller on the HQ destroyer HMS *Calpe*, whose view at critical times was largely obstructed by the air-laid smokescreens.

Allied Attempts with Dive-bombers; the Soviet Vertushka Carousel

Having consistently opposed the acquisition of dive-bombers, despite appeals by the British Army, in June 1942 the RAF began receiving the much delayed Vultee Vengeance dive-bombers ordered for it, but which it did not want. Now the Vengeances were judged obsolescent and too vulnerable for use in Europe. They were passed on to the Indian Air Force (to supplement its Hurricanes), the RAF in India, and (in 1943) the RAAF. All used them with distinction. The RAF's Vengeances were first used to support the Arakan offensive in Burma in November 1942. Attacks against Japanese-held villages and troop positions were normally made by a six-aircraft group, peeling off from echelon formation at 10,000ft. Reports of the Vengeances' successes, albeit against minimal air opposition, were received with some embarrassment by the Air Ministry in

Britain, and largely suppressed. [Smith, 1981:173] Meanwhile, that other reluctant dive-bomber operator, the USAAF, withdrew its A-24 Banshees after six out of seven were shot down in an attack on Buna on 29 July, and soon replaced its Vengeances with A-36s. But the USMC and Navy continued to operate the SBD Dauntless version of the A-24 with success into 1945. On the Eastern Front, the Petlyakov Pe-2 had mainly been used as a conventional bomber to reduce training requirements, but during 1942 it became increasingly and successfully used as a dive-bomber, but in shallow dives (up to 30 degrees). Late in 1942, the Soviet 150th Bomber Regiment, under Col.I.S.Polbin, introduced a squadron *Vertushka* or carousel for Pe-2 ground attack. With this technique, the aircraft formed a defensive circle, leaving it one after the other for a diving attack in the target area, and climbing out to rejoin the circle ready for a repeat attack. The method ensured effective coverage of the target as well as mutual defence against fighters, but subjected each aircraft to concentrated AA fire as it attacked. Meanwhile Soviet sources indicate that by 1942, VVS fighters were making 'vertical attacks' on ground targets. [Fetzer, 1973:122]

Operations in North Africa
Exploiting lax Allied intelligence security, Rommel's North African offensive drove the British back to Egypt at a rate which left the Luftwaffe behind, thanks to inadequate transport. Then, in a diversion which could be ill-afforded, the Luftwaffe flew 15,000 sorties against the Free French-held fort of Bir Hakim. But through the second half of 1942, the British built up their forces in North Africa, including the RAF's Western Desert Air Force. US aircraft began to arrive also, including a few B-17 and B-24 bombers, the first heavy bombers in the theatre; by November, the US Middle East Air Force was operating alongside the RAF. With the Battle of Alamein beginning on 24 October, the British began advancing from the east, with well-coordinated use of RAF and SAAF tactical air power. Six squadrons of Wellingtons bombed German artillery as Hurricane fighter-bombers attacked troops and armour. In November, the Operation 'Torch' US/British

landings in Morocco and Algeria were supported initially by carrier-based air power, land-based aircraft being flown in from Gibraltar as airfields were secured. But air/ground co-operation here among the new units was 'deplorable'. [D'Este, 1988:163] Prior to Torch, the British mounted a series of raids on Genoa, Milan and Turin, the aim being to keep Italy's fighters and AA units at home. But stepped-up Axis raids on Allied-held ports and airfields included raids by Piaggio P.108B heavy bombers and Reggiane Re2001 fighter-bombers from Sardinia. With Torch came the US 12th AF under Brig. Gen. J.H. Doolittle; its heavy bombers became the major component of Doolittle's North-west African Strategic Air Force.

Fighter-bombers and Light Bombers in the Desert

In North Africa, road transport was among those targets rated as unpromising for conventional bombing; the vehicles of a convoy could often disperse to either side and spread out, needing individual attack. The RAF used Beaufighters for road strafing, e.g. a flight of four splitting into two sections to head left and right along a road at low level, the section leader firing at any vehicles encountered, the No.2 following behind attacking anything missed. For small targets generally, in 1942 the RAF also began using single-seat fighter-bombers, first the Hurricane, then in March, the Kittyhawk. Compared with say, a Boston light bomber, a fighter-bomber needed less maintenance, only one crewman and no escort fighters, and eventually (1944) the 'Kittybomber' would carry the same 2,000lb bomb load as a Boston. But the Boston could fly further, and bomb with some accuracy from medium altitude when the flak was too intense for fighter-bombers. Thus the use of fighter-bombers at low level against small/mobile targets released the Bostons for higher-level use against larger targets – tank concentrations, supply dumps and airfields. Each had its place, but the Bostons were ordered to cruise at low altitude (below the radar) so as to release more escort fighters to fighter-bomber duty. On the German side, in 1942 the *Stuka* was proving too vulnerable, and the Gnome Rhône engines of the Hs129 too unreliable and prone to damage from sand and dust; to compensate, the Luftwaffe introduced the Bf109 *Jabo* for desert operations.

Daylight Bombing

Japanese Bomber Formations and Operations; the Darwin Raid

The Japanese having no modern bombsight, high-level bombing by the land-based medium bombers of the IJN, and those of the IJAAF, consisted of pattern bombing by formations led by the most skilled crews, all crews 'bombing on the leader'. HE bombs from 15 to 1,000kg were used. The normal formation size was 36 bombers, but this reduced as the war progressed. Escort fighters normally flew in three groups, two at 1,000m below at right and left, the third 1,000m above and to the rear. The bomber formation was maintained when under AA fire or fighter attack; for the latter, the formation normally tightened up, the crews only breaking away if subjected to unusual attack manoeuvres. The Japanese expansion in 1942 involved widespread bombing, including of largely undefended towns, with heavy raids on: Rangoon, Mandalay and other towns during the invasion of Burma; Colombo and Trincomalee in Ceylon; and Rabaul, Bougainville and Port Moresby. Many raids on urban areas used fragmentation bombs; given the lightly built houses and no shelters there were heavy casualties. The biggest Japanese air attack since Pearl Harbor was a mainly carrier-based strike on the shipping, port and airfield at a weakly-defended Darwin, on 19 February. The raid included low-level attacks as well as pattern bombing by formations of B5N2s, and by two waves of land-based G4Ms from the Celebes. In later weeks, further land-based raids followed. But radar and fighter protection improved; on 25 April, 24 bombers were met by P-40 Warhawks and 11 were shot down. On 21 March, raids by 230 Japanese aircraft on Magwe/Lashio destroyed most of the surviving RAF aircraft in Burma. In December, the Japanese flew small night raids (a total of 23 sorties) against Calcutta; little damage was caused but one-and-a-half million people fled.

The Allied Response in the Pacific Theatre

By January, the British were moving scarce reinforcements to the Far East. Blenheim and Ventura bombers were flown overland in stages, many being lost *en route*, others to Japanese raids on the airfields after arrival. Along with Dutch (Martin B-10) and RAAF (Hudson) remnants, surviving aircraft were pressed into action piecemeal, with inadequate ground staff and supplies, and no crew acclimatization or training. Small escorted daylight raids were mauled by the *Zeros*, and navigation by inexperienced crews without radio aids, over mountainous jungle at night, brought further losses to little effect.

In the USA, means of striking back at Japan were being reviewed. One scheme considered, in January 1942, was to try to bury large areas of Japan under layers of ash by a sustained bombing campaign against Japan's volcanoes. [B.F. Smith, 1983:101] Meanwhile, the dwindling US Pacific B-17 force had been reassigned to Java, where more were lost on the ground due to Japanese air strikes. But in the air, it was found that the high-flying B-17s could hold their own in this theatre. The Japanese had no early warning radar to enable fighters to be scrambled in time. The *Zero* fighters had poor performance at altitude and, lacking armour and fuel tank protection, were themselves much more vulnerable (than German fighters) to the B-17's defensive firepower. Even so, the effectiveness of the B-17s was limited, due to: inadequate logistics, airstrips and maintenance facilities; crew inexperience; tropical weather; and the use of the bombers in tactical and anti-shipping operations, often with small raids of five or six aircraft.

Preparation for the US Daylight Bombing Offensive in Europe

Despite the Pacific War needs, a 'Germany first' policy was adopted by the US government, the US 8th Air Force being formed on 14 January 1942 to operate in Britain, with Brig.Gen.I.C.Eaker in charge of the 8th Bomber Command. The USAAF remained wedded to daylight precision bombing, which offered a distinctive and wholly American contribution to the war. British appeals to join with the RAF in night bombing were rejected, for reasons of: the avoidance of crew retraining; the lack of flame-damped exhausts; the bomb loads being too small for the less precise bombing achieved at night; and the fact that a combination of US day and British night bombing would give the German defences no respite. On 4 July, US crews made their first bombing mission in Europe, manning 6 out of 12 RAF Bostons against targets in Holland. On 6 July, the 97th Bomb Group at Polebrook began receiving B-17E bombers. Early training flights included defensive practice against mock attacks by RAF fighters. After each flight, the Norden sights were removed and stored under armed guard.

With the prospect of large US and RAF bomber forces operating in parallel, the British airfield building programme was stepped up to become one of the largest of the war, using rubble from the blitzed towns and cities to build runways and hardstands. The runways needed to be strongly built; those at Kilbolton – built hurriedly in 1940 for fighters – were badly damaged by the impact and weight of B-17s landing on them. The 'Drems' system of electrically operated approach, runway and peri-track lighting replaced Glim lamps; a Chance Light flashed airfield code letters; and a red/green/yellow illuminated Angle of Glide Indicator aided the approach. Eventually, the RAF and 8th AF Bomber Commands were to use 180 airfields in Britain, mostly in East Anglia, with over 4,000 miles of runways and taxiways.

The Lamy Raid; the Axis Offensive against Malta; 'Tip and Run' Raids

In a unique long distance raid, on 21 January a single He111 with extra tankage flew 1,500 miles from North Africa for a surprise attack on the airbase at Fort Lamy, south of Lake Chad, destroying fuel supplies and 10 aircraft.

In preparation for a proposed airborne invasion of Malta (Operation Hercules), the Axis forces began weakening the island's defences by attacking British supply convoys and by the Luftwaffe's most intensive bombing campaign against a single target. The heavy bombing began in mid-January 1942, by Ju87, Ju88 and He111 aircraft flying from Sicily, mostly in daylight with fighter escort. The attacks were aimed primarily at the harbour and shipping at Valletta, the airfields, and the AA batteries. The raids built up during April and May, using double and triple sorties. In April, Malta and Gozo's 143 square miles received over 6,500 tons of bombs, more than the whole of Britain in any month of the 'Blitz'. Supplies of fighters from Britain were often sunk *en route* or destroyed before they could be used, and the island became near-paralysed by shortages. The bombing continued through the summer, mostly by the RA with small escorted tight formations of Z.1007bis bombers attacking the airfields from high altitude. But Malta survived, and continued its key role in the Mediterranean war.

In response to British raids on German historic towns (Lübeck, Rostock), in April 1942 the Germans themselves began surprise *Seeräuberangriff* (pirate) or 'tip and run' attacks by Bf109 fighter-bombers on largely undefended south coast towns in Britain, beginning with Torquay. The raiders swept in over the sea at low level with guns firing, dropped their bombs, turned and were heading for home by the time the air raid sirens sounded. The raids were mostly very small, but on 31 October around 60 fighters escorted some 30 Fw190s each with a 500kg bomb in an attack on Canterbury; at the speed the fighter-bombers travelled they were over Britain for less than six minutes. [Price, 1977c:142]

Eastern Front: Soviet Long-range Bomber Force; Sevastopol; Stalingrad

In the German retreat from Moscow, Soviet VVS units attacked mainly at the Front itself, making few deep strikes in the German rear. This allowed the Germans to withdraw in reasonable order, and was judged a tactical error by the Soviets. [Hardesty, 1982:88] In April 1942, a Soviet long-range bomber force was re-established within a new ADD (Long Range Aviation), under Maj. Gen. A. Golovanov. But the Soviets had not been impressed by the results of the German strategic bombing against Britain, or against Soviet cities, and the new force was given little priority despite its capability for attacking the enemy's rear areas and communications. The ADD's initial strength included Pe-2 and Il-4 bombers plus civil transport aircraft.

With Soviet defenders holding out at Sevastopol, on 2

June the Ju87s and Ju88s of *Flieger Korps VIII* began one of
the most intensive bombing assaults of the war. Each day,
600 sorties were made against Soviet positions including the
Maxim Gorky fortress, aircraft from nearby airfields making
up to 18 sorties each. At times, fully fuelled Ju88s made up
to four sorties before the crew were able to leave the aircraft
for a break. The total number of bombs dropped reached
125,000, many being 1,000kg bombs, the largest available.
Rocket AP bombs were made available in case the Soviet
fleet attempted to relieve the fortress. Despite the intensity
of the bombing, when Sevastopol fell on 4 July the
fortifications themselves showed little damage.

·The German assault on Stalingrad included heavy
bombing, a 400-plus aircraft raid on 23 August leaving much
of the city in flames. Later, with the German 6th Army cut
off, in November the Luftwaffe began a large, desperate and
ultimately futile supply airlift into the pocket. He111
bomber units, including some transferred from the
Mediterranean, plus training units, were ordered to
supplement the transport fleet. The losses of aircraft and
trained crews to the steadily tightening Soviet defences
around the pocket were severe. Göring later said 'There
died the core of the German bomber fleet'. [Air Ministry,
1983:218]

Selective RAF Daylight Raids; the Armoured Lancaster; Mosquito Raids

Although the RAF was concentrating heavily on night
bombing, thought was still being given to ways of achieving
daylight bombing with acceptable losses. On 17 April,
diversion raids by light bombers and over 500 fighters were
used to support an RAF low-level daylight raid on the MAN
works at Augsburg. The attack was made near dusk, to
allow a return flight in darkness, but only 5 of the 12
Lancasters got back home, all of them damaged. On 11 July,
44 Lancasters used cloud over Denmark and the Baltic to
reach Danzig to attack the U-boat yards at dusk in the
longest (1,500 miles) round trip yet attempted; two were
lost. On 17 October, a larger low-level dusk raid, by 94
Lancasters on the Schneider Armaments Arsenal at Le
Creusot and a nearby transformer station, was achieved by

flying around north-west France and then in from the Bay of Biscay; only one aircraft was lost, but 1,000 civilians were killed. On 6 December, 93 Ventura, Boston and Mosquito bombers of the RAF's 2 Group mounted a low-level daylight raid on the Philips works at Eindhoven. The raid caused major damage, but 15 aircraft were lost.

In May 1942 the Air Staff advocated a specially armoured Mk.III day bomber version of the Lancaster. Harris thought such an aircraft offered little reduction in vulnerability compared with an unmodified Lancaster, and rejected the proposal; the aircraft was already in production. [Webster and Frankland, Vol.I, 1961:451]

With the Mosquito, RAF Bomber Command had a bomber with the speed, altitude and manoeuvrability to outstrip existing German day fighters, plus the range to penetrate far into Germany. The first such daylight raid was at low level, by four Mosquitos against Cologne on 31 May, the morning after the first '1,000 bomber' raid. Thereafter, Mosquito bombers (disguised in Fighter Command colours) regularly flew daylight high-level nuisance and low-level precision attacks. For low-level, at times with two groups making co-ordinated diving attacks and passes to confuse AA defences, tight formations of four, six or eight aircraft released 2,000lb of bombs each, horizontally into the sides of selected buildings. Delay fuses ensured all were past before the leader's bombs exploded. The first such raid on German HQ buildings, was on the Gestapo HQ in Oslo on 25 September; four bombs smashed through the walls, but failed to explode. During 1942, the 4 x 250lb internal bomb load of the Mosquito was increased to 4 x 500lb. Telescopic fins to enable the larger bombs to fit into the bomb bay proved unnecessary; the bomb ballistics remained acceptable with cropped fins.

US Pacific Theatre Operations: the 'Doolittle' Raid; Guadalcanal

One of the boldest joint-service operations of the war consisted of a unique carrier-launched one-way raid by 16 US Army North American B-25B medium bombers, against Tokyo on 18 April 1942. The raid, led by Lt. Col. J.H. Doolittle, satisfied Roosevelt's requirement for a token strike against Japan in retaliation for the attack on Pearl

Harbor. The operation was prepared in secret. No single-engined aircraft had the payload/range needed, and twin-engined aircraft had not previously operated from carriers. The B-25 offered the best take-off performance, needed for the short carrier deck. The assigned B-25s were fitted with autopilots, given extra tankage in place of the dorsal turret, and dummy guns in the tail to help discourage fighter attack. Volunteer crews were given Navy carrier take-off training. For the mission, the B-25s were lashed to the flight deck of the USS *Hornet* since they were too large for the deck lifts. Take-off was to be made with the carrier at full speed into wind, using painted white guide lines offset to one side of the deck to ensure wing-tip clearance of the 'island'. After discovery by a Japanese patrol vessel, the raid was launched from 800 miles out, further than intended, and earlier than the alerted Japanese expected. Tokyo's barrage balloons were down, and patrolling fighters did not spot the bombers far below. The B-25s successfully dropped their 2,000lb loads of HE and incendiary bombs, from *c*.1,500ft on Tokyo, Kobe, Nagoya, and Yokohama. Although most crews were saved, all 16 B-25s were lost because of fuel shortage and difficulties in reaching the landing fields in China, in bad weather. Raid damage was insignificant, but the mission boosted US morale and caused the Japanese to assign an extra four fighter groups to the defence of the homeland. The Japanese Army mounted massive reprisals in the Chinese provinces where the US aircrew sheltered, killing almost 250,000 Chinese. [Costello, 1985:239]

In August, with a pre-landing bombardment by 5th AF B-17s and RAAF Hudsons with carrier-based air cover, US forces mounted Operation 'Watchtower', their first amphibious invasion of the Pacific war, in the Solomons. The landings on Tulagi and Guadalcanal captured the latter's near-complete new airfield, and USMC Dauntless dive-bombers and fighters were soon operating from the newly named Henderson Field. With the intermediate bases on Bougainville not yet ready, the Japanese mounted desperate raids on the beachhead and airfield using Aichi D3A dive-bombers flying from Rabaul. Since this was outside the round-trip range of the D3A, experienced crews were sacrificed.

The Flying Fortress versus Enemy Fighters; Precision Daylight Bombing

Otherwise under-utilized, RAF Fighter Command supplemented the US 8th AF's own Spitfires in providing escort cover for the 8th BC on its early daylight raids. However, fully escorted raids were limited to shallow penetration (e.g. as far as Paris or Rotterdam) by the short range of the Spitfire. For longer range raids, the B-17s were left to continue on their own. The first USAAF bombing raid in Europe was made on 17 August 1942, by 12 B-17s escorted part way, attacking marshalling yards at Rouen and Sotteville, each three-aircraft flight bombing when its leader bombed. On this and 10 further missions, no B-17s were lost, German fighter pilots hesitating to press home their attacks even when no escorts were present; the US crews joked that the B-17s defended the Spitfires. On 6 September, while unescorted, two out of 30 B-17s on the 12th US bombing mission were shot down by Fw190s, but losses on subsequent missions remained low. Despite British scepticism – noting that no attempt had yet been made to penetrate the heavy defences over Germany – on 8 October, Eaker reported his staff's conviction that even without escorts, '300 bombers can attack any target in Germany with less than 4 per cent losses' [Murray, 1985:240]. But within weeks, Eaker was enquiring about drop tanks to increase the range of escort fighters.

British PR photos of bomb damage achieved in the first 8th AF raids showed impressive bombing accuracy, well above the norm achieved on the RAF's night raids. But the US policy of bombing only when the target was clearly visible was now encountering weather problems. Between 7 September and 7 November, persistent overcast allowed only three missions. With B-24s now arriving, on 21 October a mixed force of 90 B-17s and B-24s applied the new US precision bombing against the submarine pens at Lorient. Further such raids followed, including two-phase attempts with 1,600lb AP bombs intended to crack the concrete, then 2,000lb GPs to collapse it. But despite some direct hits achieved, the 4m thick concrete roof over the pens remained intact. Evidently, some targets would require special heavy bombs, possibly ones beyond the capability of the high-altitude day bombers.

Development of US 8th Air Force Bomber Formations

During autumn 1942, largely at the instigation of Col. C. LeMay, the 8th AF began reviewing its bomber flight formations. The objective was to combine mutual defence against fighters, altitude stagger to reduce risk from ground AA fire, and a compact bombing pattern with minimum risk of aircraft being hit by bombs from aircraft above. It resulted in the most elaborate three-dimensional bomber formations of any air force in the war. Early raids had used a one-level formation for a group of three separate squadrons, each of six aircraft flying as two elements of three in an asymmetric double arrowhead or 'M' formation. In September, the Group rather than the squadron became the basic combat 'box', the 18 aircraft flying as two staggered units of nine, with each nine aircraft in a spanwise asymmetric triple arrowhead formation. By the end of the year a new formation had been devised in which the three aircraft of each element were staggered in altitude (lead, high, and low), the three squadrons flying in a similar asymmetric arrowhead, arranged the opposite way to the element, as the standard 'combat box'. To help build the formation, each Group lead crew used Aldis lamp signalling, and a flare pistol to fire a two-colour flare combination. To minimize the risk of bomb hits on other aircraft over the target, where the tracks of the three squadrons converged at their different altitudes, LeMay insisted on formation bombing, all bombardiers in each squadron releasing their bombs on seeing the lead aircraft's bombs fall. If the lead aircraft was shot down, an adjacent aircraft was required to move into the lead position.

The German Ju86R-2 High-altitude Bomber, and Countermeasures

In 1942, the Germans converted a few Junkers Ju86Ps to an even higher altitude version, the Ju86R, with very long span tapered wings, a pressure cabin, and diesel engines with turbosuperchargers and nitrous oxide injection. Two Ju86R-2 bombers, the first operational bombers with a pressure cabin, were assigned to III/KG6 at Beauvais, to fly solitary daylight raids over Britain at more than 40,000ft, each carrying just one 250kg bomb. The raids began on 24

August, and were intended as 'siren tours' to cause disruption, but the British eschewed air-raid warnings for a single raider. Standard fighters tried to get up to the intruders, but stalled and fell, a USAAF P-38 getting closest. But the British hurriedly set up a special unit at Northolt with two stripped and cleaned Spitfire IXs. At the second attempt, on 12 September the highest interception of the war was achieved. The Ju86R crew, surprised to find a fighter at their altitude, jettisoned the bomb, depressurized the cabin for safety and tried to outclimb the Spitfire. The bomber was hit, but managed to escape when one of the fighter's cannon jammed and the recoil from the other caused the fighter to slew and stall. Thereafter, the high-altitude sorties were suspended except for a last one on 2 October, with reduced fuel and no bomb, purely to test the defences. [Price, 1977b:138]

Night Bombing

The British Adopt 'Area Bombing' of German Cities; Leaflet Dropping
Early in 1942, RAF Bomber Command remained the Allies' only means of attacking Germany. But with its ability to hit small industrial targets shown to be poor and new bombing aids not yet available, 'area bombing' of German industrial towns and cities became the main objective. The Air Ministry directive of 14 February decreed that operations 'should now be focussed on the morale of the civil population and, in particular, of industrial workers', and listed the 'primary' and 'alternative' target cities. Portal wanted it made 'quite clear' that now 'the aiming points are to be the built-up areas, not for instance the dockyards or aircraft factories'. [Hastings, 1979:157] On 22 February, Air Marshal A.T. Harris took over as C. in C. Bomber Command, and was to become uniquely identified with the area bombing policy. Despite Britain's own experience of being bombed, the policy was based on a belief that

bombing of population centres would be highly damaging to civilian morale. Homelessness and fear would result in absenteeism and an exodus of refugees, which coupled with disruption of transport and communications due to the bombing, would add to the production losses from factories themselves being destroyed. In March, Churchill's Scientific Adviser, Lord Cherwell, provided a report with statistics justifying area bombing in terms of the number of people made homeless. On average one bomber should achieve 40 tons of bombs dropped during its life. If dropped on towns, these would make 4,000 to 8,000 people homeless. If only half of the bombs were dropped on target, a production run of 10,000 bombers attacking 58 German towns could make almost one third of the German population homeless. British ministerial statements continued to claim that only military targets were being attacked. [Hastings, 1979:130-4]

Meanwhile, some two million leaflets per week were now being dropped over Europe by RAF Bomber Command, aided by SOE's 'special duties' units. This output was later greatly exceeded by the USAAF effort. Leaflet dropping was still manual, the leaflets being released in bundles down the flare chute to scatter in the aircraft's slipstream. The method was slow, with large dispersion and hence poor delivery accuracy. The British MAP sought improvements via automatic dispensing, e.g. with experiments in 1942 with metal containers for leaflets, built into the wings of aircraft.

British Night Bombing Photography
During 1942, RAF heavy bombers were equipped with a ventral F24 camera for night raid photographs using a 4.5-inch photoflash bomb released from the aircraft's flare chute. Unlike post-raid coverage, raid photographs gave evidence of individual crews' performance, the marking, and the development of the raid including the spread of fires. At times they also helped to pin-point the locations of flak, searchlights, decoys, smokescreen generators etc., all lights on the ground showing as streaks across the film. The camera rearward tilt angle and timing sequence, and the photoflash fuze, were pre-set before take-off for the expected bombing altitude. Pressing the 'bomb tit' simultaneously released the bombs and the photoflash, and

activated the camera sequence. The aircraft then had to fly straight and level (for 30 seconds at 20,000ft, to the great dislike of the crews if the target was well defended) until the flash exploded. The chosen 'flash frame' remained open for 4 seconds before and after the expected time of the flash. The flash bomb itself had higher drag than the bombs, to fall with a greater trail angle, exploding in mid-air to the rear of the camera's field of view. But the 200 million candlepower flash illuminated the impact area, and the bombs still in mid-air. The next frame often picked up the flashes of the bombs exploding. The camera and photoflash were not carried if the target was known to be overcast.

The US 8th AF also soon began equipping its bombers with raid cameras. For daylight raids no flash was necessary, the camera being set to take an automatic sequence of five or six frames at intervals over the target.

'Shaker' Illumination; the Renault Raid; Flame-damped Exhausts

In February 1942, Bomber Command introduced the 'Shaker' illuminating technique, in which five successive small groups of bombers dropped flares on the upwind side of the target, progressively homing in on it, for following aircraft to mark with incendiaries for the main force to bomb. Intended to be used with Gee, it was tried first without it in a raid on the Renault factory at Billancourt near Paris, on 3 March 1942, using the Seine for navigation. This was the RAF's first attempt at a large precision raid on a target in occupied territory. The 223 aircraft bombed at 121 per hour, the RAF's highest rate yet, dropping 470 tons of bombs which caused extensive factory damage and the deaths of 231 French civilians in nearby houses. The first use of Shaker with Gee came in a raid on Essen on 8 March, 80 of the 350 bombers being equipped with Gee.

During 1942, the RAF's BSDU and FIU flew trials to evaluate bomber defence measures, including evasion tactics. The Lancaster's supposedly flame-damped exhausts were found to be visible at ranges which the night fighter crews found 'alarming' [Chisholm, 1953:119], but improving the masking – without overheating the exhaust manifolds or losing engine power through increased back pressure – was to prove very difficult.

The Lübeck Raid and Incendiaries; the German 'Baedeker' Raids

On the night of 28 March, 234 RAF bombers raided the historic German town of Lübeck, chosen by Harris because it was easy to find and to destroy, so giving the crews 'a taste of success'. The raid was the first by Lancaster bombers, the first major one against a population centre, the first to make major use of incendiaries, and the first with British liquid incendiaries. Like the Germans, who had used a 15:1 ratio of HE to incendiaries in the Coventry raid, the British had underestimated the destructive effect of incendiaries. Now, weight for weight, the incendiaries caused nearly six times the damage of HE bombs, in part because Lübeck's old buildings had a high wood content. The result led to greatly increased use of incendiaries in RAF raids, typically more than 50 per cent, as in the Hamburg firestorm raid.

Provoked by the attack on Lübeck, Hitler ordered reprisals against British historic/cultural towns as given in the Baedeker guide. These began with an attack by 40 bombers (mostly Do217s and Ju88s), on Exeter on the night of 23 April. Other raids followed, with Exeter, Bath, Norwich and York each bombed several times. Bombing was from relatively low altitude (2,000m) because of the inadequate AA defence. But thanks to frequent course changes to foil the night fighters, and British jamming of the blind bombing systems, many crews got lost. The raids petered out during September. On 30 December, eight of eleven Fw200s despatched made a token long-range night raid on Casablanca, in the hope of disrupting an Allied conference. Four crash-landed in Spain on the return.

In October, the RAF restarted raids on Italian cities. Turin received the heaviest night raids, on 20 November (232 aircraft) and 28 November (228 aircraft).

The British 'Thousand Bomber' Raid; the Bomber Stream

To encourage support for the bomber offensive, on the night of 30 May 1942 Harris implemented his 'Thousand Plan' (Operation 'Millennium'); Bomber Command despatched over 1,000 bombers against a single target, the city of Cologne. Numbers were supplemented by obsolete aircraft, damaged aircraft repaired in round-the-clock working, and aircraft from reserves, new supplies, training, conversion, target-towing and gunnery units. Given the commitment of reserves, instructors and trainee crews, the Plan was rated as a high risk by some, a confidence trick by others; but it did achieve twice the aircraft and four times the bomb load of any previous raid. Cologne was chosen because it was within Gee range, and because the bends on the Rhine would be easily visible. A total of 1,046 Wellington, Whitley, Hampden, Manchester, Stirling, Halifax and Lancaster bombers took off from 53 airfields in Britain. To saturate the air defences, the 'bomber stream' was implemented for the first time, Gee being used to achieve three concentrated streams with bombing over a 90-minute period. Gee-equipped Wellingtons led, dropping incendiaries to mark the three aiming points. The later main force crews were told to aim for gaps in the fires. Carefully planned timing and bombing directions, chosen to minimize risk of collision and risk of damage from bombs falling from aircraft at higher altitude, were largely abandoned over the target. Because of icing and other problems, only about 910 aircraft actually bombed the target, 48 being lost. It was the RAF's 107th raid on Cologne, and the city's defences now included over 500 AA guns and 150 searchlights. But this huge raid devastated large areas of the city, with over 1,000 separate fires. Later bomber crews could see the glow over Cologne from 130 miles away.

Less successful '1,000 bomber' raids were mounted on 1 June and 25 June, against Essen and Bremen respectively; there were no others until 1944.

Soviet Night Bombing: Stalingrad

On 19 July 1942, the Soviets attacked Königsberg in the first of a series of small night strategic raids; other targets included Berlin, Danzig, Stettin and Budapest. Later, night harassment bombing was used to effect against German forces surrounded at Stalingrad, the Po-2s bombing transport aircraft unloading supplies flown in at night to airfields in the 'pocket'. With their wood/fabric construction, the Po-2s had a low radar signature, making them difficult to detect at long range. At times the aircraft flew in pairs, one

using a spotlight to illuminate the target area for the second
aircraft, flying in low to drop its 200kg bomb load. In
addition, the Soviet ADD began night raids of 30 to 40
aircraft, attacking the airfields and troops in the 'pocket'.

Early US Night Raids

The first B-24 raid had been a British one, a night attack on
Tripoli on 10 January 1942 by an RAF Liberator. But
USAAF B-24s began to arrive in the Middle East in June.
On the night of 9 June, 13 B-24Ds flying individually from
Egypt attempted the first US night raid in Europe, attacking
the Ploesti refineries, but none found the target. Further
small night raids followed, against Benghazi and Tobruk. In
July, B-25s arrived and these too made some night missions,
without flame dampers.

In the Pacific, during the Battle of Midway, four B-24s
attempted a night raid on the Japanese-held Wake Island
base, but failed to find the target. A later attempt on 23
December was successful, the B-24s gliding down to 2,500ft
to bomb. In China, P-40s of the US CATF (China Air Task
Force, ex-AVG) mounted a night dive-bombing mission
against the heavily defended Hankow docks.

The British 'Pathfinder Force'; Early Techniques

New navigational aids (Gee, Oboe, H2S) brought a case for
a specialist night 'Target Finding Force' to find and mark the
target for other bombers. Each new aid would initially only
be available in small numbers and would require special
training, while some aids (e.g. Oboe) were inherently only
usable by a few aircraft. After much opposition to the idea
of 'élite crews', including from Harris, on 15 August 1942
RAF Bomber Command set up 8 Group, the Pathfinder
Force (PFF), under Grp Capt. D.C.T. Bennett. The initial
strength was four squadrons, flying Stirling, Halifax,
Lancaster and Wellington bombers respectively. A Mosquito squadron, No.109 then testing Oboe, was seconded to
the PFF. The PFF operated for the first time on 18 August in
a raid on Flensburg, using Gee and marking with flares and
incendiaries. Proposals to have SOE agents place Eureka
radio beacons to enable the RAF to find and bomb the small
and distant town of Schweinfurt were not adopted. But PFF

nnovations followed quickly. On August 28 the 'RBF' (Red Blob Fire) pyrotechnic marker was introduced, in a raid on Nuremberg; the 250lb RBF contained a mix of benzol, rubber and phosphorus coloured to burn with a red glow. Then, in he 4 September raid on Bremen, the PFF operated in three groups: 'Illuminators' dropping white flares to light up the general target area, then 'Primary Visual Markers' dropping coloured flares over the Aiming Point for 'Backers-Up' to drop incendiary markers. On 10 September, the improvised Pink Pansy' marker was introduced, in a raid on Düsseldorf. The Pink Pansy was a 4000lb MC bomb case filled with a similar mix to the RBF, and igniting with a distinctive pink flash. The Düsseldorf raid also saw red and green flares being dropped to mark the west and east boundaries of the town, he Pink Pansies being dropped in the middle. Then, on 19 September in a raid on Munich, the PFF introduced route marking, dropping flares to mark a course turning-point. Such route marking aided tight streaming for the bomber force, but was also a good way of attracting German night fighters.

Introduction of the 'Oboe' Blind-bombing aid; Skymarking

On 20 December, six 109 Sqdn Mosquito B.Mk.IV bombers, bombing at intervals, carried out the first raid to use the Oboe radar-ranging blind-bombing aid, in an attack on a coking plant at Lutterade in Holland. Similar small Oboe raids were to continue for months, despite the risk of giving its secrets to the Germans for little result. For targets obscured by dense overcast, the PFF devised blind 'Skymarking', dropping parachute flares to burst in mid-air, upwind above the cloud over the target. Following bomb aimers then aimed at the illuminated parts of the cloud. The first use of Skymarking, and the first use of Oboe for target marking, was made by a PFF Mosquito in a raid on Düsseldorf on 31 December. Skymarking was code-named 'Wanganui', and was laid using Oboe ('Musical Wanganui') or H2S ('H2S Wanganui'). Skymarking was inaccurate (the flares drifting with the wind as they descended) and required re-marking at five-minute intervals. Also, the Germans soon began sending up decoy flares nearby, to confuse bomber crews. But the technique remained in use right through the war.

V   1943

Bomber Developments

New Bombers
New bombers making their first flights in 1943 included: the twin-engined Bristol Buckingham (Britain, 4 February) which with ten 0.303in machine guns was the fastest fully armed bomber of the day; the single-engined Brewster XA-32 ground attack aircraft (USA, 22 April); the twin-engined Hughes D-2 high-speed long-range bomber (USA, 20 June), with an airframe built of 'Duramold' plastic-impregnated wood; the twin-engined Yokosuka P1Y1 *Ginga* fast medium bomber (Japan, c.August) ordered into production but with many delays; the Vickers Type 447 Windsor heavy bomber (Britain, 23 October), the only four-engined aircraft to have Barnes Wallis geodetic construction, and also featuring four separate main u/c units (one for each nacelle) and twin-gun barbettes in the rear of each outer nacelle; the twin-engined Dornier Do317 (Germany), a development of the Do217 intended to have a pressure cabin; the twin-engined experimental Myasischev DVB-102 (USSR), a further Soviet attempt to achieve a stratospheric bomber, with two separate pressure cabins; and the Heinkel He277 (Germany), a development of the He177 with four separate engines to avoid the fire problems with the He177's coupled engines.

New aircraft in service included the Yakovlev Yak-6 light bomber, the Me410 and Ju188, the Yokosuka D4Y1 ('Judy') dive-bomber, and versions of the British Typhoon, Mosquito and Beaufighter. In the Pacific theatre, USAAF B-17 and B-26 bombers were replaced by B-24s (for longer range) and B-25s (for longer range and ability to use the shorter island runways).

Bomber Developments

Among technology developments, the USAAF introduced flak curtains hung in the aircraft; these absorbed impact energy by their elasticity, and were lighter than armour plate. Deliveries of the B-17G, with a 'chin' turret to help defend against head-on fighter attacks, began in September. By November, new B-17s and B-24s had increased range thanks to internal wing-tip 'Tokyo tanks'. In Japan, heavy losses of G4M bombers, shot down in flames because of their unprotected fuel tanks, led to improvised protection in the form of sheet rubber and sponge, plus CO_2 fire extinguishers. In Britain, an interim prototype for a Mk.IV high altitude day version of the Halifax flew in March; the Mk.IV was to have had increased span and two-stage supercharged engines. In Germany, a modified Me323D six-engined transport was used in an attempt to test drop an experimental 18,000kg bomb. The aircraft was given an assisted take-off, being towed by an He111Z, but began to break up in mid-air, the result of prior enemy strafing damage. The crew released the bomb but were killed in the subsequent crash. Two new US bomb-sights were introduced, the D-8 (for low altitude) and Sperry S-1 (for night use). In Britain, the gyro-stabilized tachymetric Mk.II SABS (Stabilised Automatic Bomb Sight) was provided to 617 Squadron for precision bombing. It was first used on 12 November, aiming 12,000lb HC bombs at the Antheor viaduct. Although much more accurate than the Mk.XIV vector sight, the SABS required a 10-mile straight and level bombing run, with the target visible, and it could not use a 'false wind' adjustment for misplaced or offset markers. Hence the more versatile Mk.XIV was retained for main force use.

Advanced Bomber Projects

Bomber projects of 1943 included some interesting ones. In Britain, the four-engined Percival P.37 heavy bomber was of twin-boom flying wing design. In Japan, the six-engined Nakajima G10N1 *Fugako* was intended for round trip bombing raids on the US mainland from Japan. In Italy, the Piaggio P.133 prototype was nearing completion at the 1943 Armistice; a development of the P.108B, it carried six 20mm cannon. In Germany, the Heinkel He111Z-2 was a strategic bomber version of the five-engined 'Siamese Twin' *Zwillig* glider tug. The Junkers company began work on the Ju287 turbojet-powered high-speed heavy bomber, the proposed 25 degree sweptback wing for high-subsonic flight being changed to an even more revolutionary sweptforward one. In September, an Me210 prototype flew with modifications for the projected Me310 pressurized high-altitude bomber and *Zerstörer*, later cancelled in favour of the Me410. The highly unconventional Blohm und Voss P.163 featured wing-tip nacelles to house the crew, leaving the fuselage free for the engines (a coupled unit driving a large nose propeller), fuel and bombs. The wing-tip crew nacelle was flight tested on a BV141.

Weapon Developments

Bombing Extremes: German 'Crowsfeet'; the British 'Blockbuster'
By 1943, German bombers occasionally dropped containers which ejected large numbers of small (5 to 6cm high) four-pointed metal barbs. Known to the British as 'crowsfeet', these passive weapons were symmetrical, coming to rest on three spikes so that the fourth always pointed upwards. Dropped at night, those falling on roads and runways could puncture tyres, and so immobilize vehicles and wreck aircraft, until they were cleared away the next morning. The British also made air-drops of crowsfoot spikes, in the Far East in 1944.

The war's largest blast bomb, the British 12,000lb HC 'Blockbuster' was effectively three 4,000lb HC canisters in series, with an annular tail unit. It was intended for attacks against specific large buildings, being less effective than three 4,000lb bombs against dispersed area targets. A Lancaster bomb bay could carry a single one. It was first used on the night of 15 September 1943, by 617 Squadron Lancasters in a low-level attempt to breach the banks of the Dortmund Ems canal.

Petrol Bombs: Allied Development of 'Napalm' and 'FRAS'

The first US trial with gasoline bombs was on 16 May 1942, at Lae. In 1943, US carrier crews improvised a gasoline-filled practice bomb tied to a 100lb GP bomb so that the blast would ignite and spread the gasoline. Such attempts confirmed the need for a thickener in the fuel. In the USA and Britain, work had been under way since 1941 on firebombs made with petrol converted to a less volatile gelled form, as used in flame-throwers. A thickener, such as rubber, reduced the spread, slowed the rate of burning, and developed higher temperatures, thereby causing deeper damage. With rubber in short supply, research moved to alternative thickening agents. Work under Prof. L. Fieser at Harvard University led to a formulation of naphthenate, palmitate and lauric acid as a thickener, giving the 'napalm' jellied gasoline bomb, ignited by white phosphorus. The British gelled fuel, 'FRAS' (Fuel Research Aluminium Stearate) using aluminium stearate as the thickener, was developed for flame-throwers but later used in aircraft bombs as an alternative to napalm. Elsewhere, Soviet sources refer to VVS use in 1943 of 'self-igniting liquids "KS" in AZh-2 casings'. [Fetzer, 1973:209]

Bouncing Bombs: 'Upkeep' and 'Highball'; Kurt

In Britain, development of the Wallis 'Upkeep' anti-dam weapon was authorized in February 1943. Carried by a modified Lancaster, the 9,250lb, 50-inch diameter bomb was cylindrical, and filled with Torpex. It was fitted with three hydraulic pistols set to detonate at 30ft depth of water, plus a 90-second time fuse as back-up. Production bombs were employed in the 'Dambusters' raid on the night of 16 May. Later, Upkeep bombs were test-dropped on land for possible use against canal embankments and locks. But Upkeep was never used operationally again. Of the other British bouncing bombs, the spherical 950lb, 32-inch diameter 'light' version of 'Highball' was to have been carried by the Mosquito, two per aircraft in tandem, and also by US aircraft (Avenger, B-25, B-26). It was intended for use against shipping, starting with the *Tirpitz*, although bouncing them into railway tunnels was also envisaged. It was tested in 1943, but never saw operational use. The 'heavy' version of Highball was intended to be carried, one per aircraft, by Wellington and Warwick bombers for use against multiple arch dams and canal locks, as well as against shipping. But like the naval mortar-fired 'Baseball', it was never developed.

After the dams raid, the Germans recovered a 'British revolving depth charge' and its equipment from the wreckage of a Lancaster. Once its operation was understood, rather than copy it the Germans began experiments on basic principles, so delaying for 18 months their own bouncing bomb. This, the SB800RS *Kurt*, a 400kg spherical bomb was successfully test dropped by Fw190G and Me410A aircraft, but cancelled in November 1944. A projected variant featured a rocket boost/tail unit and gyroscopic stabilization to increase range and provide greater safety for the dropping aircraft, the rocket unit breaking away on contacting the water.

Air-to-Surface Guided Weapons

In Germany, the first operational guided bomb, the FX1400 or SD1400X *Fritz X*, and the first operational powered guided missile, the Henschel Hs293A, both entered service in July. Both were *Kehl-Strassburg* radio-controlled air-launched weapons, operated by KG100 with Do217 carrier aircraft, primarily for anti-shipping use. The unpowered, stub-winged *Fritz X* gave a steep trajectory with high impact speed for an AP role, the winged rocket-powered Hs293 allowed release from further afield. *Fritz X* had a cruciform tail with spoiler controls and a gyro for roll stabilization; the Hs293 had more conventional ailerons and elevator. But the objective with each was to achieve an accurate hit from a safe height/distance to minimize the danger from AA fire to the attacking aircraft. After release, the weapon was steered by a controller in the aircraft on a line-of-sight course towards the target, its visibility being aided by a small flare in the tail. Within months, operations with both the *Fritz X* and the Hs293 were being hampered by US NRL-developed jammers, so the Allies thought; post-war, the Germans blamed poor training, unreliable equipment and use at excessive range.

Other air-to-surface weapons under development in 1943 included the US GB and VB-series weapons; and a Japanese IR-homing anti-shipping bomb and the *Funryu 1* radio-guided missile. An Italian pre-set guided glide bomb used a glider attachment with a 1,000kg bomb; control used a gyro unit for azimuth and an air-brake for dive angle.

CBW Developments: Chemical Weapon Casualties; Soviet BW

Although they remained unused, the secret stockpiling of chemical weapons in all war theatres continued apace, bringing a risk of accidents as a result of enemy action. Some 83 people dying from escaping mustard gas were among the casualties when 96 Ju88 bombers using *Düppel* attacked the harbour at Bari, Italy on 2 December 1943. One of the ships hit, the SS *John Harvey*, was secretly carrying 100 tons of M47A2 mustard gas bombs for the 15th AF at Foggia. The bombs were themselves of unstable type, being made with the cheap but impure Levinstein H process, giving a gas build-up which had to be vented regularly. Aside from the 100lb M47, USAAF chemical bombs available at this time included the 115lb M70, 500lb M78, and 1,000lb M79. Inexplicably, details of the tabun nerve gas, provided in July 1943 by a German chemist captured in North Africa, were ignored at Porton Down.

Despite their proficiency in CW, it seems the Germans did not begin BW development until 1943, and even then the priority given remained low so that little progress was achieved by the end of the war. Information on the much greater Soviet BW work remains scant. However a Soviet Air Force germ warfare specialist, a Capt. Von Apen, deserting to the Germans, described Soviet BW experiments, including plague-spraying and the parachute-dropping of rats with containers which would break on impact to spray them with virulent bacteria. [Harris and Paxman, 1982:85,142]

Nuclear Developments; Allied Fears of German Radiation Weapons

In 1943, the Allies noted that even if the Germans failed to achieve an atomic bomb, they might use a uranium reactor to generate highly radioactive material. This could be used in bombs as a form of poison gas, or (as Groves later warned Eisenhower) applied as a 'radiation barrage' against ground troops. In Britain, the possible need to evacuate the population of London because of radiation bombs was addressed, and the Medical Research Council produced the first report on the possible long-term genetic effects of exposure to radiation. Apparently the Germans did briefly consider such radiation weapons, as a deterrent against Allied use. [Irving, 1967:182]

While the US Manhattan programme advanced, in Europe Allied efforts were directed at preventing German nuclear research, where possible, with disruption of heavy water production at Rjukan by sabotage operations, then by a bombing raid by 140 US B-17s on 16 November.

Navigation, Blind Bombing and Radar Developments

Ground Markers for Air Navigation

Radio aids being vulnerable to jamming or interference, visual aids were often preferable. In 1943, the Germans introduced two powerful searchlights shining vertically into the sky, near Dunkirk. Being visible from much of southern England, these helped German crews raiding Britain at night to find their way home. Before this, in May of 1943 alone, four Fw190 fighter-bombers had landed in Britain, apparently thanks to 'Meaconing'. The British were themselves using searchlights as navigation aids, guiding returning crippled bombers around towns and towards airfields; the airfields themselves carried homing searchlights ('Sandra').

On the Eastern Front, by 1943 the Soviet ZOS service was using a mix of tools to help guide Soviet aircraft, especially at night. As well as radio D/F and homing beacons, these included flares, searchlights, bonfires, and lights laid out in an arrowhead pattern to indicate direction. Later, large symbols painted on the ground or laid out in white fabric, and in one sector a large tethered balloon, were also used. It appears that the Luftwaffe also learned to make good use of the ZOS markers. [Boyd, 1977:146]

'*H2S*' *in Service, and German Reactions; X-band Sets*

Despite objections to the use of the Magnetron valve over enemy territory where its secret would quickly be discovered, 10cm H2S Mk.I was introduced on 30 January 1943, by the PFF in a raid against Hamburg; Bomber Command had demanded the short-term advantage. In the second raid using it, on 2 February, an H2S-Stirling was shot down near Rotterdam. The recovered H2S came as a revelation to the Germans, the resulting 'Rotterdam Commission' causing major changes to current radar projects in an effort to catch up with the Allied centimetric developments. On 22 June, a rebuilt British H2S set was test flown in a He177. The Germans tried to counter H2S using large radar decoy reflectors (wire netting and metal tetrahedrons) but the scale required made the technique impractical. The Mk.I H2S was followed by the improved Mk.II, but Allied development now favoured 3cm X-band sets, the shorter wavelength offering better resolution imaging, able to show lakes, parks, etc. in cities. The TRE 3cm H2S Mk.III was introduced by PFF Lancasters on 22 November in the opening raid of the Battle of Berlin. A US 'H2X' X-band set, was adopted by the USAAF as AN/APS-15 'Mickey' or 'BTO' (for 'Bomb Through Overcast'), for blind bombing on daylight raids.

Meanwhile, with *Heinrich* jammers now compromising Gee over much of Western Europe, the British had introduced a multiple frequency Gee Mk.II in February. Crews were given the reserve frequencies and change times in advance, and at each change, could get a quick position fix before the Germans switched the jammers.

Blind Bombing: 'Oboe' and German Intelligence; Egon; Gee-H

Despite the importance of 'Oboe', the RAF allowed the Germans opportunities to learn its secrets, by repeatedly using it on minor raids. Only after the success of the first large Oboe-marked raid, on 5 March, was Oboe banned except for target marking on major raids. Oboe radar pulses were masked by their similarity to other pulses, but the Germans picked up the course control radio signals, and by mid-1943 associated them with the high-flying Mosquitos. But the means by which the Mosquitos achieved their objectives remained unclear, and attempts to shoot one down to examine its equipment were unsuccessful. After an accurate raid through overcast on steel furnaces in the Ruhr, Hitler believed that IR-guided bombs were being used. Others suspected that agents were setting up homing radio beacons close to the targets. But eventually the signals for bomb release were noticed and then the curved flight path and the eight-minute bombing run. In December, Oboe was first countered with *Karl*, which jammed the course radio signals.

During 1943, TRE increased the potential range of Oboe by use of repeater aircraft at intermediate positions to relay the Oboe signals, but the system was never used in full. Meanwhile, apparently while the Germans were still puzzling over the British Oboe system, in mid-1943 I/KG66 began using a blind bombing aid code-named *Egon*, which operated on similar lines to Oboe, with radar-ranging from two modified *Freya* sets (designated FuSAn730 *Freya Egon I*) some 150km apart. The aircraft itself carried a two-channel FuG25a IFF-type repeater for the two radar signals. The Germans also uprated *Knickebein* to operate on 34 frequencies instead of 3.

TRE also developed the 'H' radio system, for use with 'Gee' as a combined navigation/blind bombing aid, 'Gee-H'. The 'H' part operated like Oboe in reverse, giving pulses which were picked up at two separate ground stations at known locations and retransmitted. The pulses were received back on the aircraft's Gee set, where the two time delays gave the aircraft's position by triangulation. The 'H' ground stations could handle sufficient frequencies for up to 50 aircraft simultaneously, a big improvement on Oboe. The enemy could detect and home onto an aircraft's H pulses, but sparing use (near the target only) minimized this risk. Gee-H was first successfully used on 7 October 1943.

Electronic Warning and Countermeasures

Tail-warning Radars: 'Monica'; 'Neptun'

The RAE 'Monica', the first aircraft tail warning radar, entered service on RAF bombers early in 1943. Tail-mounted and pointed rearwards, it gave the crew audible 'bleeps' to warn of any aircraft detected at the rear. But an approaching night fighter could remain unnoticed among bleeps generated by other bombers. Monica was also dangerous since night fighters could be equipped to home onto its transmissions, and by March examples of Monica were in German hands from aircraft shot down. It was argued later that with the German night fighters known to be using AI radar, the bombers could have relied on using Boozer; instead, although partly superseded by (the similarly dangerous) 'Fishpond', Monica remained in use until mid-1944, when in some estimates, it had been responsible for more bomber losses than any other single device of the war. [Gunston, 1976:11] By October, German bombers over Britain were also using tail-warning radar (FuG214 *Lichtenstein BC/R*, later FuG216 R-1 (*Neptun R-1*), but with less risk than the British use of 'Monica'; German bombers were seldom part of a stream, and evasive action could be taken whenever any aircraft registered on the radar. Late in the war, US B-17s and B-24s operating at night were fitted with AN/APS-13 tail warning radar.

Chaff (Foil) Strips for Radar Jamming: Giman-shi; Window; Düppel

With 'Window' and *Düppel* held secret and unused in Europe, in May 1943 strips of *Giman-shi* (deceiving paper), 75cm long to counter the 1.5m US gun control radars, were dropped by IJN aircraft during night raids on Guadalcanal. This use seems not to have been reported by the Japanese to the Germans, nor by the Americans to the British. But in June, Churchill accepted that the balance of advantage was now favourable for Window. As first used in the Hamburg raid on the night of 23 July, it consisted of 30cm × 1.5cm strips of foil, stiffened by backing paper and lamp-blacked so as not to show up in searchlights. Bundles were hand-dropped down flare chutes at one per minute, to burst and drift down to litter the towns and countryside below; the descent could take two hours or more. For the Hamburg raid, the RAF's losses (12 aircraft out of 791) were only 1.5 per cent compared with 6 per cent on previous raids. The blinding of the *Würzburg* radars was so complete that Göring offered a money prize for a countermeasure. Early radar devices (*Würzlaus*, *Nürnberg*) attempting to discriminate between slow-moving foils and fast-moving aircraft brought little success. The Germans' own *Düppel* foil was first used operationally on the night of 7 October, during a raid on Norwich. The 80cm strips disrupted the older type British ground and AI radars, and prevented IFF interrogation. By the end of 1943, chaff was also being used by the USAAF. Meanwhile, the first US airborne jammers had been introduced in B-17s over Italy in October 1943, AN/APT-2 'Carpet' jamming *Würzburg* AA control radars, and AN/APT-3 'American Mandrel' countering the *Freya* EW sets.

Allied Communications Monitoring and Jamming

In 1943, first RAF then US bombers carried an extra German-speaking crewman and receivers to monitor German shorter range VHF fighter R/T communications. This provided real-time information to the crews, plus valuable strategic information on the German defences. Longer range 3-6Mc/s signals were monitored from the Y-service station at Kingsdown in Kent.

One German reaction to 'Window' was *Wilde Sau*, operating night fighters on a freelance basis aided by a broadcast 'running commentary' giving the whereabouts of the British bomber stream. The British responded by changing 'Tinsel' (operated at will by the bomber crews) to 'Special Tinsel' (used under instruction from Kingsdown); and introducing the 'Airborne Cigar' (or 'ABC') R/T jammer, able to jam three different frequencies simultaneously.

Realizing that German high-altitude night raids on Britain by Fw190 fighter-bombers operated under R/T control, the British introduced ground transmitters for jamming the frequencies used, under code-name 'Cigarette'. The British also began aiding their own bombers via ground-based countermeasures, first with the 'Ground Cigar' VHF jammer introduced on the night of 30 July. The 'Corona' countermeasure begun at Kingsdown on the night of 22 October, involved using German-speaking operators to broadcast fake instructions e.g. ordering the German night fighters towards diversionary raids, or to land at distant airfields. There were heated broadcast arguments with each side claiming to be the genuine control station. When the Germans introduced women controllers, the British responded with German-speaking WAAFs. Corona eventually became an annoyance system, sending test transmissions, Hitler's speeches, etc. In December, the German Forces *Annemarie* transmitter began broadcasting particular types of music to indicate the area sector being penetrated by the main bomber stream. The British responded with 'Dartboard', jamming the music via the powerful Aspidistra transmitters. When the Germans took to using Morse, the British countered with random Morse signals from 'Drumstick' transmitters.

Bomber Support

Bomber Crew Training Developments

By 1943, Germany and Japan were experiencing increasing difficulty with training aircrews, thanks to fuel shortages, inadequate resources, diversion of aircraft and instructors to operational duties, and short-cutting of training in order to speed the provision of urgently needed replacement crews. The inexperience of the new crews led to increased combat and accident losses. In the USSR, the early war phase of expediency was giving way to longer and better training. For the Western Allies especially, extensive training programmes in the USA and Commonwealth countries were long since established, with much emphasis on operational training on actual service aircraft types.

For the Allies, much ingenuity was expended on training, including improving on the Link Trainer simulator. In Britain, the Silloth Trainer employed a complete bomber fuselage, with a realistic control system operated by air bellows, and with fully operating radio, electronics and systems; it was used to simulate complete flights. In 1943, Cambridge University devised a simulator for PFF crews to train on, aiding them to assess the MPI (Mean Point of Impact) of existing markers, to enable accurate back-up marking. Later, the British introduced the Jordan Trainer for training Master Bombers. To represent a position orbiting a German city under night attack, the trainee sat in darkness in a bomber cockpit, high above an elaborate revolving model of a city, the model using lights, steam and pyrotechnics to simulate defences, marking, cloud and smoke.

For the USAAF, daylight bomber crew training, with its great need for gunnery expertise, included novel approaches to gunnery training. These ranged from the use of truck-mounted turrets for firing at targets as the truck sped past, to a purpose-built gunnery training aircraft (Fairchild AT-21). Also, 1943 saw the introduction of RP-63A 'live target' conversions of Bell P-63 Kingcobra fighters. These 'Pin-Ball Targets', which flashed lights to record a hit, were given thick skins, armour plate and bullet-proof glazed areas. They were used in simulated attacks on bombers, the gunners firing at them with a lightweight frangible practice ammunition.

US 'Wing-tip Escort' Bomber Conversions

US prototype four-engined heavy 'wing-tip escort' fighters, the Lockheed Vega XB-40 and Convair XB-41 – conversions of a B-17F and a B-24D – appeared in 1943. Compared with the normal bomber version, each carried additional armour, 16 guns, twice the ammunition, and special supply tracks to feed ammunition to the waist and tail positions. There was a plan for the other bombers to be fitted with additional, dummy, gun installations to mislead the enemy fighter pilots. Thirteen YB-40s were built, apparently with up to 30 guns in some cases. The 8th AF 92nd Bomb Group flew the first YB-40 mission in a raid on St Nazaire on 27 May. But the YB-40s proved to be too heavy, tail heavy, slow and unmanoeuvrable, and unable even to defend themselves adequately. They were withdrawn in August.

Long-range Single-engine Escort Fighters; the P-51B Mustang

Belatedly, in 1943 the Allies began using fighters with drop tanks for extended sweep and escort operations. The British introduced 108-gallon laminated plastic/paper tanks, but although the 8th AF in Britain also began using these on P-47s (on 28 July), the US Wright Field rejected the British tanks as unsuitable and began developing aluminium ones. For really long range, greatly increased internal fuel was also needed. Thus, the Soviets increased the internal tankage of the Yak-9, giving the Yak-9D with a radius of 700km. Needing a long-range escort fighter in Britain, US Gen. H.H. Arnold had three Spitfires specially modified and flown across the Atlantic in stages to Britain (the only single-seat fighters to do so) to try to convince the British to convert some of their under-utilized Spitfires as escorts for the US bombers [Webster and Frankland, Vol.II, 1961:43]. Thanks largely to Portal's scepticism that any long range escort could operate against short-range interceptors, and despite the proven long-range performance of PR Spitfires, the British did not respond, and left the US to develop its own long-range fighter. This appeared in December. The North American P-51B with drop tanks offered a combat radius of 880 miles, allowing fighter escort deep into Germany. The first escorted long-range mission, against Kiel 500 miles away, was flown on 13 December. The balance of power in the Western Front daylight air war was shifting dramatically.

Allied Weather Reconnaissance to Support Bombing

The weather over Europe being crucial for bombing operations, during 1943 the Allies introduced weather flights specifically to support the bomber offensive. In April, RAF Bomber Command's new 1409 Met Flight, with Mosquitos, began long-range meteorological sorties, code-named

'Pampas', over enemy territory. Soon, each raid was preceded by a Mosquito flying to the target zone (indirectly to avoid giving away the target) to radio back weather data; missions were also flown for the USAAF. In addition, on each RAF raid 'Windfinder' H2S bomber crews radioed back information on wind speed and direction; averaged winds ('zephyrs') were then broadcast to all crews. By mid-1943, prior to each major 8th AF raid, a B-17 'weather ship' climbed to operational height to report on cloud, icing and contrail formation. In September, the 8th AF began long-range B-17 met. flights from Cornwall out over the Atlantic. Later, in 1944, the 8th AF began flying 'Scout' over-target sorties 15 minutes ahead of the bomber force, to report on the weather, smoke, defence activity, etc. The Mosquitos used were later replaced by P-51s since these were less distinguishable from escorts.

Planning routes and Targets: PR and PI; US 'Flak Analysis'

The Allied CIU (Central Interpretation Unit) at RAF Medmenham assigned specialist photo-interpretation groups to different target types, new constructions, bomb damage, camouflage, decoy sites, etc. They used the growing stock of aerial photos (eventually over 15 million), comparing recent with earlier ones to detect signs of change. One group's task was to prepare a detailed information folder for each coming raid, giving annotated photomosaic target maps, plus details about the target, flak defences, decoy sites, etc. Reproduction, to provide a copy to each bomber crew, was a major task for a large raid.

Deceptive routing was needed for PR sorties over highly sensitive targets, so as to avoid triggering increased defences around the site. For the 'Dambusters Raid', pre-raid photos were taken from high altitude while appearing to be on course for another target, which was duly overflown before the aircraft turned for home. The pilot was instructed to bale out in an emergency, so that the photos would be destroyed in the crash.

In February 1943, Dr L.E. Bayliss of the US Army Operational Research Group produced the first mathematical analysis of Anti-Aircraft fire from the standpoint of its avoidance by aircraft. This analysis gave a 'Curve of Total Probability' of an aircraft being hit as a function of its slant range from an AA gun. Using careful plotting of the locations and strengths of German AA sites, this start to the science of Flak Analysis led from March onwards to optimized routing and bombing run directions for 8th AF raids, to minimize exposure to guns within a critical 2,500yd radius. A noticeable reduction in flak damage and bomber losses was obtained. [Hogg, 1978:115]

Allied Air-sea Rescue; Emergency Airfields

With the expansion of British and US bombing operations in Britain, new ASR provisions for the Channel and North Sea included: the use of fighters (RAF Spitfire, 8th AF P-47) – able to operate close to the enemy coast – to search and drop supplies; the British parachute-dropped powered Mk.1 Airborne Lifeboat; and the British 'SARAH' VHF radio emergency beacon. Later the P-47s flew patrols over the Channel routes whenever the 8th AF was operating. On 6 September, RAF launches picked up 118 US crewmen after twelve 8th AF bombers ditched in the Channel out of fuel.

With increasing numbers of RAF and USAAF aircraft, especially bombers, returning badly crippled, or in trouble because of fog, the British created a special 'Emergency Landing Ground', RAF Woodbridge ELG at Sutton Heath in Suffolk. The site was chosen for being low lying and flat, by the east coast, and relatively fog free. The first emergency landing there was made by a US B-17 on 18 July 1943. Two further ELGs were built at Manston and Carnaby. These 'crash dromes' had few buildings or other obstacles to hit, and an oversized runway 4,500yd long (i.e around twice normal length) and 250yd wide (i.e five times normal width) to aim at – vital for aircraft that were scarcely controllable as a result of battle damage. Eight dispersal loops provided parking for 50 aircraft each. An abundance of ambulances, crash tenders, mobile cranes and bulldozers provided for crash attention and removal, and later these included US-supplied fire-appliances having remotely controlled telescopic arms capable of insertion right into the wreckage to spray foam. The runway was divided into three parallel strips, with green, white and amber lights for the south, centre and north lanes, respectively. When possible, crippled aircraft were directed to the south lane where a foam bed was laid for wheels-up landings; less damaged and partially powered aircraft to the centre lane; and aircraft low on fuel or diverted by bad weather to the north lane. By the end of the war, a total of 4,115 aircraft had made emergency landings at Woodbridge.

Ground-attack Developments

German Anti-tank Developments; Use of Heavy Bombers

In 1943, the Luftwaffe made major efforts to increase its 'tank-busting' capability: Soviet tank production was increasing steeply, and more heavily armoured tanks (KV variants and the *Josef Stalin*) were being developed. Specialist anti-tank units (*Panzerjäger-Staffeln*) were introduced, variously equipped with Ju88P, Bf110, Hs129B and especially Ju87G aircraft; and there were further experiments with heavy calibre cannon and new high-velocity ammunition with tungsten-hardened cores. Service 30mm cannon were being replaced by the 37mm BK 3.7 Flak 18. Even this was unable to penetrate the thick frontal armour of the T-34 or KV-1 tanks, but was effective in attacking them from the side or rear. While some units took to using 4kg SD4 hollow-charge bombs against tanks, other and bigger anti-armour weapons were being tried, the 50mm BK 5 cannon entering service on the Ju88P-4. More impressive still, the Ju88P-1 saw limited service with a 75mm PaK 40 cannon, which was made jettisonable in the event of fighter attack because it made the aircraft so unwieldy. The *Düka* 88 U-Boat gun was apparently also proposed for the Ju88P, but not adopted.

Despite the great size of a four-engine bomber for ground attack, the Germans used several Heinkel He177A bombers, each with a 50mm BK 5 cannon under the nose, in desperate attempts to relieve troops cut off at Stalingrad;

this led to five He177A-3/R5 conversions having a 75mm BK 7.5 cannon under the nose. Elsewhere, and at less risk, British SOE Halifax crews, returning from night supply drops, took to train busting using the rear turret guns in a low, slow, parallel pass.

Soviet Ground-attack Aircraft

In the USSR, the Sukhoi Su-8 or DDBSch twin-engined *Shturmovik* had heavy armour plate protection, four 37mm anti-tank cannon, and a 600kg internal bomb load. But it was not adopted. New ground-attack versions of the Yak-9 fighter included the Yak-9T with a 37mm anti-tank cannon firing through the propeller hub, and the Yak-9B with a fuselage bomb bay for four 100kg bombs. Meanwhile, the Pe-2 was now being used in dives of up to 60 degrees. The Kuban conflict saw the first major Soviet use of western Lend-Lease aircraft: the Bell P-39, Curtiss P-40, Vickers Spitfire VB, and Douglas A-20 bomber. The P-40 and Spitfire were not greatly liked, the VVS believing more robust, more heavily armed aircraft were better for ground-attack operations. By contrast, the P-39 Airacobra – neglected by the Western Allies – was judged adequate as an interceptor, and with its central engine location giving good pilot view, and its 37mm cannon, near ideal for hedge-hopping ground-attack operations. Reportedly, the VVS assigned its best pilots to the P-39 *Kobry*. [Hardesty, 1982:141, 235]

US Ground-attack Developments: 'Big Single' Aircraft, and Big Guns

In the USA, the Curtiss A-25 Army version of the Navy's SB2C-1 dive-bomber entered limited service in 1943; like the RAF, the USAAF had remained sceptical of the merits of the dive-bomber. Meanwhile, almost uniquely, the US was pursuing development of large and powerful single-seat, single-engine ground-attack aircraft. The Brewster XA-32 was impressive enough, with a 3,000lb internal bomb load and four 37mm cannon. Two bigger ones, the Kaiser Fleetwings XA-39 and Curtiss XA-40 had been cancelled, but a third eventually flew in 1944. This, the Consolidated Vultee XA-41 could carry a 7,000lb war load internally, and had four 37mm and four 0.5-inch guns in the wings. But the A-36 dive-bomber version of the P-51 was now showing its worth, while fighter-bombers were thought capable of defending themselves, as well as delivering adequate ordnance. The Americans were also interested in very large ground-attack guns. Trial nose installations included a 75mm cannon in an A-26 Invader, and US Army 75mm M4 field gun in a Douglas B-18A. The M4 was adopted for B-25G bombers late in 1943.

Ground-attack Techniques and Operations

British Desert Air Force Close Air Support at El Hamma

In North Africa, Woodall's close air support system was fully implemented by AVM H.Broadhurst for DAF operations with the 8th Army. Innovations to aid Montgomery's offensive at El Hamma on 26 March included: lines of yellow smoke to show forward troop positions; a creeping shell barrage giving a visible line of dust and smoke as a 'moving bomb line'; DAF pilots in tanks, acting as FACs (Forward Air Controllers, being used for the first time); and a 'flying FAC' monitoring the battle as a whole. Twenty-two squadrons of fighters and fighter-bombers provided close support. Night bombing was followed by pattern bombing by light/medium bombers, then strikes on gun positions and armour by relays of fighter-bombers while Spitfires flew top cover. The ground forces then advanced behind an artillery barrage creeping forward at 100ft per minute which served as the moving bomb line for the continuing air attacks. The German defences were overwhelmed by the intensity of the assault. Despite this success, RAF opposition to such full close support continued, but the concepts used became features of Allied tactical air warfare.

Eastern Front Ground Attack: the Shturmovik; Night Operations

VVS techniques with the Il-2 *Shturmovik* used a low-level approach for strafing and firing RS-82 rockets against infantry or vehicles, or a shallow dive against a specific target requiring accuracy. In group attacks, some crews were assigned to AA suppression, if necessary holding back to observe where the flak was coming from. The offensive at Krymskaya on 26 May, saw the first Soviet use of an air-laid smokescreen to hide the armoured and infantry assault, 19 Il-2s in two groups laying the smoke. On 2 June, Snr Lt. N.P. Dedov introduced an Il-2 attack carousel, in an attack on German positions near Moldavanskaya; the Il-2s flew in columns of six to the target area where each column formed a defensive circle, the aircraft leaving in succession to attack and rejoin the circle.

For Soviet night bombing raids close to the front, searchlights and tracer shells fired by ground forces were used to indicate the direction of the targets; the aircraft themselves dropped 'bombs that gave off light' [Fetzer, 1973:209] to aid visual attacks, and controllers in observation aircraft monitored the attacks. With the Po-2 harassment bombers suffering increasing losses to German mobile 'flak circuses', the pilots took to flying in pairs. If one was picked up by searchlights, he attempted evasion by sideslipping or 'shamming dead' in a spin, while the second moved in unnoticed to bomb the searchlights and guns. In a copying move, in December the Germans set up *1.Ostfliegerstaffel* with volunteer Soviet crews and captured Po-2s, to fly harassment raids against the Soviets. Meanwhile, the Germans were also stepping up other night ground-attack operations. With the *Stuka* now too vulnerable by day, some Ju87D-7s were adapted for night use, with flame-damped exhausts and night-flying equipment.

The Kursk Tank Battle

The greatest tank battle and greatest aircraft versus tanks battle of the war came with the German Operation *Zitadelle* offensive at Kursk. Some 2,000 German aircraft flew over 37,000 sorties, many helping in the total of 1,100 Soviet

tanks claimed destroyed. On the first day, 5 July, *Hptm*
H.U. Rüdel of 1/St.G.2 used his Ju87G's twin 37mm cannon
to destroy all 12 T-34s in a Soviet column, by aiming at the
rear of each tank, which had limited protection and housed
the engine and fuel. Rüdel went on to become the
Luftwaffe's tank-busting ace, credited with 519 Soviet tanks.
On 5 July Soviet Il-2s made the first use of PTAB 2.5kg
hollow charge bombs and on 7 July, destroyed 70 tanks of
the 9th Panzer Division in 20 minutes. Lavochkin La-5
fighter-bombers also flew many sorties against German
tanks, firing RS-82s or dropping PTABs and climbing to
provide cover for the Il-2s. The VVS also extended the
Okhotniki freelance fighter concept to ground-attack
operations, with Il-2s operating in groups of two or four,
roaming at will to attack enemy trains, vehicles and infantry.
By late 1943, with the Germans pulling fighters back into
Germany to counter the US day raids, the Soviets were able
to convert more fighter squadrons to ground attack.

Air Operations Lessons in the Allied Invasion of Sicily

The 'Operation Husky' invasion of Sicily was the first major
Allied invasion in Europe, notable for its use – and misuse –
of air power. For the ill-fated night airborne landings on 9
July, Wellington bombers flew diversionary raids while
cannon Hurricanes escorted the low-flying transport aircraft
and gliders, to attack any AA searchlights used. Later, the
first major use was made of A-36 dive-bombers, attacking
reinforcement columns; and a successful offensive was
achieved against road transport, the Germans having to use
mules across country. The Luftwaffe managed only a few
raids, achieving surprise by exploiting the radar cover
provided by Mount Etna. But the Allied air support was not
co-ordinated with Army and Navy requirements, requests for
air strikes needing 12 hours notice [D'Este, 1988:175]. US
commanders were critical that although fighter cover kept
the Luftwaffe away, the landings received little air support
against ground opposition, while communications and
support thereafter also remained poor. Later air strikes were
confined largely to inland interdiction, including the
'asinine' [Fuller, 1948:266] destruction of towns and villages,
obstructing the Allied advance. Allied fighter-bombers also

repeatedly attacked Allied units, despite pre-arranged recognition signals; incensed US troops deliberately shot down one attacking P-38. Further, while there were four destructive raids on Messina, there was no bombing of the access roads and landing sites to disrupt the Axis evacuation to Italy, while bombing of the ferry fleet was wholly ineffective; barrage balloons and flak ships kept the fighter-bombers high. Some 10,000 vehicles and 119,000 troops were evacuated, with only one soldier killed by Allied air attack. [D'Este, 1988:514]

Allied Operations in Italy; 'Cab Rank' Close Support
The invasion of Italy in September was preceded by widespread bombing of railways and airfields, plus RAF night raids on Milan, Turin and Genoa. Although communications had improved little, carrier-based, DAF and US aircraft provided effective close support for the landings at Reggio di Calabria, Taranto and Salerno. The Germans could offer little air opposition, and the weather quickly became the main operational problem – overcast cloud, rain, and mud on the airfields. On 8 September, 131 B-17s of the 15th AF attacked Kesselring's Army HQ at Frascati, destroying much of the town but putting the HQ out of action for only six hours. On the 13th, a German counter-attack against the Salerno bridgehead led to a bomb carpet laid by Allied bombers north and south of the area; the ruins of Pompeii became more so. By the 15th, Kittyhawk fighter-bombers were operating from Italian airfields. In November, the DAF implemented a 'Rover David' rapid-response version of the close-support system. Instead of waiting to be scrambled, the Kittyhawk fighter-bombers flew 'Cab Rank' standing patrols over the Front, usually in line astern, peeling off singly or in groups when called down to attack particular targets, identified on photographic maps with grid references. If there were no 'request' targets, the aircraft attacked pre-selected targets before returning to base. 'Rover Frank' was a variation for use against enemy artillery; 'Rover Joe' was a US derivative.

Allied Ground Attack in South-east Asia
In South-east Asia, RAF Hurricanes flew roving 'rhubarb' search/strike sorties over the Burma jungle, while a new US

5th AF specialty was the use of heavily armed A-20 and B-25 'gunships' to strafe Japanese positions. These could be difficult to identify from the air, friendly and enemy troops often being hidden under the jungle canopy. Hence ground marking by coloured smoke shells was desirable, as were ground reports on the success of air attacks. Casualties under trees could be high, due to bombs detonating in the tree tops and dispersing the shrapnel further. As the US offensive against Japanese-held islands progressed, support for the actual landings was mostly provided by carrier-based Navy aircraft. As airfields became available on the islands, AF and Marine aircraft were flown in to assist. RAAF operations included attacks by Beaufighters on Japanese positions at Nassan Bay, and support by Vengeances for the Australian landings at Langemak Bay.

China was the only war theatre where an air force operated extensively in an army support rôle with almost no tactical co-ordination with ground forces. Language, liaison and training difficulties prevented the setting up of ground-to-air communications by the US 14th AF and the Chinese until late in the war. Instead, the aircraft operated without ground direction, attacking targets in the Japanese rear, well clear of Chinese troops. [USSBS, 1945–49: No.67] Throughout South-east Asia, Allied air operations against the Japanese Army's supply system included strafing attacks to destroy the pack/cart animals used, horses especially, but also bullocks and elephants. Aircrews found the task distasteful, but the US 14th AF alone claimed 19,941 horses killed by the end of the war. [USSBS, 1945–49: No.67]

Daylight Bombing Techniques

Revised 8th Air Force Formations
In Britain, 8th AF bombers introduced LeMay's revised three-dimensional box formation in a raid on St Nazaire on 3 January 1943. That month, the 8th AF received its first US single-engined escort fighters, P-47s, but these offered little

range improvement over the Spitfire. Self-defending Task Forces remained the key to survival on deep penetration missions. The multiple staggered arrowhead formation was now extended to cover a Combat Wing of three Groups, giving the largest combat formation (54 aircraft) used during the war. Each Group consisted of three squadrons in lead, high and low position, each squadron having two elements of three aircraft in the lead and high position. In January, the 'Javelin' formation was adopted, the Groups being echeloned upwards to the rear and towards the sun. In February, the 'Wedge' put the Groups in lead, high and low position. In April the groups were moved closer, with the elements and squadrons echeloned the opposite way to each other. This revised formation was used for the rest of the year. For the bomb run, the Combat Wing maintained formation up to the IP (Initial Point – a chosen visual/radar landmark). It then split, the three Groups proceeding independently, with course changes to avoid heavy flak, then a 70-second steady run-in over the target to release the bombs. For a large Task Force, the several Combat Wings flew with five-minute gaps between them. Building up the formations with many aircraft taking off from different bases required much time and fuel, reducing the bomb load and giving the Germans ample warning of a raid on the way. To help, in May the 8th AF began using the RAF's 'Splasher' ground radio beacons as rendezvous points, then in October their own 'Buncher' beacons when more were needed; the frequencies used were changed daily to counter German jamming. Since climbing through cloud in formation was dangerous, the bombers normally climbed individually and formed up above the cloud. On their return, crews with damaged aircraft or wounded on board fired red distress flares for priority in landing. The remainder retained a loose formation in a holding pattern, peeling off to land at 20-second intervals in a set sequence: low, lead, then high squadrons.

Weather Problems for the US 8th Air Force

On 27 January 1943, the 8th AF mounted its first mission into Germany, 64 B-17s bombing Wilhelmshaven when the primary target was overcast. Use of the British Gee was soon implemented for overcast conditions, but the weather continued to give the 8th AF serious problems. Mud on the British airfields, thrown up onto the ventral 'ball' turret during take-off frequently made it all but impossible for the gunner to see out. Rain had a hazard of its own. On 4 February, 86 aircraft climbed through heavy rain into the cold upper atmosphere where the rainwater collected then froze the bomb doors shut and locked the turrets in one position; almost half the crews aborted the mission. The intensely cold and rarefied upper atmosphere was also a hazard for the crews, since the aircraft were unpressurized and unheated, with open windows through which guns were fired. Fur-lined clothing was provided, plus oxygen including in portable flasks to enable movement within the aircraft. But the oxygen masks could freeze up from breath moisture, or the supply be damaged by gunfire. The electrically heated suits were unreliable and the aircraft's electrical system could not power one for every crewman. As a result, after spring 1943, when aircrews began receiving personal body protection in the form of 'flak vests' of canvas with overlapping steel plates, often more men were disabled by anoxia and frostbite than by battle wounds.

US Leaflet Operations; the 'Leaflet Bomb'

Whereas RAF Bomber Command gave low priority to leaflets, the 8th AF assigned two squadrons of B-17s solely to leaflet raids, plus two aircraft per squadron carrying leaflets while accompanying the rest of the force on bombing raids. In September 1943, B-17s of the 305th BG began night leaflet raids. But carried in external boxes and released from 25,000ft, the leaflets could scatter up to 100 miles from the intended drop zone. Use of bundles fastened with a barometric release did not work well. But a more satisfactory Monroe T-2 'leaflet bomb' was introduced in 1944, the cylindrical case being opened by a time fuse towards the end of the drop. The 'Bumph Bomb' was eventually adopted by the British as well.

8th Air Force Bombing Techniques; AFCE; Pathfinders

The preferred 8th AF method was direct visual bombing in clear weather. With the bombardier training the Norden bombsight on the AP (Aiming Point), the required course corrections were signalled on the pilot's display. When the target was obscured by partial cloud, 'grid bombing' and a stopwatch were used, the lead bombardier choosing on his map grid a prior visible AP with an estimated time delay for releasing the bombs. The Automatic Flight Control Equipment (AFCE) introduced in March linked the Norden sight to the autopilot, so enabling the bombardier to take over flying the aircraft during the bomb run, to give a more accurate track over the target. With overcast conditions common over Germany, British blind-bombing aids were adapted by the 8th AF for daylight use. Oboe received limited use, on B-17s; H2S was soon replaced by H2X. The 482nd (Pathfinder) Group, formed to provide the H2X formation leadships ('Mickey ships'), operated for the first time on 27 September, in a 305 aircraft raid on Emden. But success with H2X was limited by reliability problems. Other aircraft bombed when the leadship was seen to drop its load, which could include target marking incendiaries. Because of the time delay for other crews to react and release their own bombs, the lead bombardier normally aimed just short of the true AP. Efforts to enhance the visibility of the leadship's bomb drop to other crews included painting the bombs in bright colours (yellow or red and white) and attaching cloth streamers or smoke flares to them. Finally, the M87 100lb Smoke Streamer was introduced to provide the visual signal, the coloured smoke trail beginning one second after release. The M84 100lb Target Identification Bomb, an air-burst red smoke skymarker, was also introduced for marking the bomb release line in overcast conditions.

Daylight Bombing Operations

The Allied 'Combined Bomber Offensive'
At Casablanca in January 1943, Roosevelt and Churchill authorized a co-ordinated US/British 'Combined Bomber Offensive' (CBO). Its main objective, later restated in the

Eaker Plan and Pointblank directive, was the destruction of the German fighter industry. Eaker suggested that US day bombers could use incendiaries to start fires on key targets as markers for RAF bombers to attack that night. But Harris gave priority to area bombing, and the CBO became 'more of a bombing competition'. [Webster and Frankland, Vol.II, 1961:5] Eaker was now claiming that US day bombing was five times as accurate as British night bombing, while – since the German night defences had improved considerably – the US bomber loss rate by day was actually lower than the RAF's at night. But a missing B-17 represented 10 crewmen lost as against 7 for a Lancaster, and US penetrations into enemy-held airspace were still much shorter than those of the RAF.

Medium Bomber Operations: Mosquitos and Berlin; US 9th Air Force
On 30 January 1943, six of the RAF's fast, high-flying Mosquito Mk.IV bombers made the first Allied daylight raids on Berlin, timed to disrupt speeches by Göring and Goebbels at a Nazi rally.

The US 9th AF had been formed in the Middle East, with a first raid (by B-24s) on Naples on 4 December 1942. During 1943, the 9th's medium bombers performed many small daylight raids, some against shipping. Most raids against land targets were made at dusk to allow a return in darkness, landing by the light of truck headlights or flares. Pattern bombing was used, by small formations from 30,000ft, where flak was severe – as at Naples. Against airfields, several small groups were assigned to bomb different hangar or dispersal areas. From Britain, 12 unescorted B-26s attacked Ijmuiden power station at low level in daylight on 14 May, achieving little damage. After a repeat raid on 17 May, when the defences were ready and all 11 B-26s were lost, the policy changed to shorter range escorted missions at medium altitude. In November, the 9th AF was combined with the RAF's 2nd Tactical Air Force to form the AEAF (Allied Expeditionary Air Force). By D-Day, 2TAF itself comprised some 75 squadrons, including Polish, French, Czech, Dutch, Belgian and Norwegian as well as Commonwealth (especially Canadian) squadrons.

Pantelleria – the First Use of a Statistical Bombing Plan

The Allied invasion of Sicily in 1943 required the prior subjugation of the nearby Italian island bases of Lampedusa and especially Pantelleria, with its fortifications and underground facilities. Under Operation 'Corkscrew' US 9th AF pattern bombing of the island's town, airfield and harbour began on 18 May. But British advisor Dr S. Zuckerman devised instead a statistical bombing plan aimed at the 16 gun batteries which could oppose Allied landings. It was based on the calculated density of bombs needed to be aimed at the batteries to achieve 30 per cent probability of destruction, leaving the rest mostly unserviceable as a result of secondary effects; the airfield and harbour were to be left usable by the Allies. This, the first such bombing plan, was implemented on 30 May, the achieved bombing density being monitored by PR and careful plotting. When the landings began on 11 June, only two batteries could mount significant opposition. The rapid capitulation of the garrison was largely credited to the prior bombing. It was the first time that a fortified base had fallen to air power.

Eastern Front: the Soviet Kursk Raid Disaster; Finnish Raid

By 1943, the Soviets were using fewer escort fighters, reassigning them to other duties; to compensate, the bombers flew in larger groups of 50 to 60. But Soviet tactical bombing at the front now included the use of escorted Pe-8 heavy bombers, some against German tank concentrations prior to the Kursk battle. Forewarned by Intelligence, on 5 July (the first day of the German Kursk offensive) the Soviets mounted their largest bombing raid yet, an attempted dawn pre-emptive strike at five Luftwaffe bases near Kharkov, all crowded with aircraft for the offensive. But the raid became a disaster that 40 years later was still not recognized in Soviet war histories. The 400 bombers of the VVS 2nd and 17th Air Armies were detected by German radar, and met by waves of Bf109s. Some 120 bombers were shot down, and few others got through to bomb the target airfields. [Hardesty, 1982:159]

The Finnish bomber force of four squadrons had remained committed to the support of ground forces throughout the Continuation War, but with increasing losses to Soviet AA and fighters. On 19 September, a rare major raid was attempted, a unique mix of 30 Ju88, Do17, Blenheim and Ilyushin DB-3 bombers being despatched to attack the Soviet base on Lavansaari Island. But in poor weather, few crews found the target.

The US Ploesti Oil Refinery Raid

On 1 August 1943, the 9th AF in North Africa mounted Operation 'Tidal Wave', a one-off large-scale daylight low-level attack on seven individual targets in the Rumanian oilfields at Ploesti. Only unescorted B-24s had sufficient range, the flight being made at low level to avoid early radar detection. Low-level bombing was practised beforehand. For the raid, the 179 B-24s flew from airfields near Benghazi, in two formations. But the defences were ready, thanks to the decoding of a US radio message and, in part, because of a delay when the lead group made a turn at the wrong landmark. The B-24s formed large, slow and steady targets, and many of the 52 lost fell to the intense light flak over the target area. The damage caused to the refineries was considerable, taking eight months for production to return to pre-raid levels. But the price paid in aircraft and crews had been prohibitive.

The US Schweinfurt and Regensburg Missions

The town of Schweinfurt, with its five ball-bearing factories, was top of the Allied 'Pointblank' list of 76 key German targets. It was the one to fully test the theories of selective precision daylight bombing and the self-defending bomber formation. It required a much deeper daylight penetration into Germany than had been attempted before, unescorted for most of the way, and under attack by relays of German fighters, there and back, such that consumption of ammunition was itself a major problem for the bomber crews.

Operation 'Double Strike' on 17 August 1943 was the biggest 8th AF operation yet, and the first with shuttle bombing. For deception, the Schweinfurt task force, with LeMay himself flying, was preceded by another one attacking the Messerschmitt factory at Regensburg and then heading southwards over the Mediterranean to North Africa. In the two forces, 363 B-17s eventually crossed the mainland coast, with initial and return escort provided by US P-47s and RAF Spitfires. Beyond escort range, both forces came under almost continuous attack, including by air-to-air bombing and rocket mortars, many fighters achieving several sorties from different bases as the running battle progressed. The turn southwards by the Regensburg force was not expected by the Germans and only two further aircraft were lost from it. But for the combined missions, a total of 60 bombers were lost, an unacceptable 16 per cent. PR checks showed impressive bombing accuracy at Regensburg, and serious damage to the ball-bearing plants at Schweinfurt. But machine tools were difficult to destroy, and production at Schweinfurt was restored within four weeks. The Germans expected repeat raids and the path to Schweinfurt became better defended than that to Berlin. [Coffey, 1978:267]

In the second Schweinfurt mission on 14 October, 291 B-17s crossed the mainland coast. Most of the German fighter units waited until, near Aachen, the P-47s turned for home. Thereafter, attacks on the bombers were continuous on both outward and return legs. Including several due to fog, 65 B-17s were lost (a rate of 19 per cent) and many others badly hit. Heavy damage to the ball-bearing plants was achieved, but production was virtually restored within six weeks. With 8th AF crew morale deteriorating – and diversions to Switzerland increasing – this second Schweinfurt mission brought acceptance that the concept of self-defending formations was not viable. From now on, US day bombing missions would be constrained by the availability and range capability of escort fighters. The percentage of German fighters in Western Europe had increased from 43 per cent in January to 60 per cent in October, while those on the Eastern Front declined from 33 per cent to 19 per cent.

US Bombing Operations in the Mediterranean; the 15th Air Force

The heaviest raids on Italy were by the RAF at night, notably one by 504 aircraft on Milan on 12 August. But US

day raids, tactical and strategic, were increasing. After RAF
Wellingtons dropped 800,000 warning leaflets during the
night, on 19 July 270 US B-17s and B-24s made the first
Allied raid on Rome, attacking rail targets and airfields.
The fall of Corsica to the Allies made its 17 airfields
available. Then on 27 September, the 13 vital air bases on
the Foggia plain in Italy fell to the British 8th Army. From
these airfields, bombers could strike at targets in southern
Germany, Eastern Europe and the Balkans. From Foggia,
the new US 15th AF carried out its first raid on 2 November,
attacking the Wiener-Neustadt Bf109 factory. The 15th AF
had a mix of medium and heavy bombers and concentrated
on a variety of selected small targets – factories, bridges, etc.
By the end of the war, it had grown to 85 squadrons of
bombers and 22 of escort fighters.

Bombing Operations in the Pacific/CBI Theatre
While RAF bombing was largely confined to Burma, US
bombing attacks on the airfields, bases, ports, depots, etc. of
Japan's expanded empire were also mostly small scale but
now spread across six Air Forces, having one to four Bomb
Groups each: the 5th AF (based in Australia and New
Guinea); 7th (Central Pacific); 10th (India); 11th (Aleutians); 13th (New Hebrides); and 14th (China). The 5th AF
operations were supported by RAAF Bostons, Beauforts
and Beaufighters. Bombing missions were also flown by
USN PB4Y-1 (B-24) patrol bombers, while PB4Y-1P
'photo-bomber' Liberators usually dropped bombs on one
or other of their PR targets. Air operations were variously
hampered by heat and damp, monsoon rains, flooding of
airfields, aircraft lost in violent thunderstorms, and cyclonic
winds able to lift and overturn a B-24. Nevertheless, the US
advance in the Pacific was accelerating with an island
leap-frogging approach, seizing weakly held points and
establishing new airfields to use in attacking Japanese bases
and supply shipping. After weeks of heavy 5th AF bombing
of airfields on Bougainville, US forces landed in November.
Then, with bombing support by the 7th AF from Funafuti in
the Ellice Islands, the capture of key islands in the Gilberts
was begun. But the landings on Tarawa atoll brought heavy
casualties; the bombing by carrier-based aircraft had failed

to destroy the concrete defence positions. Japan itself being still out of reach, strategic bombing operations remained fewer and smaller than in Europe. In a notable one, on 13 August nine 5th AF B-24s flying from Darwin carried out the longest duration round trip raid of the war, a 17-hour, 2,400-mile mission to bomb the Balik Papan oil refineries in Borneo. Japan's own ability to mount long-range raids was already in severe decline, because of the rapidly increasing Allied fighter defences, and the vulnerability of the Japanese G3M and G4M bombers. But, operating in primitive conditions at Buin in Bougainville, the Japanese flew D3As and D4Ys on dive-bombing missions against US bases. In Burma, Japanese raids on the Chittagong airfields included one in which the bombers glided down with engines off, the attack setting fire to the elephant grass around the bomb dumps.

Night Target Marking Developments

Area Bombing v. Marking Small Targets; 'Target Indicator' Marker Bombs

With the RAF's night bombing offensive increasing, Harris remained committed to area bombing of Germany's industrial towns and cities. He argued that because of German industrial dispersal, selective bombing of supposed key strategic targets ('panacea targets' he called them) would not have the impact claimed, while Bomber Command did not have the capability of finding and marking such small targets at night. But the Pathfinder Force, and later also 5 Group, were in fact developing a range of techniques for finding and visually marking targets in night raids. The emphasis was on ground marking by coloured pyrotechnic marker bombs, dropping them visually, using the light from parachute flares, or blindly using radio/radar aids.

The British 'TI' (Target Indicator) marker bomb was first used on the night of 16 January 1943 in the RAF's first raid on Berlin since 1941. Designed to appear distinctively different from incendiary or other fires, the TI used a 250lb LC bomb case to house sixty 12-inch pyrotechnic candles. With barometric ejection and ignition in mid-air, the candles cascaded to the ground like a spectacular firework Christmas tree, burning for some three minutes. Red, green, yellow or white candles were available. Later, the 250lb 'Red Spot Fire' type was introduced, able to burn for ten minutes with an intense crimson flame; and then green and yellow versions. The Spot Fire was conspicuous and much less likely to be obscured by smoke than were the distributed small candles of the normal TI. For use with Oboe (which needed six minutes for a back-up Oboe drop), TIs were later modified as 'LBTIs' (LB for Long Burning) having time delays for some candles. For greater accuracy against small targets, non-cascading TIs of both candle type and white-burning magnesium type were later introduced, some incorporating small explosive charges to deter fire fighters. The TI colours used were varied to keep the defence forces guessing. However, yellow TIs were preferred as 'long stops' to indicate the limit of the target area, and to 'cancel' inaccurately laid markers. 'Back-up' markers were normally of a different colour, and crews were instructed to aim in preference for the initial markers if they were still visible.

Blind Dropping of Target Indicators; Night Raid Colour Photography

Blind dropping of TIs was code-named 'Paramatta'. Blind dropping using Oboe was named 'Musical Paramatta'. It was first used in a raid on Düsseldorf on 27 January, the Oboe Mosquito dropping a salvo of four TIs, with back-up marking by other aircraft. On that raid the glow of the TIs could be seen through the 10/10ths cloud layer. Reportedly, Hitler refused to believe that the RAF could mark and bomb accurately through continuous cloud, and accused his Air Staff of falsifying their reports. [Musgrove, 1976:26] Blind dropping of TIs using H2S was named 'H2S Paramatta', first used by PFF Stirling and Halifax bombers in a raid on Hamburg on 30 January. This was the first operational use of the H2S ground-imaging radar, which for the first time allowed blind bombing or marking at any range, free from any constraints from ground stations. But with its poor image resolution, the 10cm H2S was better used for blind dropping of proximity flares to allow a visual search for the target before marking with TIs.

The RAF now needed colour film for night raid photography, to show the locations achieved with the various coloured TIs. With the Kodakolor film insufficiently sensitive to show ground detail also, 'composite film' strips were adopted: two frames of colour to show the TIs, 10 of normal monochrome to show ground detail. Meanwhile, some bombers occasionally carried movie cameras to record complete passes over the target area, some with colour film. Since the Mosquito had no facility for dropping photo-flashes, a special TI was devised to allow Oboe Mosquito crews to photograph their marking. This 'TI Flash' replaced 20 of the 60 candles with a photoflash which ignited two seconds after the TI burst. A Mosquito crew used a TI Flash to achieve the highest night photo of the war, Osnabrück from 36,000ft on 18 April 1944.

German Decoys: Target Indicators; the Mythical 'Scarecrow'

The Germans introduced two types of decoy TI to divert bomber crews away from the real markers. A simple ground-burning type was followed by a rocket-launched version, fired up from the ground to burst and cascade down like the real TI. The decoys were weaker in colour, with a shorter burn time, but were sufficiently like the real TIs to cause problems. As a countermeasure of sorts, PFF crews at times fired Very pistols to indicate when the real markers were being released. But in the coming months RAF crews repeatedly reported bombing red TIs when none had been dropped. Eventually, the Germans also introduced 'Spot Fire' decoys.

By autumn 1943, RAF bomber crews were reporting a new German deception device, fired to the bomber stream's height and then exploding to simulate a bomber falling in flames. Apparently intended to scare crews, these 'scarecrows' became accepted in Bomber Command reports. But post-war research failed to find evidence of the Germans having such a device, and it seems that the British crews were probably seeing bombers themselves exploding, as a result of unseen *Schräge Musik* attacks. [Middlebrook, 1982:174] However there were reports of scarecrows being seen during missions when no bombers were lost. [W.E. Jones, 1983:98] ,

Use of Proximity Flares ('Newhaven'); Re-marking to Avoid 'Creepback'

The PFF adopted the code-name 'Newhaven' for dropping flares in the target area to try visually to identify the target itself for marking. The flares were standard 4.5-inch type, time-fused to pull the pyrotechnic from its container, deploy the parachute and ignite the flare, which burned for three minutes with a red or green light. Later a type which ejected 'stars' of a different colour (green, orange or red) was introduced, to help defeat decoys. The LNSF used a different 'White Drip' parachute flare of great brilliance, dripping a 1,000ft tail of white molten magnesium while descending, but with too short a burn duration for general use. Blind dropping of flares using Oboe was called 'Musical Newhaven', but Oboe was usually considered accurate enough for dropping marker bombs directly. Blind dropping of flares by H2S was called 'H2S Newhaven', first used in a raid against Wilhelmshaven on 18 February 1943. Unfortunately, the use of flares also attracted enemy night fighters and helped illuminate the bombers for attack. On the night of 31 August, the Germans themselves began dropping 'fighter flares' over the bomber stream to aid the night fighters.

Accurate re-marking was essential during a long night raid to counter the phenomenon of 'creepback', crews tending to bomb early rather than late with the result that the centre of bombing gradually moved away from the intended Aiming Point. For an attack on the long narrow town of Wuppertal-Barmen on 23 May, the approach and aiming point were chosen such that the creepback spread down the length of the town. The massive Hamburg raid of 27 July introduced elaborate re-marking procedures, with 53 back-up marking aircraft distributed through the main force, and using a two-second overshoot to try to re-centre the attack. Even so, a seven-mile creepback developed during the raid. Later, in 1944 Bomber Command planners introduced some allowance for creepback by selecting the Aiming Point beyond the required target area.

Night Bombing Techniques and Operations

Raids on U-boat Pens

When the reinforced concrete U-boat shelters in France were under construction and vulnerable, the British Admiralty's priority for bombing attacks had been the *Scharnhorst* and *Gneisenau*, not the shelters. Now the 8th AF had shown the completed shelters to be unpromising targets for conventional bombs. However, the U-boats were causing grievous losses to Allied convoys. Therefore, at Admiralty insistence, and with most civilians having fled after earlier raids, the RAF mounted heavy Oboe-marked raids on the U-boat bases at Lorient (13 February, 466 aircraft) and St Nazaire (28 February, 437 aircraft). The objective was to destroy if not the shelters themselves then all the surrounding infrastructure supplying them. The raids demolished the towns ('No cat or dog is left' reported Grand Admiral Dönitz), while the shelters remained intact. [Webster and Frankland, Vol.2, 1961:97] For the Germans, the disruption was minor, and their comment that the shelters provided valuable air-raid protection for Germany stopped further such raids. But the failure led eventually to the Admiralty development of the Terrell rocket bomb, even though the Navy had no aircraft to carry it.

The Lorient raid was the first to exceed 1,000 tons of bombs dropped. A raid on Dortmund on the night of 23 May was the first to exceed 2,000 tons.

The 'Battle of the Ruhr'; Night Shuttle Bombing Missions

The first of the RAF's three major bombing campaigns against Germany in 1943 was the Battle of the Ruhr, in the period 5 March–12 July. It began with a hugely destructive

Oboe-marked attack by 443 aircraft on Essen. During the campaign, Bomber Command flew 18,506 sorties, dropping 58,000 tons of bombs in 43 major attacks on heavily defended cities, mostly in the Ruhr. The battle cost Bomber Command 872 aircraft missing. But despite the devastation caused in industrial as well as residential areas, it seems there was only about one-and-a-half months loss of production. The giant Krupps steel works at Essen had been a frequent target for the RAF, but to little effect until an Oboe-marked raid on the night of 25 July 1943, when 627 aircraft dropped 2,032 tons of bombs on it. On seeing the damage, Dr Gustav Krupp collapsed, and never recovered; but the plant itself did.

With the onset of short summer nights, the RAF were unable to make deep penetration raids and return while still in darkness. Accordingly, in the first shuttle bombing mission, on the night of 20 June, Lancasters raiding the Zeppelin plant at Friedrichshafen flew on to land in North Africa, with a return raid on Spezia three nights later. But maintenance work on the bombers at distant temporary bases proved difficult without a major logistics/support effort. In the Zeppelin raid, the target area was quickly obscured by smokescreens, but as planned, later crews substituted time and bearing bombing runs from landmarks on the shore of Lake Constance.

New German Night Raid Techniques against Britain
On 16 April 1943, 28 Fw190s of SKG10 inaugurated German high-altitude night fighter-bomber raids against London, with navigation aided by D/F stations in France. But the attacks were too small and inaccurate to achieve much success. With its 500kg bomb and wing tanks gone, an Fw190 could outrun a Mosquito night fighter; but with no radar or RWR, it was vulnerable to surprise attacks when cruising. On the night of 4 May, the Germans used a new tactic for a raid on Norwich, the Luftwaffe's bombers simply joining the returning RAF bomber stream. This obviated any defence action until the bombs began falling. A new Pathfinder unit, I/KG66, flying Do217 and Ju88 bombers then Ju188s, made its first mission over Britain on 18 August. Target marking used 50kg Type LC50 marker

bombs, which burned for four minutes, the flame colours being green, white or yellow. The marking technique involved: a target finder (*Zielfinder*) dropping flares over the target area; a target marker (*Zielmarkierer*) dropping the marker bombs; then two illuminator (*Beleuchter*) aircraft dropped further flares to light the target area for the start of the main force attack.

Night Bombing on the Eastern Front

On the night of 20 April, the Soviet Air Force mounted a rare large-scale strategic raid, some 200 medium bombers attacking Insterburg. German strategic raids on the Eastern Front were also rare. But a series was begun on the night of 3 June, 168 bombers (mainly He111s) attacking the Molotov Collective Combine T-34 tank-production centre at Gorki. Navigation was aided by use of the Moscow public broadcast transmitter, and the bombing was carried out using marking by KG100, and the new *Lotfe 7D* bombsight. In August, the Germans began belated plans for a strategic bombing corps to fly small precision raids against Soviet armaments factories and power stations. The new corps was to include the pathfinder unit KG100, and would use Ju88 and He111 bombers, eventually He177s. But instead, priority was given to countering the ever-growing Soviet ground force juggernaut; and with the German retreat, the prime strategic targets were soon out of range anyway.

The Dambusters' Raid

On the night of 16 May 1943, the RAF carried out Operation 'Chastise', one of the most innovative bombing raids of the war, a precision low-level night attack on a complex of five dams providing hydroelectric power to Germany's Ruhr industrial area. To breach a massive concrete dam (the Möhne was 100ft thick at its base) a large weight of explosive needed to be placed right against the upstream side of the dam wall prior to detonation, a requirement far beyond the capability of conventional bombing at the time. The Barnes Wallis 'Upkeep' spinning/bouncing bomb was purpose-designed for the task. Modified Lancasters, designated 'Type 464 Provisioning Lancaster', were to carry one bomb each with its axis across the underside of the fuselage. It was to be spun up to 500 rpm, and then dropped at a precise height, speed and distance, to skip its way over the water surface, slowing down to hit up against the dam wall and sink down to explode. Mid May was chosen for the raid, when the dams would be fullest (for maximum flood damage) and there would be moonlight for visibility.

For the raid, No.617 Sqdn was specially formed with élite crews, under Wing Cmdr G.Gibson. Attacks were practised over similar reservoirs in Britain, with simulated moonlight flying carried out in daylight, using a US-devised combination of amber goggles and blue perspex over the cockpit glazed areas. Bomb release at the right distance and 60ft height was achieved with a wooden sighting frame for the dam end towers, and two Aldis lamps mounted fore and aft under the fuselage, angled to give light spots on the water touching in a lateral figure of eight at a point 60ft below. Fighter Command type VHF R/T sets were installed in each aircraft for voice communications, allowing Gibson to act as 'Master Bomber', directing the raid. This was the first use of the Master Bomber technique.

The raid was carried out by 19 Lancasters; only 11 returned. Of the 5 dams, only the Möhne and Eder were successfully breached. The Upkeep was quite unsuitable for the shallow-sloped Sorpe earth dam; dropped on top to make a breach at the crest, it rolled down to make an ineffective crater far from it. Overall, some 1,200 people drowned, many of them Soviet POWs, and little interruption was caused to the Ruhr power supplies. But with spectacular PR photos taken the next morning, it provided a tonic for Allied morale, and boosted Wallis's standing; the 24-year old Gibson was awarded the VC. Given the aircraft and crew losses, the raid was never repeated, and by September the dams had been repaired, with greatly increased defences. Wallis himself was critical that no attempt was made to use conventional bombing to disrupt the repair work on the dams.

The 'Firestorm' Phenomenon; Krefeld; the Hamburg 'Firestorm' Raid

The *Feursturm* (firestorm) phenomenon had been predicted

in Germany in 1927 [Rumpf, 1963:93] but it took the war to bring realization – the RAF night raid on Krefeld on 21 June 1943 providing the first major example. A firestorm resulted from a distribution of fires with a concentrated central one of such intensity that the updraught caused radially inflowing winds of hurricane velocity, uprooting trees, carrying burning debris, feeding the fires and forcing them beyond all possible control. The level of devastation and civilian casualties was unprecedented. This amplification of damage was not possible with HE bombs. Nevertheless, a factor in achieving it was the deliberate associated use of HE bombs. GP bombs gave craters and heaps of rubble (impeding fire trucks), broken gas mains (to feed the fires), and broken water mains (to hamper fire fighting). Blast bombs destroyed windows and roofs, giving the following incendiaries a good air supply to build the fires.

Operation 'Gomorrah', Bomber Command's second major campaign of 1943 was the Battle of Hamburg in which repeated saturation bombing was used to achieve for the first time the near-total destruction of a major city. Hamburg's coastline ensured a good H2S image, allowing accurate marking whatever the weather. After weeks of dropping leaflets warning people to leave the city ('There is peace now, then it will be eternal peace') [Whiting, 1987:145], the campaign began on the night of 24 July, with bombing by 791 aircraft, and using 'Window' for the first time. The US 8th AF flew 235 day sorties to Hamburg on the 25th and 26th, aiming at the docks and shipyards. Then, the night of 27 July saw the great 'firestorm raid'; 787 RAF bombers used mainly incendiaries to destroy large areas of the city, with fires visible from 140 miles and the smoke forming an anvil-shaped cloud topping 20,000ft. Many of the victims died of suffocation and carbon dioxide poisoning, giving rise to fears that the British had embarked on poison gas warfare. The 'firestorm' raid was followed by two further heavy RAF raids, 777 aircraft on 29 July, and 740 aircraft on 2 August. In the campaign against Hamburg, a total of 9,000 tons of bombs caused over 30,000 dead and millions of tons of rubble. Goebbels rated it 'a catastrophe', but the concentration and repetition which caused such destruction was not repeated for other German cities. Despite

Hamburg's devastation, survivors returned and industrial production was gradually restored.

Use of a 'Master Bomber'; the Peenemünde Raid

The PFF had long sought to use a 'Master of Ceremonies' or 'Master Bomber' to control a raid and so increase its effectiveness. After its use on the Dams raid, the technique was sanctioned for the PFF. Grp Capt. J.H. Searby, as Master Bomber, tried it in a raid on Turin on 7 August, and then used it for the first time in a major raid for the attack on Peenemünde. The Master Bomber arrived with the lead aircraft and then loitered over the target area throughout the attack, giving marking and bombing instructions by VHF R/T. The raid instructions particularly aided inexperienced replacement crews, despite some disruption by German jamming. By mid-1944, on major raids the PFF usually operated a Deputy as well as the Master Bomber. These took turns, one making a marking run while the other observed and instructed the 'backers up'. Further PFF aircraft headed each wave of bombers, to remark the target, again under the direction of the Master or Deputy. Also in 1944, a 'Long Stop' crew was introduced to take over the task of dropping yellow TIs to cancel bad markers or as a boundary line to limit the spread of bombing.

Concerned at intelligence reports of German progress with secret weapons, on the night of 17 August 1943 the British despatched 596 heavy bombers on Operation 'Hydra', against the rocket/missile establishment at Peenemünde. The raid was the RAF's only full-strength precision night raid, attacking three separate targets within the Peenemünde complex. These were the experimental works, the A-4 missile production works, and the housing estate for the technical staff – making this the first RAF raid specifically intended to kill civilians. Innovations included: first use of the Spot Fire marker; first use of a Master Bomber on a large raid; and first shifting of marking – done by aiming at the same markers but using a calculated false setting on the bombsights – for the second and third targets. The raid was not wholly successful, the initial marking being two miles off due to poor H2S imaging; many foreign workers in a nearby labour camp were killed. After the raid, amid the fire and rescue activity, work teams began painting, dynamiting and shifting rubble in key areas to create simulated damage in time for the early morning PR flight. But decentralization of work away from Peenemünde was quickly implemented.

US Attempts with Night Bombing

Having suffered heavy losses in unescorted daylight bombing raids, in the autumn of 1943 the US 8th AF experimented with night bombing, using B-17s with flame dampers and gunflash eliminators. For five weeks, the 422nd Bomb Squadron flew night missions (with 5 B-17s) with RAF Bomber Command. But two were shot down, the Norden sight proved unsatisfactory for this role, and with the retraining and aircraft modifications needed, the USAAF judged it preferable to press for escort day fighters instead. In October, a further attempt was made by the 492nd BG, using the Sperry S-1 sight.

In the Pacific, small night raids were flown by US Navy PB4Ys and 13th AF B-24s from Henderson against Japanese bases, often using flares for target illumination. Flying from Buin, the Japanese themselves made some night raids either on moonlit nights or timed for a dawn or dusk attack. Over Burma, the Japanese had been flying small night raids without flame-damped exhausts and were now experiencing losses to RAF Beaufighters.

Blind-bombing Developments: Gee-H, H2S, Oboe and SABS

The RAF's first successful operational use of the new 'Gee-H' blind bombing aid was made by Mosquito aircraft in a raid on Aachen on 7 October 1943. The first use by Lancasters in a major raid (589 aircraft on Düsseldorf) followed on 3 November. Following criticism that H2S had not been tried for blind bombing directly (as opposed to blind marking), on 17 November 83 PFF aircraft attacked Ludwigshafen, all using H2S for blind bombing; no markers were carried, and the decoy TIs lit by the Germans were ignored. The first attempt at a large scale RAF night raid without PFF marking did not come until 12 August 1944, when only 23 of the 373 H2S-equipped heavy bombers managed to bomb the target, Brunswick. At 10cm., H2S imaging was very poor, especially for the area directly below the aircraft, the operator having to judge his position from the image around the screen periphery. The first raid to combine PFF Oboe marking with 617 Sqdn's precision bombing using the new 'SABS' (Stabilized Automatic BombSight) came on 16 December 1943 against a V-1 site at Abbeville. The bombs averaged 94 yards from the centre of the markers, but that centre was itself 350 yards from the target. This experience led 617 Sqdn, under Wing Cmdr L. Cheshire, to begin developing low-level marking techniques for 5 Group, Bomber Command.

The Battle of Berlin

RAF Bomber Command's third major bombing campaign, the Battle of Berlin, lasted from 18 November until 30 March 1944. Despite the 'Pointblank' directive to concentrate on attacking the German aircraft industry, the campaign against Berlin derived from Harris's claim that with 8th AF assistance, Bomber Command could bring about the collapse of Germany by wrecking Berlin 'from end to end'. The campaign saw 9,111 sorties in 16 major raids on the German capital. But Berlin was a much more difficult target than Hamburg: much bigger; more spread out; without a clear H2S image, and hence much more difficult to blind mark. Further, the much greater range meant greater vulnerability to night fighters and a smaller bomb load because of the extra fuel needed. Armour was reduced to increase the bomb load, and take-off was made at high weight, giving difficulty in climbing; cases of crews dumping their largest (4,000lb HC) bomb in the North Sea to gain height were countered by wiring the raid camera and photoflash to operate automatically when the large bomb was released. Over Berlin, thick overcast usually prevented accurate marking and bombing, and also daylight PR raid assessments. Successive raids damaged different parts of the city without achieving really heavy concentration, and the lack of photos allowed Bomber Command chiefs to exaggerate the effectiveness of the campaign. In reality, the results did not justify the heavy losses in aircraft and crews.

VI 1944

Bomber Developments

New Piston-engined Bombers
New piston-engined bombers making their first flights in 1944 included: the twin-engined Junkers Ju388K (Germany, January), a further development of the Ju88, with turbosupercharged engines and a ventral bomb pannier; the single-engined Ilyushin Il-10 *Shturmovik* (USSR, January); the Consolidated Vultee XA-41 big single-seat, single-engined ground-attack aircraft (USA, 11 February); the twin-engined Tachikawa Ki-74 (Japan, c.March), a high-altitude reconnaissance-bomber with a pressure cabin; the twin-engined Douglas XB-42 Mixmaster (USA, 6 May), of unorthodox 'pusher' design, but out-performing a Mosquito on the same power; the twin-engined Beech XA-38 (USA), an attack bomber with a nose 75mm cannon; the four-engined Avro Lincoln heavy bomber (Britain, 9 June), a development of the Lancaster; the twin-engined Polikarpov NB(T) night bomber (USSR, July); the twin-engined Myasischev VB-108 (USSR, summer), a high-altitude bomber with a pressure cabin; the four-engined Junkers Ju290B (Germany, summer) a strategic bomber version of the Ju290 transport; the four-engined Nakajima G8N *Renzan* land-based Naval heavy bomber (Japan, 23 October), potentially a formidable aircraft, with turbosupercharged engines, a high aspect ratio laminar-flow wing, and a defensive armament of six 20mm cannon and four 13mm machine guns in power-operated turrets; the Boeing XB-39 (USA), effectively an 8-engined B-29, the four nacelles housing Allison V-3420 double engines.

New bombers and ground-attack aircraft entering service in 1944 included the Yokosuka P1Y1 Ginga ('Frances'), SAAB-18, Mitsubishi Ki-67 ('Peggy'), Hawker Tempest,

Bell P-63 (with the Soviet VVS), Nakajima J1N ('Irving'), Tupolev Tu-2, and Douglas A-26 Invader. Due to systems problems it was April 1944 before the first operational B-29s could be sent to China. The US declined to provide the USSR with the B-29, by far the most advanced strategic bomber in the world. But when three B-29s force-landed on Soviet territory after raids on Japan, Stalin ordered them impounded, two of them to be dismantled and 'reverse engineered' in every last detail. The Soviet copy emerged post-war as the Tupolev Tu-4.

Technology Developments on Bombers

New bombsights included the Soviet OPB-1D for horizontal and PBP-4 for dive-bombing; and the British Mk.III low-level angular bombsight provided to the RAF's specialist bombing unit, 617 Sqdn. This latter device avoided any need for estimating the bomber's height at bomb release, by measuring the rate of increase of angle of the line-of-sight to the target, below the flight path during the approach. Among armament developments, the British gyro-gunsight – effective during evasive movements as well in level flight – was introduced on RAF and US bombers. The new British Rose Brothers' hydraulic turret featured twin 0.5-inch guns, heating, easier exit, a gyro-gunsight, and room for a second crewman to help with settings if required. To counter the new Me262 jet fighters, some B-24 bombers of the US 392nd BG were fitted with a fixed rearward-firing Army M6A1 'Bazooka' each side of the rear fuselage, to be fired by the tail gunner. Reportedly some were used operationally, with no great effect. Other improvisations included a conspicuously large dummy gun mounted in the tail of a US B-29. Among other developments, US wing de-icing trials included some with the XB-25E (hot air system) and XB-25F (electrical heating). The experimental Pe-2RD version of the Soviet Pe-2 bomber featured a tail-mounted auxiliary RD-1 rocket engine for take-off or to boost speed and altitude when needed. The British introduced a tail-mounted Infra Red identification system, enabling an RAF bomber to identify itself as friendly to RAF night fighters.

New German Attempts at a Strategic Bomber

By 1944, continuing difficulties with the He177 led to further hurried projects and proposals for a new German strategic heavy bomber. One was for a long-range version of the four-engined Me264, achieving take-off at overload condition using assisted take-off rockets under the wings and a jettisonable extra wheel for each main u/c. Another, the four-engined Junkers Ju488, was largely improvised from existing Junkers aircraft parts to simplify production. Two others were for bomber conversions of large Junkers transports, the four-engined Ju290B and the ultra-long range six-engined Ju390A. In both these cases, the fuselage structure was unable to take the large cut-outs needed to incorporate a bomb bay, so the weapon load was to have been carried on external racks under the fuselage and wings. Finally, there was a new project for a six-engined high-altitude bomber, the Junkers Ju286. All came to nought as the priority for defence increased.

German Turbojet Bombers Enter Service

Apparently piqued by the exploits of the Mosquito, Hitler insisted that the twin-turbojet Me262 fighter be used as a high-speed bomber, ignoring its potential against US bombers or the Mosquito itself. Accordingly, the Me262A-2a *Sturmvogel* fitted with bomb equipment (fusing/release/sight) and fuselage pylons for 1,000kg of bombs, became the first operational turbojet-powered bomber, with raids over Northern France with KG51 in August 1944. Despite the drag of the bombs, the Me262 could evade standing patrols of Spitfire XIV and Tempest V fighters at will, in making shallow dive attacks on the Nijmegen bridge. But bombing accuracy was poor. The Me262A-2a/U2 was an experimental high-level bomber, with an extended nose housing a prone second crewman with a *Lotfe 7H* bombsight.

The Ar234B *Blitz* version of the twin-turbojet Arado Ar234 introduced a conventional u/c plus bomb attachments under the fuselage and nacelles. The Ar234 was the first aircraft to have a braking parachute as standard, and the only bomber of the war to make routine use of rocket-assisted take-off, with Walther 109-500 LP units jettisoned on parachutes after burn-out. For the bombing run, the single crewman flew the aircraft using the *Lotfe* 7K sight linked to the autopilot. In December, II/KG76 began operations with Ar234B-2 bombers against Allied positions during the Ardennes offensive; but they were too few and too late. The four-engined Ar234C had BMW003 turbojets in separate or paired nacelles, but none reached service.

Turbojet Bomber Projects; the Sänger-Bredt Rocket Bomber Project

The first turbojet-powered heavy bomber, the Junkers Ju287 featured six BMW 003A turbojets in clusters of three under the leading edges of a unique swept-forward wing. It was cancelled in July 1944 because of priority for Germany's emergency fighter programme, but the Ju287 V1 four-turbojet aerodynamic test bed was test flown to evaluate the wing with its adverse aeroelastic behaviour. Projected German turbojet bombers included mixed-power versions of the Me264 bomber (four radial engines plus two Jumo 004 or BMW 018 turbojets), plus a version powered by two BMW 028 turboprops; and the Heinkel He343 four-turbojet medium bomber. With the USA now also developing a more fuel-efficient axial-flow turbojet (GE J-35), US interest in turbojet bombers was increasing. The proposed Boeing Type 413 four-jet version of the B-29 was rejected, but in March the first US jet bomber was ordered, flying in 1946; derived from the piston-engined XB-42, the Douglas XB-43 light bomber was powered by two J35s in the fuselage. For the XB-42 itself, a proposed auxiliary turbojet under each wing to boost maximum speed was tried post-war (XB-42A). A requirement for a heavy jet bomber brought proposals for four competing designs, all flying post-war: the North American B-45, Convair B-46, Boeing B-47 and Martin B-48.

An August 1944 report, 'On a Rocket Drive for Long Range Bombers' by Dr Eugen Sänger and Dr Irene Bredt of the *Deutsche Luftfahrtforschung* covered a highly imaginative project for a 'suborbital' or 'antipodal' bomber, but one needing technology that was far out of reach. This rocket-powered, hypersonic boost-glide 'aerospace-plane' was to have taken off on a rocket-boosted sled along a 3km monorail, climbing above the atmosphere to burn-out at a speed of 22,000km/hr. At such speeds, centrifugal lift would allow a long coasting glide, the aircraft proceeding further by skipping in and out of the denser atmosphere while gradually slowing down, to give a total range of 23,500km. The skipping trajectory aimed to help dissipate the intense kinetic heating experienced during periods in the atmosphere. The Soviets, including Stalin, became very interested in the Sänger-Bredt project when they obtained the report at the end of the war.

Weapon Developments

New Blast Bombs; Mid-air Detonation; SBX

The new bombs of 1944 included the largest operational US HE bomb of the war, the 4,000lb M56 LCHE blast bomb, carried in two pairs under the wings of a B-29; and the largest German bomb, the 2,500kg SC2500 'Max', carried one under each wing of the He177. The Germans also introduced the SB1000 blast bomb, dropped clean for accuracy but deploying a parachute to slow it just prior to detonation; the /410 variant was shaped to fit the bomb bay of the Me410. Finding fragmentation bombs effective against Japanese forces in jungle areas, in 1944 the US 11th AF also used larger GP bombs fitted with a precision time fuse; dropped from a pre-set altitude the bombs exploded 25–50ft above the ground. US, German and British attempts were made to develop an 'SBX' (Slow Burning Explosive) bomb, noting that industrial and mining explosions damped by solid particles like coal dust could cause greater damage than that given by a normal 'sharp' explosion. Trials confirmed the validity of the observation, but only for confined spaces; in a typical building, doors and windows burst early in the explosion and vented the rest of the blast, leaving the main structure intact. Related US work led post-war to the FAE (Fuel-Air Explosive) bomb.

The British 'Tallboy' Penetration Bomb

In Britain, concern at German construction of reinforced concrete V-weapon sites revived interest in the Barnes Wallis penetration bomb project of 1940. Development began on the 10-ton weapon, but when the Germans adopted simpler V-weapon launch sites, work changed to a six-ton version which could be carried further to targets in Germany. Streamlined, with a machined pointed nose casing, the 21ft long RDX-filled 12,000lb MC or DP/HE 'Tallboy' was accurately and strongly made for a precision drop and deep penetration. It was to be dropped by Lancasters of 617 Sqdn, from 18,000ft, using the SABS for accuracy. After initial test drops, it was given angled fins to impart a spin-up as it descended, to counter instability through the transonic speed range. It was first used on the night of 8 June 1944, caving in the Saumur railway tunnel. Subsequent targets included U-boat pens, V-weapon sites, and the *Tirpitz*. Although not expected to penetrate thick concrete in a direct hit, on occasion Tallboys did so, bringing down 1,000 or more tons of concrete. A smaller 4,000lb version was used at times; it could be aimed much more accurately than a normal 4,000lb bomb.

Incendiaries: the British 'J'; US Fuel Tank and Napalm Bombs

Probably the largest incendiary bomb of the war was a 1944 British 2,700lb petrol/gel weapon in a 4,000lb HC case, for low-level attacks against fortified positions; it was not adopted. The unusual British 30lb 'J' (Jet) liquid incendiary bomb used thermite to heat a solution of methane in petrol, forcing it through a tube to form a 15-ft flaming jet. It was released in clusters, deploying individual parachutes. But many of the 400,000 dropped failed to ignite, and the Germans extracted the contents for use as a fuel. A 20-lb version used cordite to vaporize solid naphthalene to form the jet. A 10lb 'J' bomb was also developed but not used.

With ignition failures and storage problems delaying service use of napalm ('gel-gas'), US P-51 pilots began using their part-filled drop tanks as incendiary weapons, dropping them in a low-level skip bombing run, to burst across the target. The return strafing pass needed to ignite the fuel was later obviated by attaching a magnesium incendiary to the tank, or by fitting an impact fuse in place of the tank filling cap. The purpose-built napalm bombs ranged from the 25-USgal Mk.65 to the torpedo-sized 200-USgal Mk.68. Also introduced were a napalm version of the 100lb M47, and the 6lb M69 napalm/magnesium incendiary bomblet, dropped in a 500lb cluster. The M69 had a cloth streamer in place of a tail, plus a powder charge for tail ejection to spread the contents, making the weapon highly effective. In addition, jettisonable fuel tanks were filled with napalm and fitted with igniters. USAAF P-38 bombers made the first operational use of napalm bombs on 17 July, attacking fuel depots south of St Lô. Because they spread burning jelly which clung to any surface, napalm bombs were to prove effective, if peculiarly nasty, e.g. against personnel in gun emplacements and bunkers. The napalm burned off vegetation and camouflage, and penetrated trenches, bunker openings and pill-box slits, killing the occupants by asphyxiation if not incineration. But the M69s were also to be used in the US area bombing of Japanese cities where they proved more effective than the conventional 4lb M17A1 magnesium-thermite bombs. The napalm M47s were to be used as markers.

German Bomb-towing Trials

In 1944, the Germans devised a method of enabling the Me262 twin-jet fighter to carry a large bomb by towing it. The 500 or 1,000kg standard bomb was fitted with wooden wings and a wheeled dolly to be jettisoned after take-off. The bomb/wing assembly was coupled to the aircraft's tail by a *Deichselschlepp* tow bar. In operation, the Me262 was to enter a shallow dive towards the target, the pilot releasing the bomb and then the wings and tow bar. Flight tests showed stability and control difficulties, especially with the larger bomb, so severe that on one occasion the pilot had to bale out. The concept was abandoned as too dangerous for the Me262, but was also evaluated for the Arado Ar234C using a 1,500kg bomb.

US Guided 'Vertical Bombs': 'Azon'

The US VB (Vertical Bomb) series of radio-guided free-fall bombs were adapted conventional bombs. The only one to see major use during the war was the VB-1. This was a 1,000lb M44 bomb with a new tail assembly having control surfaces and actuators, a vertical gyro for roll stabilization, a radio receiver, and a tracking flare. Named 'Azon' (for AZimuth ONly), it was controllable in direction (left or right), but not in range (undershoot or overshoot), the latter being much more difficult to judge anyway. This made it advantageous for long, narrow targets like bridges, the attack being made in line with the target. It gave much greater accuracy than an unguided bomb, but training proved difficult. First used by 8th AF B-24s on 31 May 1944, the Azon was soon rejected for the European Theatre of Operations (ETO) because of frequent cloud plus bomber vulnerability to flak; for controllability the Azon needed to be released at intermediate height. However, the VB-1 was later successfully used by the 7th and 14th AFs, against bridges and viaducts in south-east Asia. The VB-2 was a 2,000lb version.

US and German Glide-bombs

The US Aeronca-built GB-1 winged pre-set glide bomb was a 2,200lb stand-off weapon intended to enable bombers to attack a target from outside the range of most flak units protecting the target; but without active guidance its accuracy was poor. It used a 2000lb M34 GP bomb, with a 12-ft span twin-finned airframe. B-17 bombers carried a GB-1 under each wing. In the first operational use, 58 8th AF B-17s launched over 100 GB-1 'Grapefruit' at a Cologne marshalling yard on 28 May 1944, but most were dropped early because of the fierce AA fire and so impacted short of the target. Of the other GB-series glide bombs, only the GB-4 saw service in the war, becoming the first operational guided weapon to use TV. The 2,500lb GB-4 used the GB-1's airframe, with a nose-mounted vidicon camera for TV-assisted radio-command guidance from the launching aircraft. Under Operation 'Batty', the 388th BG at Fersfield launched two GB-4s against E-boat pens at Le Havre on 13 August, four others against targets in France and Germany up to 13 September, but operational difficulties proved severe.

The German Blohm und Voss Bv226 (later Bv246) *Hagelkorn* was a high-performance guided glide bomb of sailplane-like configuration for shallow glide angle and hence long range, but heavy (with reinforced concrete wings) for high speed. The range was 200km if released at 10,500m altitude. Carrier aircraft included the He111 and Fw190. Guidance systems tried included radio command, an IR homer, and eventually the *Radieschen* radio homer – the latter for attacking Allied 'Loran' transmitters. Many test rounds were launched by Fw190Fs from Karlshagen in 1944, but it did not reach operational use. Planned developments included a CW version.

Chemical Weapon Developments: a Third Nerve Gas

By 1944, the German stockpile of nerve gas weapons included 12,000 tons of tabun-filled aircraft bombs. During 1944 the Germans developed 'soman' (fluoromethylpina-colyloxyphosphine oxide), a third nerve gas. It was more lethal than sarin but also much more persistent, and again difficult to make. Little had been produced by the end of the war.

In Britain, Churchill briefly advocated chemical warfare against Germany in retaliation for the V-1 attacks, and several Bomber Command squadrons were diverted for CW training. At this time, poison gas could be carried by Mustangs, Typhoons, Vengeances and Bostons, using 250lb and 500lb SCI canisters, or an adapted US 400lb M10 spray tank.

BW Developments: Anthrax BW Bomblet; Brucellosis and Botulinus Toxin

In Britain, anthrax (code-named 'N') was rated by Cherwell as 'a weapon of appalling potentiality', being 300,000 times more toxic than phosgene. While attempts to develop an aircraft spraying technique for anthrax continued, a 4lb Type 'F' anthrax bomblet developed at Porton Down was adapted for mass production in the USA under a security curtain rivalling that for the A-bomb. The first 5000 production E48R2 bomblets were completed in May 1944. A hundred of them could be carried in a 500lb cluster bomb, and released during the descent to scatter and burst in mid-air to spread the anthrax spores. Reportedly, one plan for a decisive 'knock-out blow' called for some 4.5 million bomblets to be dropped over Germany by 2,700 US and British heavy bombers, wiping out Germany's urban population. [Harris and Paxman, 1982:104] But while production progressed, the rapid Allied advance following the D-Day invasion kept the plan in abeyance.

As a more acceptable/humane alternative to anthrax, the US developed a brucellosis weapon which offered high casualties but with low mortality and contamination lasting only a few days. Meanwhile however, botulinus toxin – rated as the most virulent BW agent of the war [Hersh: 12,97] – was also isolated, at Fort Detrick in 1944. Eight ounces of the agent, distributed appropriately, could wipe out the world's population; and it was non-persistent, being destroyed by 12 hours of exposure to air, so avoiding the uncontrollability of most BW agents. Allied chiefs feared that the German V-1 flying bomb might be used to launch botulinus toxin into British cities, and the arrival of V-1s with only HE warheads came as some relief.

German Work on an HE/Thermonuclear Bomb

Early in 1944, under Dr K. Diebner, the German weapons establishment at Kummersdorf carried out experiments towards an HE/thermonuclear bomb. The tests used conventional explosive surrounding a silver spherical container filled with deuterium. It was hoped that the melting silver and converging shock waves generated by the explosion would momentarily achieve the enormous temperatures and pressures needed to cause nuclear fusion (hydrogen atoms forming helium) with great release of energy. Success at small scale would be shown by radioactivity after the experiment, but none was found and the programme was abandoned. In mid-1944, the appearance of extra-large craters (presumably from the RAF's 'Tallboy' bombs) led to German fears that the Allies might themselves have developed an HE/Thermonuclear bomb, perhaps using hollow-charge explosive. Technicians with Geiger-Müller counters examined the craters, but found no radioactivity. [Irving, 1967:216, 226] In November, the Allies became concerned at major construction at sites around Hechingen, the centre for German nuclear physics. The plants were quickly found to be for the extraction of oil from shale, and the Allies bombed them anyway.

Navigation, Blind Bombing, Radar and Countermeasures

Navigation: German use of 'Gee'; SS Loran; H2S and Fishpond

With their own beam systems jammed, in 1944 the Germans made limited use of the British 'Gee' to navigate on raids over Britain. For secrecy, to avoid the British changing the Gee transmissions, only I/KG66 pathfinders carried a receiver, normally a German *Truhe* set but one Ju188 shot down over Britain contained a captured RAF Gee set (re-labelled FuG122). Meanwhile, in autumn 1944 the Germans built a powerful new jammer for Gee, on the Feldberg hill near Frankfurt. But within days of becoming operational, it was located and destroyed by RAF fighter-bombers.

Using a short wavelength with a long time-base, Loran radio waves could be reflected from the ionosphere at night, giving ranges of up to 12,000 miles. This 'SS' Loran (for Skywave Synchronized) technique was of little value for the USAAF's day bombing, but usable for RAF night raids. Accordingly, in August LNSF Mosquitos began using it over Germany with combined Gee/Loran sets, Loran being used when beyond the range of Gee. Despite its lower accuracy, Loran was used for blind bombing of Berlin.

British developments with the 'H2S' ground-imaging radar included a gyro-controlled roll stabilizer to hold the display while the aircraft was banking or taking evasive action; and the 'Fishpond' aircraft warning facility. Fishpond used a second CRT to show bearing and range of any echoes at intermediate heights below the aircraft, so picking up any bombers or enemy night fighters below. Fishpond gradually replaced Monica.

Blind Bombing: Centimetric Oboe Mk. II and Deception; Micro-H

On 7 January, the Germans achieved the first Oboe Mosquito shot down, and by studying its equipment were able to improve their jammers for Oboe Mk.I. But the British were now ready with a new centimetric Oboe Mk.II (the major version being Mk.IIM, code-named 'Album Leaf') which was more accurate than Mk.I, and more difficult to jam. When Oboe Mk.II was implemented, Mk.I was kept operating in parallel, for deception. A *Naxburg* set picked up Oboe Mk.II signals on 30 January, but their significance went unrecognized as the Germans redoubled their efforts to jam the already successfully jammed Oboe Mk.I, and the RAF were able to use the unjammed Mk.II unhindered. This deception remained successful until 3 July when an Oboe ground station operator mistimed the 'spoof' Oboe Mk.I signals, and the Germans noticed that the Mosquito accurately dropped its markers some four minutes prior to receipt of the apparent release signal. Work on a new jammer was quickly implemented. In April, Oboe Mk.III introduced a 'multiple pulse recurrence frequency' facility enabling use by up to four aircraft on one wavelength; and a 'delta approach' facility, allowing aircraft to approach a target from different directions, the dot-dash audio control being based on rate of approach to the target.

A Gee-H derivative, the US AN/APA-40 Micro-H (i.e. Microwave-H) navigation/blind bombing system for the 8th AF displayed the return pulses from the two ground stations as two spots on the H2X screen. The aircraft course was corrected to keep the spots equidistant from the centre, the spots coinciding with it at the target. Fitted to B-17s and B-24s, Micro-H was first used for navigation on 1 November, and for overcast blind bombing on 18 December. Unlike Gee-H, Micro-H was never jammed.

Airborne Countermeasures: New Jammers; 100(SD) Group; 803 BS

During 1944, the Allied RCM effort supporting the bombers increased rapidly in sophistication and extent. New airborne jammers for use against ground and night fighter radars included: derivatives of Carpet (the British 'Carpet II' and

'Carpet Sweeper', the US AN/APQ-9 'Carpet III',
AN/APT-5 'Carpet IV' or 'Robe', AN/APQ-2 'Rug', and
AN/APQ-21 'Mat'); derivatives of Mandrel (AN/APT-1
'Dina', AN/ARQ-8 'Dinamite', and 'Piperack'); and
'Airborne Grocer'. The British 2,000W 'Jostle IV' VHF
jammer was the largest airborne jammer at that time, carried
in the ventral turret well of B-17 and B-24 bombers.
Introduced in July, it forced the Germans to revert to the old
3-6Mc/s communications. In November 1943, the RAF had
formed No.100(SD – for 'Special Duties') Group, to
'confound and destroy' the enemy with electronic warfare
operations. By mid-1944 the 'destroy' part of 100 Group
consisted of seven squadrons of Mosquito night fighters
equipped with Serrate, Perfectos and Monica, roaming over
Germany on intruder missions. The 'confound' part
consisted of one squadron (No.192) for radio/radar
intelligence-gathering missions, flying Wellington, Mosquito
and Halifax aircraft; and four squadrons (with Halifax,
Stirling, Fortress and Liberator aircraft) of defence
suppression RCM aircraft, using Jostle, Mandrel, Piperack
and Window. These jamming aircraft joined the RAF's night
raids. The Fortresses (B-17F and G), painted black and
fitted with flame dampers, could operate at higher altitude,
giving longer range jamming and reduced vulnerability to
night fighters. In January 1944 the US 8th AF set up its own
RCM unit (later, the 803rd BS), to work alongside 100
Group. The 803rd had five B-17s equipped with Gee, Carpet
and Mandrel, plus a ferret B-17. After operations in support
of RAF Bomber Command, and re-equipping with B-24s,
the unit flew daylight Mandrel Screens and jamming
missions against radar-directed flak, supporting the 8th AF.
On 1 November, the 803rd provided 'spoof' VHF R/T traffic
to simulate a second 8th AF raid forming. Then on 25
November, it provided the first 'VHF screen', using Mandrel
to mask the 8th AF's R/T traffic during formation build-up.

'Mandrel Screen' Operations; the British 'Special Window Force'

From May onwards, bombers of 199 Sqdn were assigned to
'Mandrel Screen' operations, jamming EW radars. Each
Halifax carried up to eight Mandrel jammers for different

frequencies, plus 'Shiver' jammers for use against *Würzburg* radars. The extra electrical power for all the jammers was provided by special alternators on the outboard engines. To cover the D-Day invasion, Mandrel Screens were flown over the Channel by pairs of jamming aircraft flying on opposite sides around 10-minute 'racetrack circuits'. Later, a 'Creeping Mandrel' variation was introduced, to provide a screen moving slowly forward by flying the racetrack circuit with alternate shorter and longer legs. On D-Day, 'Window' was used to aid the Operation 'Taxable' simulation of two invasion fleets heading for the Pas de Calais while the real fleets approached Normandy; Lancaster bombers flew two racetrack patterns above launches, dropping 'Window' to boost the radar image. As a further distraction, 100 Group mounted a 'spoof' bomber stream along the Somme, with Lancasters and Fortresses using ABC and Window. On 14 July, 100 Group implemented a Special Window Force (SWF) for spoof missions, the SWF aircraft dropping Window to appear as a large bomber force. Thereafter, combined Mandrel/SWF operations penetrated deeper and deeper into Germany to keep the enemy's defences at full stretch. Typically the SWF formation and the real bomber force would emerge from the Mandrel screen in different places, heading in different directions.

Bomber Support

Flight Refuelling Developments
During the war there was limited interest in using in-flight refuelling for achieving long-range bombing missions. The USAAF evaluated the pre-war British Flight Refuelling 'Looped Hose' system, using a B-24 as tanker and a B-17 as receiver. But the technique needed fine weather, and firing a line from the B-17 to engage a line trailed by the B-24 was judged too cumbersome. Later planned tests with a B-24 and a B-29 were cancelled, and the system was only adopted by the USAAF after the war. In 1944, the Germans considered

using the six-engined Ju390 transport as a tanker for flight refuelling a Ju290A or Me264 for bombing New York from bases in Europe. Although successful day trials were carried out with the Ju390, refuelling at night would have been needed and the concept was not adopted. In 1944 the British authorized conversion of 600 Lancasters to tankers, to refuel 600 Lincoln bombers for long-range bombing of Japan by the RAF 'Tiger Force' from bases in south-east Asia. A possible stop-gap, a large dorsal dummy 'saddle' tank of 1,200-Imp.gal was tried on two Lancasters but rejected when flight tests showed unacceptable take-off performance and handling. In the event, the advance of US forces in the Pacific was rapid, and few Lancasters had been converted for in-flight refuelling by VJ-Day.

Alternative concepts tried for carrying additional fuel for long range included towed unmanned 'fuel gliders' (e.g. the US Cornelius XFG-1), and a towed winged fuel tank tried with the Me262 and Ar234C in Germany.

The British 'FIDO' Fog Dispersal System

Fog was a special hazard for returning bomber crews. One night in 1941, the crews of 30 Whitleys all baled out because they were unable to see to land; and in December 1943, six out of seven Halifaxes trying to land at Woodbridge ELG in fog crashed with great loss of life. Prompted by Churchill, Britain's PWD undertook work on fog dispersal for airfields, under FIDO (Fog Investigation and Dispersal Operation). Pre-war work on fog dispersal by moisture-absorbing chemicals, by refrigeration, by intense noise, and by electrical discharges, was superseded by direct heat methods. Some tests used lines of coke braziers, others raised petrol pipelines which were finally adopted with a trial airfield installation at Gravely. FIDO became operational at Woodbridge in June 1944. The pipelines each side of the runway carried petrol to burners at intervals along the pipe. When operating, the intense heat generated at the burners caused great up-draughts which cleared the fog locally. Disadvantages included the fuel cost, initial black smoke, and handling difficulties at final approach caused by the up-draughts and turbulence, while the flames themselves were a hazard to aircraft veering to one side. But FIDO could raise ground visibility from 100 yards to 2,000 yards, and gave Allied bomber crews confidence that they could return and land safely even in thick fog. At Woodbridge, it was to enable over 100 aircraft to land safely during one foggy night in January 1945, and the total there reached 1,200 by the end of the war. FIDO installations were made at 15 airfields in Britain, one in France and one (by US Navy CBs) on Amchitka Island in the Aleutians.

Ground-attack Developments

The Decline of the Dive-bomber; New Ground-attack Aircraft

By 1944, the steep-diving dedicated land-based dive-bomber was being replaced by fighter-bombers which were more versatile but able to use only a less accurate, intermediate dive – as did the Soviet Pe-2 still well used on the Eastern Front. Even in Burma where air opposition had greatly declined, the RAF replaced its Vengeances with Spitfires and so lost its precision 85–90 degree dive capability against point targets. The USAAF, too, phased out its A-36s in favour of P-51Bs. But the USMC and RNZAF were operating Douglas SBDs with success, and in March the USMC began using the Chance Vought F4U Corsair, dive-bombing at angles of 70 to 80 degrees.

But there was continuing interest in other forms of ground-attack aircraft versions and conversions, some with formidable weapons. In Japan, the Ki-102b ground-attack version of the Kawasaki Ki-102 twin-engined fighter had a 57mm Ho-401 cannon and two 20mm cannon. In the USSR, the Ilyushin Il-10 *Shturmovik* superseded the Il-8, both being higher-powered derivatives of the Il-2; the Yak-9K was given a 45mm cannon; and a Tu-2 bomber was tested with a 75mm cannon for use against rail targets. German ground-attack aircraft in service included the Ju88P-4 and Ju288, each with a 50mm BK 5 cannon; the Henschel

Not rockets, but smoke-streamer bombs: apparently seldom used, smoke streamers released by 8th AF lead aircraft provided a clear visual signal to other crews to release their bombs; here, they all have. All the bombs are arcing down, but only those with smoke trails can show the trajectory. The aircraft are B-17G Fortress bombers, identifiable by their 'chin' turrets.

Mosquito low-level precision raid: 2TAF Mosquito bombers attacking the Gestapo HQ housed in two adjacent four-storey buildings in the University of Aarhus, Denmark, on 31 October 1944. One HQ building, centre, has largely been demolished, and a staff vehicle below it is on fire. The other building at left is also damaged, and did not survive the next few minutes.

Inferno: a fire with fuel, ammunition and bombs aboard usually needed the autopilot for control, and a quick exit. This B-24 has its engines and main tanks ablaze within seconds of a fighter attack over Austria in September 1944, the crew having little chance. The B-24 was not especially fire-prone, but it had other problems: the bomb-bay doors tended to cave in when ditching, while at impact in a crash-landing the high wing with its great weight of engines tended to slam forward and down, crushing crewmen in the front fuselage.

Hell on earth: a dramatic view from 12,500 ft of a hugely destructive RAF raid on Pforzheim, on the night of 23 February 1945. Bomb bursts mingle with incendiaries, and scale is given by the Lancaster bombers silhouetted against the smoke and fire. Some 380 bombers dropped 1,825 tons of HE and incendiaries in 22 minutes; around 17,600 people were killed.

Bombs for all targets: a 1945 photograph showing some of the RAF's range of HE bombs; reall large bombs (12,000 lb and up) were unique to the RAF. The tai of the 8,000-lb HC is the open cylinder at the far end. The Grand Slam's tail fins are canted 5 degrees to provide spin-up during descent. The bomb labelled 2,000-lb MC appears to be a 2,000-lb AP.

Oil target: despite opposition from ACM Harris of Bomber Command, the Allied raids on refineries and synthetic oil plants in German and occupied territory eventually became a major factor in winning the European war. A direct hit could be spectacularly self-evident, as here with the Pardubice refinery in Czechoslovakia, under attack by 15th AF B-24s.

Above: *Confounding the experts*:
combining the performance of an
interceptor with the range of a
bomber, the Merlin-engined P-51
Mustang escort fighter had a
dramatic effect on the Western Fr
air war. These 8th AF P-51s have
drop tanks and D-Day invasion
stripes. One is a P-51B, the others
P-51Ds, having a bubble hood and
lowered rear fuselage for pilot rea
view. The loss of rear fuselage side
area gave reduced directional
stability, later restored with a fin
extension, as on the aircraft neare
the camera. Left: *Rockets and
debris*: since RPs arrived ahead of
the aircraft, crews using them with
HE warheads in low-level attacks
could find themselves flying into a
lethal cloud of debris. Here an
SAAF/BAF Beaufighter has just
the middle one of three small
locomotives, in Yugoslavia in 194
Two further RPs are visible,
streaking over the top of the
locomotive.

Shipyard attack: the yards at Monfalcone on the Gulf of Venice under attack in 1945, showing smoke from the bombing, plus craters and a capsized ship from a previous attack. The RAF Liberator has just been hit by a bomb from an aircraft above, causing the No. 2 engine to lose its propeller and to stream smoke; the crew managed to get it back to base. The Liberator's very efficient long-span Davis wing is evident in this plan view.

Grand-slam success: water-filled craters – many from previous raids – surround the Bielefeld railway viaduct, showing seven spans destroyed after the RAF attack on 14 March 1945. 617 Squadron dropped 12,000-lb Tallboys and a 22,000-lb Grand Slam in its first operational use; this did much of the damage, with the large crater near the right of the breach. The sizes of the craters can be compared with the houses (foreground and top right).

The War's ultimate in devastation: central Hiroshima after the A-bomb attack on 6 August 1945, and some road clearance. A few reinforced concrete buildings (like the newspaper offices here at right), within a few hundred yards of ground zero, survived as shells, vantage points for international observers to come and ponder the new age of warfare.

Everywhere destruction: as in many other German cities at the end of the war, Stuttgart's roofless and ruined buildings were largely the result of the British policy of 'area bombing' to achieve 'de-housing' as a means of disrupting German war production. Against Japan especially, the USAAF also adopted area bombing.

B-29 Superfortress: the B-29 was only used in the Pacific theatre, primarily to exploit its great range. But at short range, its bomb load was unprecedented, as shown by these two B-29s of the US 20th Bomber Command unloading during an attack on a Japanese supply depot, near Mingaladen airfield, Rangoon, April 1945. The instability of the bombs is noteworthy.

Superbombers being prepared: The ten (or more) crew B-29 Superfortress, the War's most advanced heavy bomber, in a busy between-raids scene at Isley Field, a US 21st Bomber Command base on Saipan in the Marianas. The B-29 in the foreground shows to good effect its two dorsal and two ventral gun barbettes, the guns in minimum drag (rear-pointing) position. For later night raids, all except the tail guns were deleted.

The Pacific Island War: US Marine Corps F4U Corsair fighter-bombers preparing for take off at a Central Pacific island base, late in the War. Each carries a single 500-lb bomb under the belly for a strike at a Japanese target, probably a base on another island. By 1945, the Japanese had few ships left to attack.

The RAF's bomber stream: the size of the stream for a major raid, usually only evident from the noise, became visible when the force was assembling late in a summer evening, or on a daylight raid late in the War. The 7-man Lancaster became the RAF's standard heavy bomber, and this still shows almost 100 of them filling the sky, setting out on a daylight raid in summer 1944.

'Little Boy': this unique uranium bomb was the first nuclear weapon to be used operationally, dropped on Hiroshima. It had a yield equivalent to 20,000 tons of HE, whereas the slightly heavier RAF Tallboy had just three tons of HE. The projections on the side near the nose are aerials for the radio altimeters carried by the bomb.

Hs129B-3 with a 6m long ventral 75mm BK 7.5 gun was successful even against the *Josef Stalin* tank. The US Consolidated Vultee XA-41 was built in prototype form only. In Germany, work was extended to more exotic ground-attack aircraft. The Berlin B.9 research aircraft had shown that a prone position (lying, stomach down) enabled a pilot to withstand higher 'g' in a pull-out manoeuvre, while offering low frontal area and therefore low drag. Early in 1944 the Henschel company adopted this approach for the Hs132 turbojet-powered ground-attack aircraft. Meanwhile, the Dornier Do335 'push-pull' fighter was evaluated as a fighter-bomber; an Me262A-1 jet fighter with a 50mm BK 5 nose cannon was tested against ground targets; and the projected Blohm und Voss P.191 eight-engined aircraft was apparently intended for flak suppression. In Japan, the MXY5 glider was adapted as the Yokosuka/Mizumo *Shinryu* anti-tank suicide glider, carrying a 100kg impact-fused warhead. It was to be given a rocket-assisted take-off for operations right at the front, or be towed to the battlefield area by a Yokosuka P1Y bomber. The crewman was then to make a steep dive to impact on an enemy tank. Only one was built.

Rocket Projectiles

By 1944 the RP had become a major RAF ground-attack weapon. The normal installation on Typhoons was eight 3-inch rockets, a bank of four under each wing; a double-stack 16 RP installation was less rigid/accurate. In 1944 P-51s in Burma and 14th AF P-40s in China were fitted with Bazooka-type launcher tubes for M-8 4.5-inch RPs, in a cluster of three under each wing. They were used for close support and against Japanese armour. The US 5th AF in New Guinea field-fitted 12 such tubes (4 clusters of 3) to some A-20G Havocs, for low-level attacks. One German response to the huge Soviet armoured offensive on the Eastern Front was hurried development work on tank-busting RPs. In October, the *Panzerschreck* 88mm anti-tank RP was introduced, the Fw190F-8 carrying three launcher tubes for it under each wing. It was quickly superseded by the 70mm *Panzerblitz Pb1* (four under each wing) and then the 55mm *Panzerblitz Pb2* version of the R4M (six or seven under each wing), the Pb2 having a hollow charge warhead. These rocket weapons were also tested on the Hs129B. In addition, a Ju88P-4 was tested with a 22-round magazine for an RZ65 rocket launcher.

Experimental/Unorthodox Weapons

Notably in Germany, 1944 saw trials with a variety of new and unorthodox weapons and devices for ground-attack operations. A Ju87C was tested with an 88mm recoilless gun mounted under the fuselage to fire through the propeller disc, but severe damage was caused when the rear-firing rocket charge (to absorb the recoil) failed to fire with the gun. The *Gero* flame-thrower was tested on the Henschel Hs129B. The *Werfer-Granate 28/32* 280mm mortar was tested – with little success – as an anti-tank weapon for the Fw190F-8 and Hs129B, with one or two carried under each wing. The SG116 *Zellendusche* anti-bomber weapon was flight tested (unsuccessfully) on an Fw190F-8 in the rôle of an anti-tank weapon, with the MK103 barrels firing downwards. Finally, the SG113A *Förstersonde* automatic mortar, using 77mm recoilless guns, was tested as a pair of barrels on each wing of the Fw190F-8, and as a group of six in the fuselage of the Hs129B. The guns fired downwards when triggered by a nose-mounted 'magnetic anomaly detector' (MAD) sensing the magnetic field changes created by a tank hidden in woodland or under camouflage below. The device apparently destroyed a T-34 tank in one test, but reliability was poor. The British also tested an airborne MAD (the US ASQ-1 intended for locating submarines) for detecting tanks; and tried the H2D night tactical adaptation of H2S, intended to detect movement on the ground below, but it showed poor ability to discriminate between moving and stationary objects.

Ground-attack Operations

Allied Use of Airpower for Invasion Support;
Operations in Italy

In 1944, the Allies made further amphibious landings in Axis-held territory. In Europe, 11,000 land-based aircraft supported the huge Normandy invasion. Carrier aircraft supplemented land-based aircraft in covering the Anzio and south of France landings. In the Pacific, the rapidly expanding USN carrier force provided the bulk of the air support for the landings there (Marshall Islands, New Guinea, Marianas, Palau and Caroline Islands, and the Philippines – Leyte, Mindoro). Land-based bombers aided in the prior bombardment, which included bombing and shelling of the beach defences and minefields, the craters providing cover for the troops coming ashore. AF and USMC fighters, fighter- and dive-bombers were flown in as soon as airfields had been captured and repaired; e.g. on 22 June, 7th AF P-47s were catapulted from CVE escort carriers to land on Saipan, flying their first close support operations that day.

In Italy, the luckless citizens of Civitavecchia found themselves subjected to heavy Allied decoy bombing prior to the Anzio landings, the bombing being purely to give the impression that the landings would be here, north of Rome. At Anzio itself in February, DAF and US tactical aircraft did much to disrupt the German counter-offensive to the beachhead, but failed to silence the 'Anzio Annie' railway gun. Further south, Allied tactical airpower failed to dislodge German troops from steel and concrete bunkers high in the hills near Cassino. In June, the Allies set up the Balkan Air Force to provide tactical airpower to support partisans in Albania and Greece, and especially in Yugoslavia; some fighter-bombers were used for supply drops. In November, fighter-bombers were used in the Operation Bingo' assault on transformer stations for the

electrified Brenner Pass rail line. In December, BAF
fighter-bombers were used to aid Greek forces against rebe
units in a civil war.

Allied Operations in South-east Asia

RAF ground attack strikes in Burma used Vengeances
Beaufighters, Mustangs, and especially Hurricanes, witl
bombs, rockets and cannon. Troops, including each Chindi
unit had an RAF officer to direct air attacks. The
Vengeances were employed, e.g. in pin-point dive-bombin∤
attacks against Japanese earth bunkers, using a mix o
delay-fused GP bombs to explode deep down, and 'NITI
(Nose Instantaneous, Tail Instantaneous) fused rodded
anti-personnel bombs. The wide-ranging Beaufighter earned
its RAF name 'Whispering Death' from quiet, fast, low-level
surprise attacks against road, rail and river traffic. The
Mosquito was also used, but its glued/wooden structure
proved susceptible to the hot, damp climate. US P-38s and
P-51s made strikes on Japanese forward airfields. Wel
lington and Mitchell bombers airlifted munitions for ground
attack squadrons with Allied forces cut off in the Impha
valley, the Hurricanes flying incessant attacks against the
besieging Japanese. During the drive southward in autumr
1944, the US 10th AF alone flew 12,000 close suppor
strikes, mostly by P-47s, some reportedly within 35 yards o
Allied troops; just one Chinese and two British soldiers were
killed. [USSBS, 1945–49: No.67] In December, co-ordinated
attacks were made on all Japanese staging and forward
airfields in Burma, catching aircraft on the ground
refuelling. Features of the Allied operations included
employing Hurricanes to spray the malaria-ridden Kabav
valley with DDT ahead of Allied troops; use of a Spitfire
('The Looker') to confirm that a target area was cloud free
before despatching the attack aircraft; the use of nets and
frames under parked Hurricanes so that pilots could safely
jettison their bombs and take off as fighters should the field
come under attack; US use of liaison aircraft to help direc
close support bombing; the use of Vengeance dive-bomber
dropping first delayed action bombs in close suppor
operations and then – as the Allied troops attacked –
unfused bombs, the Japanese remaining under cover to

await the bomb explosions; similar use of Spitfires to make strafing passes, and then dummy strafing passes as the Allied troops attacked.

Eastern Front Ground Attack

By 1944, Soviet close support operations were being directed by radio via a central command post at the Front, and local controllers in tanks; the artillery used coloured smoke shells to mark the targets. The Soviet operations included: in the Crimean mountains, bombing by Il-2s to cause landslides, cutting off roads and destroying convoys to obstruct German forces; heavy bombing against the fortifications and minefields built by the Finns across the Karelian Isthmus; the strewing of incendiaries in the Steppes in high summer, the resulting grass fires forcing the German troops to move positions; and set-piece attacks against major targets, with two or three bomber regiments (of 30 aircraft each) bombing from 3,000m, then two or three ground-attack regiments, and finally two or three fighter-bomber regiments attacking at low level. With the huge Soviet offensive – supported by 7,000 aircraft – on the third anniversary of 'Barbarossa', the scale of the Soviet ground-attack operations rivalled those by the Allies on the Western Front; and the losses to German flak were equally large.

Faced with Soviet armour breaking through the German lines, daily Luftwaffe operations began with reconnaissance sorties to establish where the Red Army had moved to during the night. These were followed by bombing and strafing attacks by Fw190 fighter-bombers. Where Soviet tanks were engaging German troops, they became priority targets, a frequently used technique being a fast, low skip-bombing attack, releasing a 250kg bomb with a one-second delay fuse, to bounce off the ground into the tank or to hit it directly. Where Soviet columns were moving forward unopposed, the priority targets were the fuel supply vehicles, which could easily be knocked out by strafing; without them the tanks would have to halt anyway.

Allied Fighter-bomber Operations for the Normandy Invasion

In the Allied air operations pre- and post D-Day in support

of the invasion, 8th AF fighters not needed in escorting the day bombers were assigned to clearing the skies and airfields of German aircraft in Northern France. This gave the British 2TAF and US 9th AF fighter-bombers almost unrestricted freedom for ground-attack operations. Prime targets were coastal radars, trains, tanks, troop units, military vehicles, and (once the landings had begun) bridges around the beachhead, to isolate it. Rocket-firing Typhoons were used for systematic attacks on the radars. Intended for the small *Würzburg* sets, the 'Abdullah' radar homer fitted to a Typhoon proved ineffective; the radar operators could switch frequency or even switch off altogether when aircraft were coming directly towards them. For the invasion itself Bostons laid smokescreens over the beaches ahead of the approaching landing-craft. By D-Day plus 1, the Allies were constructing forward airfields (Emergency Landing Strips, Refuelling and Rearming Strips, then operational Advanced Landing Grounds) in the beachhead. Flying from these, the Typhoons and P-47s continued their destruction. The Germans tried giving false voice instructions to direct the aircraft astray, one such try being foiled by a suspicious US flight leader demanding that the controller sing the words of the 'Mairzie Doats' popular song of the period. But German light flak took a steady toll of the Allied fighter-bombers. The losses were greater for low-level than for dive-bombing, but without dive-brakes, fighters built up too much speed in a dive for really accurate/low dive-bombing. Overall, the immense Allied air operations in support of the Normandy invasion were highly successful, but 4,100 aircraft were lost from the 480,000 sorties flown between 6 June and 31 August.

German Attacks Against the Normandy Beachhead

With inadequate resources (and its ground-attack units all on the Eastern Front), the Luftwaffe's response to the D-Day invasion was late and improvised. Features included: initial unescorted daylight sorties by Ju88s, with inevitable losses; small scale night raids by Ju88, Do217 and He177 bombers, with further losses to flak and night fighters; attempts, with pilots untrained for ground attack, to use Fw190 fighters as fighter-bombers, some with 21cm rocket mortars; restricting night bombing to high altitude, thereby reducing losses but rendering the bombing ineffective; diversion of the bombers to minelaying; assigning night fighters to aid in ground strafing; and the return of the Ju87 for night attacks. Overall, the German losses in France were heavy, 931 aircraft by 30 June.

Allied Close Support; 'Column Cover'; 'Horsefly'
The Allied advance after D-Day was spearheaded by air-supported armour, the lead tanks carrying fluorescent coloured panels to aid recognition from the air. Close support, including 'cab-rank' standing patrols, relied on target marking by coloured (usually red) smoke mortar shells, the air-to-ground fragmentation rocket attacks being directed by Forward Air Controllers (FACs) in armoured 'contact cars'; German troops at times fired their own red smoke shells as decoys. An exceptionally large operation came on 22 June with the US assault on Cherbourg, supported by 14 Wings of AEAF fighters and fighter-bombers providing a bomb-line carpet. The attack was opened by rocket-firing Typhoons and also included Window drops, and precision strikes by B-26 Marauders using Oboe. On 26 July 1944, the US 9th AF began 'Column Cover' missions, P-47s patrolling in relays of four over advancing US armoured columns. The tank commander could call down strikes when required, or to ask for searches ahead, the fighter-bombers seeking out and attacking German positions that were camouflaged or hidden in trees. The US 'Horsefly' variation employed an artillery officer in a Piper L-4 (Cub) using the same radio frequency as the controller and having a better view of each airstrike. When on 7 August, the Germans finally mounted a counter-offensive, near Mortain, the tanks were spotted, allowing the Allies to prepare a 'terrible welcome' [Terraine, 1985:660]. Relays of Typhoons quickly destroyed 90 tanks and 200 other vehicles, the first time that a Panzer unit had been destroyed by air-to-ground RPs. Reporting to Hitler on the Allied air operations, Gen.von Kluge declared, 'I see no way of developing any strategy that will cancel their annihilating effect ...' [Piekalkiewicz, 1985:371]

Use of Heavy Bombers for Close Support; Casualties
The 30th of June 1944 saw the first large scale use of heavy
bombers in a tactical operation against armour, 256 RAF
bombers using 'Controlled Oboe' wiping out a concentration
of German tanks near Villers Bocage, in a 15-minute
daylight raid. On 7 July, in Operation 'Charnwood', the
RAF made the first night close support use of heavy
bombers. But the ground to air signals which had been
practised and agreed, were not used. Instead, with PFF
marking and a bomb line 6,000 yards beyond the front line to
avoid hitting friendly troops, the bomb carpet laid by the 450
Lancasters also largely overshot the German positions,
destroying much of north Caen with heavy civilian losses.
The 1,000lb MC bomb craters also hampered subsequent
ground movement. But although the RAF insisted on the
Army accepting 'cratering' to avoid having to change bomb
types [Carrington, 1987:159], 2,000 US bombers attacking
the same sector used blast and fragmentation bombs to
prevent further deep craters. After Allied bombers dropped
a further 7,700 tons in the Caen area under Operation
'Goodwood' on 18 July, Eisenhower – and the bomber
chiefs – fumed at the average of 1,000 tons of bombs being
expended to advance Montgomery's forces each mile.
[Terraine, 1985:656] More effective bombing came with
Operation 'Totalize' on the night of 7 August at Falaise;
with PFF marking on flare shells fired by artillery, 100 RAF
bombers rendered the road impassable, enabling a major
defeat of German forces. Some 1,113 bombers supported
the paratroop and glider landings for Montgomery's 'Market
Garden' leapfrogging move to Arnhem in September. But
bad weather soon prevented both supply drops and close
support operations. Appeals by Bennett [:251] to have the
PFF use Oboe to blind drop supplies to the beleaguered
troops fell on deaf ears.
    Heavy bombing for close support – used with inadequate
briefing, liaison, and ground-to-air signals – brought risks of
casualties among friendly troops. US troops were killed by
USAAF bombing in Operation 'Cobra' at St Lô on 25 July.
Then on 14 August under Operation 'Tractable', RAF
bombers caused heavy casualties among Canadian troops.
Here, the troops under attack showed their positions as they

would for Army co-operation aircraft, firing yellow smoke markers and lighting celanese strips (which looked like TIs), unaware that Bomber Command were using yellow TIs. Some crews bombed these markers despite identification of the correct ones by Master Bombers. Having failed to implement available procedures to avoid such a result, Bomber Command now backed away from close support, while the USAAF strove to improve techniques for future operations. For Operation 'Queen' on 16 November, the 800 RAF bombers took the furthest targets, destroying the towns of Düren and Julich, while Americans took the closest ones. [Carrington, 1987:188]

Ground-attack Techniques

Allied Use of Rocket Projectiles; Attack Techniques
In Europe, the RAF was the principal user of RPs for ground attack, particularly with 2TAF Typhoons on the Western Front; in the Mediterranean and the Balkans, rocket-firing Beaufighters flew longer range missions striking buildings, bridges, trains, etc., as well as ships. The US 9th AF made its first use of RPs on 17 July with P-47s carrying four apiece, and was to fire many thousands by the end of the war. The 8th AF made little use of RPs, judging six or eight 0.5-inch guns with AP ammunition, plus GP or M41 frag bombs, adequate for most targets. Typhoon RP attacks were made in a dive of 30 degrees (or greater, if AA fire was fierce), firing the aircraft's cannons to force the AA gunners to take cover. The rockets were aimed using the gunsight, preferably directly up or down wind to avoid deflection, but pilots learned to allow for wind and gravity drop and could often hit a tank or a locomotive with one pair of RPs. To avoid accidents on the ground, it became RAF practice to position an armourer at the end of the runway to arm the rockets just before 'brakes-off'.

US Strafing Attacks on Airfields; Allied Use of Flak Suppression

As air opposition declined, 8th AF fighters went over more and more to a roving offensive against ground targets, plus systematic attacks against airfields, mostly with strafing. P-47 pilots adopted a diving attack, using the pull-out to provide a swath of bullets. For a planned attack, three squadrons would approach at low level for surprise, the first climbing to 3,500ft as top cover, while the second strafed AA gun positions. Then as the third squadron strafed aircraft and installations on the airfield, the second climbed to replace the first, which then attacked anything left undamaged by the other two. For fixed, defended targets, flak suppression became a separate support role. Approaches used included: a preceding strafing sweep against the AA positions, by fighters; bombing of AA positions by medium bombers at altitude before fighter-bombers swept in low; and split attacks, e.g. with Typhoons, four with RPs would attack the target while others attacked the AA defences with cannon. Flak suppression at the front line was also performed by ground forces; as Allied bombers flew overhead to attack targets further to the rear, Army field guns pounded enemy AA positions in the front line to minimize the AA response.

Allied Dive- and Low-level Bombing Attacks

In 1944, P-40, P-51, P-47 and Typhoon fighter-bombers each began carrying 2,000lb bomb loads. Key buildings targeted by Allied Intelligence were marked with phosphorus rockets by lead Typhoons; 'Bomphoons' then bombed singly or side-by-side, at roof-top height, the bombs smashing through the side of the building. Such targets included the German 15th Army HQ at Dordrecht on 24 October 1944 (when a conference was known to be taking place), and the Gestapo HQ in Amsterdam on 26 November. For well-defended targets, the leader marked then climbed to direct the raid by R/T, splitting the attack to approach from two or more directions. In similar US attacks, e.g. on the German Army HQ at Peltre on 8 November, P-47s used skip bombing with 500lb GP bombs. Bombs were also used by Typhoons and P-47s against V-1 sites and solidly-built bridges, RPs being judged too light. The 9th AF tackled most bridges, but 197 Sqdn RAF Typhoons also specialized in this role, using 30-degree dives, releasing 1,000lb bombs with 11-second delay fuses. On 5 May, DAF Kittyhawk and Mustang fighter-bombers successfully breached the Pescara dam in Italy.

Allied Techniques Against Transport

Attacks against transport were usually made in a shallow dive at right angles, the RAF using RPs or cannon; US pilots found 0.5-inch AP incendiary ammunition effective, even setting tanks on fire from a rear attack. Against a train, the locomotive was usually attacked first, to immobilize it. Munitions trains often had a locomotive at each end and sometimes one in the middle, plus flak wagons for defence. But fighter-bombers could bomb the line ahead and behind the train, to stop it while other aircraft were summoned; the flak defence was met with longitudinal strafing runs. Against road convoys the approach was, again, to destroy vehicles at the front and rear to halt the column for further attacks. Air attacks materialized so quickly that the Germans removed the doors from vehicles to allow a rapid escape, and travelled with personnel lying on top, scanning the sky.

When the Germans resorted to night movements to escape the day attacks, 9th AF P-47s began making evening drops of bombs having 1–12 hour delay fuses, e.g. at road junctions; this made night convoy movements hazardous. In addition, RAF Mosquitos attacked trains, convoys and other targets at night, sometimes with Mitchell bombers dropping flares to illuminate them. With a locomotive's steam visible from five miles at night, train crews were forced to stop when aircraft were around, making the journeys very slow. US 9th AF P-61 Black Widow night fighters were also diverted to night strafing and bombing operations against transport.

Daylight Bombing Techniques

Revised 8th AF Formations; Formation Building
With long-range escort fighters and H2X becoming
available, in January the 8th AF revised its formations to
suit. The Combat Wing of 54 aircraft was replaced by the
Group of 36 aircraft in three squadrons in lead, high and low
positions, each squadron flying in close formation on four
levels. This more compact formation was easier for the
fighters to protect, and offered more accurate radar
bombing. With US raids now involving hundreds of bombers
taking off from different bases, efforts were made to
improve the building up of the formations at the outset of a
raid. One approach used war-weary, stripped and unarmed
B-24 'assembly ships', each with flare guns, fuselage lights to
flash the unit code, and a distinctive bright colour scheme
(e.g. yellow with large red polka dots, or black with orange
lightning stripes), on which other crews would formate. The
assembly ship returned to base once the formation was on
course. An alternative was the 'monitor ship', normally a
P-47, flown by an officer giving voice instructions to the
bomber crews. Formation building was in stages, aircraft
from each base joining up as a sub-formation while flying a
designated out and return leg, and then moving off to join
the main formation.

*8th and 9th AF Pathfinder Techniques; 'Synchronous
Bombing'*
The new 8th AF formation was first used with radar on 11
January, the 482nd (Pathfinder) Group's new H2X-
equipped B-24s leading 650 US bombers in attacks on
aircraft factories around Brunswick. For conditions of
partial cloud cover, c.March the 482nd introduced 'H2X
Synchronous Bombing', with both the radar operator and
the bombardier following the bombing run to the target. The
bombardier made the drop if the target proved to be visible,

otherwise the radar operator ordered bomb release. By April, 8th AF B-24s were using the British Gee-H system for blind marking through overcast, dropping marker flares in attacks, e.g. on V-weapon sites.

US 9th AF medium bomber formations were now led by bomb-leader aircraft (e.g. A-20J and K) having frameless transparent noses for improved bombardier's view. In February, the 9th AF formed the 1st Pathfinder Squadron (Provisional) to provide lead aircraft for medium bombers for daylight overcast conditions. On the first mission, on 21 February, a pathfinder B-26 used Gee for 17 others to bomb Coxyde Furnes airfield. Later, the 9th AF pathfinders also used Oboe and H2X. In the attacks on transport targets in France in May, the need for accuracy to minimize civilian casualties led to 9th AF visual bombing in compact flights of six aircraft on converging lines of attack.

US Bombing on the Leader; Bomb Release by Radio; Use of Escort Fighters

8th AF use of 'bombing on the leader' had its disadvantages. If the leader released early by accident (as on 28 January 1944), by short circuit (6 February), or as a result of flak damage (25 February), all or part of the formation would also release, short of the target. If on the other hand a rack malfunction prevented release (as on 5 February and 2 March), the rest of the formation also failed to bomb.

But the quest for a more compact bomb pattern continued. Around March 1944 some 8th AF B-24 bombers were equipped with a 'Marker Beacon' radio bomb release (RBR) system, in which the Norden sight's automatic bomb release on the lead aircraft also caused a radio transmitter to send a signal which was picked up by receivers on the other aircraft, to activate simultaneous release of bombs on the other aircraft. In the autumn, B-17s were being fitted with an improved 'Crawfish' RBR, using the 'Azon' radio system with three frequencies in parallel to avoid jamming.

In the Pacific, by 1944 P-38Js with long-range tanks were providing escort for 5th AF B-24s attacking distant Japanese-held island bases. On a much larger scale in the ETO, the initial US use of escorts required groups of fighters to rendezvous with the bombers and accompany them until relieved by other fighters. But in January 1944, the 8th AF began using an area relay system, in which fighters were assigned to patrolling a given area (P-47s for the near areas, P-38s and P-51s for the further ones) until the bombers had passed through. Initially, the escorts flew close to the bombers to provide protection. But during February, as the escort force grew rapidly in strength, an increasing proportion was able to leave the bombers and actively seek out the Luftwaffe. By the end of 1944, some P-51s were being fitted with 'Rosebud' transponders enabling long-range identification and control by an MEW station at Gulpen in Holland.

US Formation Bombing by Fighter-bombers

Single-seat fighter-bombers were economical in terms of bomb weight delivered per crewman, and had less need of escorts. But the German use of fighter-bombers for high-level bombing had made no provision for achieving accuracy. Now the USAAF proposed using a tight formation of them, bombing accurately by means of a suitably equipped lead aircraft, all bombing when the leader bombed. A B-24 was tried for leading a formation of P-47s, but its low speed made the formation vulnerable to flak at the 24,000ft the laden P-47s could reach. Accordingly, a few P-38J Lightnings were converted as two-seat 'droop snoot' pathfinder lead aircraft, with a lengthened nose housing a bombardier and a Norden bombsight. Later a radar bombsight was added for raids through cloud cover. The first two 8th AF 'B-38' raids were made on 10 April 1944, by the 20th and 55th P-38 Groups with other P-38s as escorts, attacking airfields in France. Further missions followed, but were eventually phased out with the reducing threat to the heavy bombers.

British Daylight Bombing Techniques

For its new daylight bombing operations in June 1944, RAF Bomber Command transferred its night techniques. The target was marked as at night, and crews bombed individually, the raid being controlled by a Master Bomber. If cloud or smoke from the bombing or from defence smokescreens obscured the target and/or markers, later crews bombed blind using H2S, or even a Gee fix. The British bombers flying at 18,000ft were judged too vulnerable to flak to use large USAAF-type tight formations, so loose 'gaggles' were normally used. But tight formations were judged practical at small scale, and in July 'Oboe Formation' and 'Gee-H Formation' were introduced for precision daylight/overcast bombing. This employed a tight group of six heavy bombers, led by an Oboe or Gee-H equipped aircraft, with 'bombing on the leader'. Range was limited by the leader flying at the lower altitude of the other bombers, but forward movement of mobile transmitters as the Allied troops advanced towards Germany eased this problem. Since an Oboe-Mosquito offered no height advantage here, Oboe-equipped Lancasters were also used. But Gee-H was preferred, since it could be used by more aircraft, so allowing more targets to be attacked. To achieve close bomb grouping with larger numbers of bombers using the technique, rearward crews released their bombs after a pre-chosen delay, or when passing a Smoke Puff sky marker released by the lead aircraft. By such methods, the RAF attacked Duisburg with 1,063 bombers by daylight on 14 October 1944, following up with 1,005 bombers that night. The combined raids were the heaviest of the war, around 9,000 tons of bombs being dropped on the one city in 24 hours.

US Preparations and Training for Dropping A-bombs

While development of the two types of A-bomb proceeded at Los Alamos, preparations for delivering them were begun under code-name 'Silverplate'. A special USAAF unit, the 393rd Heavy Bombardment Squadron, was assigned in September 1944, 15 crews under Col. P.W. Tibbets beginning secret training at Wendover Field, Utah. Only Tibbets knew the true nature of their mission. The B-29s were given an enlarged forward bomb bay to take the plutonium type A-bomb, carried on a British 12,000lb HC bomb hook. Because a fighter escort would probably draw enemy attention, Tibbets planned an unescorted mission. The B-29s were stripped of armour and all except the tail guns, for increased performance to reduce the risk of interception and help to achieve a rapid getaway from the nuclear blast. The crews practised drops of dummy bombs, each drop being tracked and filmed. Rather than have the aircraft continue forward in the same direction as the bomb as it curved downwards, bomb release had to be followed immediately by a 155-degree high 'g' diving turn at full power, calculated to take the aircraft the greatest distance (seven miles) from the explosion point at the instant of detonation. In December, the 393rd and its support units became the 509th Composite Group.

Daylight Bombing Operations

Allied Tactical/Precision Raids: V-weapon Sites; Cassino; Mosquito Raids

In December 1943, the 'Crossbow Committee' invoked heavy Allied bombing of the huge new German Fi103 (later V-1) and A-4 (later V-2) weapon sites (code-named 'No-Ball'), aided by trials on replicas built in Florida. But in 1944, the Germans changed to much simpler 'modified' launch sites for the V-1, in woodland and camouflaged; plus a wholly mobile launch system for the V-2. Systematic air strikes were made on the V-1 sites. But the mobility of the V-2 units made attacks on them difficult; Spitfire fighter-bombers were sent to search for and attack them, with little success. Their elimination came with the advance of Allied ground forces. The huge underground *Mittelwerke GmbH* V-2 production facility near Niedersachswerfen was judged an impractical target even for a Tallboy, and the site was never bombed, even though vital power and other installations were above ground.

The first major Allied use of heavy bombers for direct support to ground troops came in Italy on 15 February, with the controversial US 15th AF attack on the fortress-like mountain-top Benedictine monastery of Monte Cassino. Bombing by formations of 142 B-17s and 87 medium bombers destroyed the monastery, which Allied forces believed (erroneously) was being used as a stronghold by German troops. Heavy bombing of the town of Cassino followed, converting it to rubble and craters which provided defensive positions for the Germans while hampering any Allied advance – a practical lesson that was proving difficult to learn. In December, RAF Bomber Command flew eight major tactical raids, blind marking through thick fog to disrupt the German Ardennes offensive.

After practising on a mock-up of the target, under Operation 'Jericho' on 18 February, 19 Australian, Canadian and British-crewed RAF Mosquito VI bombers carried out a special low-level daylight raid for SOE. Three waves of bombers attacked Amiens jail, breaching the walls. Around 100 prisoners were killed, but 285 others (many of them Resistance members) were able to escape. Other such raids included one on an art gallery housing personnel records at The Hague on 11 April; and one on the German Gestapo HQ at Aarhus University in Denmark on 31 October, by four waves of six Mosquitos; bombs with one-minute fuses were dropped at two-second intervals.

Renewed 8th AF Deep Penetration Raids: 'Big Week'
Under Operation 'Argument', in February 1944 the US 8th AF resumed deep penetration missions into Germany, the bombers now supported by P-51B long-range escort fighters. In Operation Pointblank's highly successful 'Big Week' (19–25 February), the 8th and 15th AFs flew 3,800 sorties against the German aircraft factories, with support from 5 RAF night raids. The 8th AF had now overtaken RAF Bomber Command in having the world's largest force of heavy bombers, and as the RAF were doing already, began flying co-ordinated missions against several targets at once, to split the German fighter defences. Although increasingly using blind bombing against German cities, the US continued to give priority to precision attacks on key strategic targets when the weather permitted. Favoured targets were ones the Germans would be forced to defend, notably oil plants and aircraft factories. The result was the greatest air battle of the war, in which the German losses mounted steeply, and the inadequate training of replacement pilots left the Luftwaffe even less able to

counter the US bombers and fighters. US daylight bomber losses again dropped below the RAF's night losses. On 7 May, the 8th AF mounted its first 1,000-bomber combination of raids.

The Allied Railway/Transportation Plan
The Axis reliance on rail transport for troops and supplies made railways desirable targets for Allied attack. But with bridges difficult to hit with high-level bombing, Britain's Dr Zuckerman had advocated instead systematic attacks on railway centres, to destroy their stores, rolling stock and repair facilities. For the Allied invasion of Sicily and Italy in 1943, southern Italy's rail system had been 'practically paralysed' by the bombing of just six main rail centres. [Zuckerman, 1978:245] But the later 'Operation Strangle' interdiction against the much larger rail network in north Italy was less successful because of the scale of operations needed to outpace repair work. Despite opposition from British and US bomber chiefs, and fears of civilian casualties, in March 1944 Allied heavy bombers were diverted to attacks on 93 rail targets in France and the Low Countries to support the Normandy invasion. Belatedly, fighter-bombers were used successfully against the rail bridges. The total effort (66,517 tons of bombs) was criticized as wasteful, but in two months rail traffic dropped by almost 80 per cent, making this 'Transportation Plan' a major factor in the survival of the Allied bridgehead in Normandy. By June, the US 15th AF was striking at the Rumanian and Hungarian rail systems, to aid the Soviets. But an Allied 'Transportation Plan' for Germany itself was rejected. The heavy bombers returned mainly to bombing cities (RAF) and aircraft and oil plants (USAAF), even though dispersal of production was now making the bombing of German cities and known factories less effective, and transport had become vital for bringing components to the assembly points. German production continued to increase until, late in the war, the oil shortage and air attacks brought such transport disruption that little of the Ruhr's daily output of 30,000 tons of goods could be moved out.

The Allied 'Oil Offensive'

On 5 April, the US 15th AF restarted bombing the Ploesti refineries with escorted raids from Foggia; these included a low-level one by P-38s, each carrying a 1,000lb bomb. Then on 12 May, the 8th AF implemented one of the crucial policies of the war, Spaatz's plan for the systematic destruction of German oil installations, notably the 12 main synthetic fuel plants. Thanks to opposition from Harris, the RAF joined in belatedly but continued the oil attacks even when the appearance of the Me163 rocket fighter and Me262 jet fighter in July caused the 8th AF to revert temporarily to attacking aircraft and engine factories. US bomber losses to flak were now increasing as the Germans, finding radar-controlled AA fire against night raids severely compromised by British jamming, instead moved AA units to the factories and oil plants being attacked by US day bombers. But German aviation fuel output dropped progressively from 175,000 tons in April, to just 10,000 tons in September; the Germans virtually ceased pilot training in powered aircraft. But the Allied offensive then eased, due to bad weather (making precision attacks difficult) and over-optimistic interpretation of raid damage photos. Plant repairs enabled an increase in production, to 39,000 tons in November, so delaying defeat.

Allied Use of Heavy Bombers for Invasion Support

While the bombing of rail targets for 'Overlord' progressed, on 11 May the 8th AF and 2TAF also began attacks on the 40 main airfields within 150km of Caen, aiming primarily for maintenance and repair facilities. For the Normandy landings on 6 June, RAF and US heavy bombers were assigned to direct support to the landings. During the previous night, all 1,136 RAF bombers available were used to drop 5,000 tons of bombs, the largest amount ever in one night, on Atlantic Wall targets. By morning, only 1 of 10 German coastal gun batteries remained operational. On D-Day itself, the 8th AF alone despatched 882 B-17s and 409 B-24s stacked in precise formations for dawn attacks on beach targets, but early morning mist led to bombing on a Gee fix (with a safety margin), so reportedly the main casualties were cabbages inland from the beaches. More effective heavy bomber raids on targets in and around the beachhead followed that day and subsequently.

After bombing attacks, notably against the Toulon naval base, on 13 and 14 August US 12th AF heavy bombers from Italy attacked gun emplacements, bridges, rail centres etc., in southern France in preparation for the 'Operation Dragoon' Allied landings on the 15th.

Eastern Front: German Bombing; US Shuttle Missions to the USSR

On the Eastern Front, c.May 1944 the Germans themselves began a daylight bombing campaign with heavy bombers, the 90 He177s of KG1. The attacks were of relatively short range against Soviet supply centres and troops rather than against strategic targets, bombing from 6,000m. Reportedly, Soviet fighter pilots treated the heavy defensive armament of the He177 with respect and few of the bombers were lost. [Smith and Kay, 1972:287]

After long negotiations and preparations (including the strengthening of Soviet runways with steel planking, under US supervision), the first US 'Operation Frantic Joe' shuttle bombing to the USSR took place on 2 June. Some 130 B-17s with 70 P-51 escorts from Foggia raided rail targets in Hungary and flew on to land at Poltava, Mirgorod and Piratyin, in the Ukraine. On 21 June, B-17s and P-51s flew the 8th AF's first shuttle bombing from Britain to the Ukraine. On the return flights, the US bombers used Soviet 250kg bombs and 0.5-inch ammunition. Later, Yak-9DD long-range fighters were flown from the Ukraine to Bari and used to escort US bombers on shuttle missions. But US requests to use Soviet bases in Siberia for bombing Japan were refused.

The British Restart Daylight Heavy Bombing; French Daylight Bombing

Encouraged by diminishing German day fighter activity, the RAF restarted large daylight raids on 14 June, 234 aircraft attacking the docks at Le Havre. On 5 September, the RAF began further such raids on German-held French ports (Le Havre, Boulogne, Calais), now cut off by Allied forces. By October, Bomber Command was carrying out many daylight raids, including into Germany, with relatively low losses. To hamper German ground forces, on 3 October, 247 RAF bombers breached the perimeter dyke of Walcheren in Holland, flooding the 'island'. In November, the new *Forces Aériennes Françaises de l'Atlantique* began raids on the Biscay ports using captured Ju88 bombers.

Allied Interdiction Against Rail Bridges in South-east Asia

By 1944, a huge Allied air build-up (on over 200 new airfields) in East India, with the US 7th AF and RAF units integrated to form Eastern Air Command (EAC), was being used in the drive against the Japanese in Burma. Bombing operations included night 'Rhubarbs' against vehicles, and especially a stepped-up offensive against the railway system. Mitchell bombers dropped spike bombs at intervals along the tracks, but the railway's many bridges were judged the most vulnerable points and most difficult to repair. Fighter-bombers attacked the nearer ones, B-25s, B-24s and RAF Liberators took those at longer range, with some Wellington missions at night. Despite trip-wires and mines exploded by remote control, many attacks were made at low level, using delay-fused bombs. Wooden trestle-type bridges were easiest to repair and needed repeat attacks when PR sorties showed them nearing completion. Additional attacks were also necessary when the Japanese built by-pass bridges alongside existing ones. At the end of December, Azon guided bombs dropped by B-24s destroyed 24 bridges in one day. Overall, 277 bridges including the 1,650ft Sittang bridge were cut during the 1944 offensive, severely hampering Japanese supply operations. Elsewhere, the US 14th AF mounted a similar offensive against rail targets including bridges, in Indo-China and later in Northern China.

US B-29 Operations in the CBI/Pacific Theatre

While US bombing operations continued across much of the Pacific theatre, in April 1944 B-29s of the new 20th AF arrived in China, putting Japan itself within range of heavy bombers. But the four bases near Chengtu had to be supplied by air, over the 'Hump' of the Himalayas from India, hence the B-29 itself was diverted to supply operations. Two B-29s made their first Hump cargo missions on 24 April, and in May the first B-29 tanker conversions were made, to fly fuel over the Hump. The first B-29 bombing mission, 100 aircraft attacking the Bangkok marshalling yards was made from India on 5 July. Thereafter, the initial B-29 bombing campaign from China was a night one. But the supply system was judged 'fantastically uneconomic and barely workable' [USSBS, 1945–49], and only 20 B-29 missions were flown from China, ten of them to Manchuria, nine to Japan and one to Formosa.

In July, with major use of USN carrier-based air power, US forces captured Saipan and Tinian in the Marianas. These islands were within the B-29's flight radius of Tokyo, and the US 'SeaBees' (CBs) began building bases: first on Saipan; then on Tinian, the world's largest bomber base, North Field, with four parallel runways each nearly two miles long. B-29s of the 21st AF arrived on Saipan in October, on Tinian in December. Meanwhile, on 10 August, B-29s flew their first missions in what would become a major mine-laying programme. In August, LeMay revised the B-29 daylight bombing tactics, replacing the four-plane diamond formation by a 12-plane 'combat box', and introducing 'synchronous bombing' when visibility was in doubt. On 8 September, a raid by 18 Japanese bombers on Chengtu destroyed 18 B-29s. But after successful daylight B-29 reconnaissance overflights, 21st AF daylight raids against Japan were begun on 24 November, 100 B-29s being sent to bomb the Musashi engine factory near Tokyo. On 18 December, the 20th AF sent 77 B-29s to firebomb Hankow, the main supply port for Japanese forces in China; the fires burned for three days.

Soviet 'ADD' Operations

The Soviet 'ADD' (Long Range Aviation) grew to some 1,500 aircraft during 1944, mostly medium bombers (Il-4, US A-20 and B-25) operating mainly in a tactical support role, bombing rail targets, supply dumps etc. at up to 300km beyond the front. Most raids were made in daylight with fighter escort. Successes included the destruction of hundreds of German aircraft while being transported by rail because of Germany's increasing shortage of aviation fuel. For the Operation 'Bagration' offensive in June, ADD missions included many bombing sweeps against German rear areas including Luftwaffe airfields. VVS fighters were used to clear the area of German fighters beforehand; to provide diversions; and to provide escort for the bombers, which often flew in a wide arc to approach the target from an unexpected direction. Other operations included leaflet raids over Finland and Eastern Europe, and supply drops to partisan groups, but little strategic bombing. Reportedly several US B-17s and B-24s were provided to the USSR c.1944, but it is not clear if or how they were used. In December, the ADD was re-organized as the 18th Air Army.

Night Bombing

German Night Bombing Against the USSR
In January 1944, the Germans restarted bombing Soviet rail targets in an effort to slow the Red Army's westward offensive. Soviet day fighter defences were now too strong for daylight operations, while their night fighters were still without radar direction. Accordingly, the German raids were made at night using flare illumination by pathfinders. The Soviets limited the damage to the trains themselves, by moving them out of stations and marshalling yards when approaching bombers were reported. On the night of 2 June, after an He177 had followed a USAAF shuttle bombing mission to Soviet airfields at Poltava and Piratyin, 200 He111 and Ju88 bombers attacked these airfields; KG4 bombers dropped flares for illumination. US officers were incensed at the inadequate Soviet response, four Yak-9s being scrambled out of some 40 night fighters stationed nearby, as 43 B-17s and 15 P-51s were destroyed in the 90-minute attack. [Piekalkiewicz, 1985:356]

The Soviets themselves were engaging in limited night bombing, some ADD units apparently using Li-2 transports converted for bombing.

Operation Steinbock; Ground Radar Direction;
V-weapons
On the night of 21 January, 227 German bombers attacked
London in the first raid of Operation *Steinbock*, the 'Little
(or "Baby") Blitz' in retaliation for the British bombing of
German cities. It included the first use of He177
four-engined bombers against Britain, and the first use of
SC2500 bombs, carried by the He177s. Most units used an
RAF-style stream, turning at *Lux* sea buoy and flare-marked
way points. The He177s used a new tactic, approaching the
target in a shallow high-speed dive from high altitude; this
and *Düppel* kept losses low. But only 32 tons of bombs hit
London. In a subsequent raid on 23 February, German
bombers used a 'fan' or 'compass rose' tactic, approaching
from different directions simultaneously to saturate the
defences. The Allies had noted the exceptional pointing
accuracy, and pulse and frequency stability of German
radars, and during *Steinbock*, the Germans exploited this
feature for directing bombers, using a *Freya* set on the
Channel cliffs. An Fw190 fighter-bomber flew along the
radar beam, aligned with the target. An IFF-type FuG25A
set carried by the Fw190 provided an amplified blip, watched
by the *Freya* controller who radioed steering instructions to
the pilot, ending with the order for bomb release. But the
British found they could use the FuG25A's blips to track the
German aircraft, even through *Düppel*. The *Steinbock* effort
declined as the Germans became more hard pressed. During
the four-month campaign, the Luftwaffe dropped 2,000 tons
of bombs on Britain, while the RAF dropped 25 times as
many on Germany. [Middlebrook, 1983:76] With raids on
Britain by German bombers becoming rare, day and night
missile attacks aimed at London began on 13 June with
ground launches of the Fieseler Fi103 (V-1) flying bomb,
supplemented from 9 July onwards by night air launches
from He111 carriers from over the North Sea. Attacks by
the Army A-4 (V-2) ballistic missile began on 8 September.
V-2 attacks on Antwerp followed.

British Flare and Marker Developments; Deception
Techniques
With the brightness of a flare blinding crews' eyes to detail

on the ground, in January the British introduced a hooded flare having an opaque umbrella-shaped canopy to shield the light from observers above. The PFF also began using cluster flares, with seven 4.5-inch flares in a 1,000lb case, or four in a 500lb case; delay capsules allowed deployment in a vertical chain with up to 600ft separation between them. Also in January the PFF introduced a TI 'Floater' skymarker which ejected 25 candles on separate parachutes, to float down in a group. Later, German successes with decoy markers led the British to introduce other new TIs to try to keep ahead. One type had candles tied in bundles of three, giving fewer but brighter light sources. A Change Colour type had layered candles giving colours alternating every 15 seconds. Another had candles giving two Morse letters alternately. A Multiflash type gave repeated four-second red flashes. In April, a much larger TI was introduced, consisting of a 1,000lb bomb casing containing 200 candles; delayed ignition of different candles gave four optional burn times of up to 20 minutes.

To stem increasing bomber losses, the RAF implemented further deception measures: broadcasting fake test signals prior to raids, and when Bomber Command was not operating; mounting two-phase raids; flying low over the North Sea to delay being picked up by German radar; and having training crews fly part-way simulated raids over the North Sea. Deception became a major PFF task, to draw German night fighters away from a real raid. On 28 January, a spoof raid by Mosquitos dropped false 'fighter flares' as well as Window and spoof route markers. Later, spoof raids were mounted purely to activate the German night fighter force, tiring them when there were no real raids; on 9 November, Mosquitos dropping Window kept six *Gruppen* of night fighters airborne for two-and-a-half hours. For a large (700-plus aircraft) raid on Bochum on 4 November, the PFF exploited the German practice of aiming a flak barrage towards skymarkers; after dropping their TIs, the PFF crews dropped flares to one side, to draw flak away from the main force.

No.5-Group 'Visual Dive Marking'
With the PFF opposed to low-level marking because of the risk to the crews doing it, Bomber Command's 5 Group

began investigating it themselves; the goal was higher accuracy. Proximity markers were blind dropped in the target area, other aircraft then dropping flares over the markers, with the Master Bomber at low level using the light of the flares to identify and mark the actual target. Marking used 30lb incendiaries which did not need the altitude of TIs. Sq. Ldr. H.B. Martin introduced more accurate release of markers by dive-bombing. The resulting 'visual dive marking' was introduced on 8 February 1944, Grp.Capt. G.L.Cheshire as Master Bomber dropping 30lb incendiaries from a Lancaster at 200ft right onto the target, the Gnome-Rhône engine factory at Limoges. Much of the factory was then destroyed by 12,000lb HC bombs dropped by Lancasters using SABS. A heavy bomber being ill-suited to dive-bombing, and vulnerable to AA fire at low level, on 5 April Cheshire began using a Mosquito. Later Cheshire dispensed with a navigator and used a long-range P-51 Mustang, with the markers on underwing racks. Cheshire was obliged to make his first mission in the P-51 without a practice flight, and with no previous experience – even in daylight – with a single-engined fighter. The 5-Group Visual Dive Marking reached its ultimate with the PFF 'false wind' technique adapted as 'Offset Marking'. To avoid them being destroyed or obscured by smoke from the bombing itself, the markers were deliberately dropped 400 yards upwind to the side. A 'false wind' correction for this offset was then calculated by the Master Bomber, and broadcast to the main force, to be allowed for in bomb aiming. No.5-Group's low-level marking set new standards for precision night attacks. But it was unsuitable for major raids on heavily defended targets (the main force having to orbit while the Master Bomber assessed and corrected the marking), nor for when there was low overcast.

The Mosquito as a Strategic Bomber; 'Siren Tours'

In December 1943, 2-Group Mosquito bombers had begun 'Flower' support operations, flying ahead of the main force to attack the night fighter airfields, while Mosquito intruders sought the night fighters themselves. Meanwhile, the Mosquito Mk.IV was adapted to carry a 4,000lb HC bomb in a bulged bomb bay, with a first operational drop on 23

February 1944, on Düsseldorf. Beginning on 13 April, and using 50gal drop-tanks to achieve the range, LNSF Mosquitos regularly carried 4,000lb bombs to Berlin, a greater bomb load over that distance than was achieved with the four-engined B-17. [Bennett, 1958:203] To give new crews experience in navigation by H2S, on 23 December single LNSF Mosquitos began nightly nuisance 'Siren Tours' over Germany, setting off air-raid sirens in each town they approached. Each aircraft normally dropped one 500lb bomb on each of four different towns.

Bomber Command and Precision Targets; 3cm H2S; 'Controlled Oboe'

Harris believed the better image resolution of the new 3cm H2S might enable Bomber Command to find and bomb the small town of Schweinfurt at night. Accordingly, after a successful USAAF daylight raid, on the night of 24 February Bomber Command mounted a much larger raid on Schweinfurt, but success was limited. For shorter ranges, raids on rail centres in Belgium and France during March confirmed the RAF's new ability to find and hit even small targets at night. In a further advance, the PFF introduced 'Controlled Oboe' in an attack on the Aulnoye marshalling yards on 10 April. Oboe Mosquitos dropped green TI's as proximity markers. Master Bombers then used flares to visually check the area around the green TIs and, having positively identified the target, dropped red TIs on it for the main force to aim at. Sometimes the RAF now achieved better accuracy than the 8th AF managed by day; individual bombing against accurately placed markers could give a closer bomb grouping than the US pattern bombing. In addition, even well camouflaged sites could usually be discovered and located by systematic PR/PI study. Once pin-pointed, such camouflaged sites were as vulnerable to Oboe raids as any other sites within range. In August, four oil dumps hidden in forest areas in France were destroyed by RAF bombing using Oboe. But despite the evident capability against 'key' targets, Harris continued to place emphasis on area bombing.

PFF Route Planning; the Nuremburg Raid; Bomber Command Losses
For major RAF raids, the PFF normally planned the flight routes. Multi-leg ones were usual, the course changes helping to disguise the target, but the increased distance reduced the bomb load which could be carried. TIs dropped to mark the turn points had been phased out, since they attracted enemy night fighters, and without them course changes made navigation more difficult. On moonlit and short summer nights, more direct routes could reduce exposure to night fighters and flak. For the Nuremburg raid on 30 March, the proposed PFF indirect route was rejected for the first and only time, for a straight 265-mile run-in to the target, favoured by other Groups. Thanks to this, and to condensation trails which formed at exceptionally low altitude and showed clearly in the moonlit skies, 96 of the 782 bombers were lost, the line of burning wreckage helping to show the night fighters the track of the bombers. It was the RAF's most disastrous raid of the war, and signalled the end of the single bomber stream.

The Battle of Berlin cost Bomber Command 1,047 aircraft missing, the PFF alone losing 150 per cent of its November 1943 strength; aircrew morale declined. Just as the US day bombers needed fighter escorts, the British night bombers now needed heavy support by intruders to counter the German night defence. With only limited support available, while the Americans were gaining ascendency by day, the British were losing it by night; the Germans could afford to assign some of their night fighters to day operations.

The Problem of Upward-firing Guns: Schräge Musik
RAF bomber crews occasionally flew a paired 'Thatch weave' (crossing each other's tails) to help watch for night fighters. But with an attack imminent, the standard evasion manoeuvre was the FIU/BSDU-devised 'corkscrew', chopping the throttles one side and using full rudder and aileron to enter a violent alternating banking dive and climb. But while this could foil an expected attack, German night fighter pilots often achieved total surprise and some began racking up large scores. With *Schräge Musik* upward-firing guns, the night fighter's normal approach was from the side

and below (outside of the 'Monica' detection cone), rising up directly under the bomber, which had no ventral viewing facility or ventral armament. Thus the night fighter remained unseen and safe from attack, its pilot taking a leisurely no-deflection shot against a full plan target, aiming, e.g. for the inboard tanks in one wing; tracer ammunition was not necessary. It was well into 1944 before the British deduced the reason for their increased losses, a few bombers having survived by luck and immediate violent evasion, and struggled home with damage clearly due to strikes all at the same upward, oblique angle. [Gunston, 1976:122] Seeing a night fighter against the dark earth below could be very difficult anyway, but the Canadian 6 Group began equipping its Halifaxes with ventral turrets. Otherwise, the RAF did nothing to provide its bombers with a downward viewing or shooting capability. Later, 'Fishpond' offered early warning of a fighter below, but even that was a mixed blessing since its use enabled the night fighter to home onto the bomber in the first place.

In the Pacific, Japanese successes with upward-firing guns were less apparent, mainly because of the smaller scale of the night bombing and Japan's limited night defence capability. But US heavy bombers also usually had ventral guns.

US B-29 Night Raids Against Japan; Japanese Night Raids

On the night of 15 June 1944, 68 B-29 bombers from Chengtu in China made the first raid by heavy bombers on the Japanese homeland, attacking the Yawata steelworks. There were no hits on target, but the raid provided an enormous morale boost to the people and war effort in China. [USSBS, 1945–49:No.67] Because of the 'hump' air supply task involved, further night raids could only follow at intervals, and by monitoring the 'hump' air traffic, the Japanese were able to judge the likely date and size of the next raid. But this was the start of a major bombing offensive, which escalated sharply when bases in the Marianas became available.

By late 1944, US day fighter superiority was forcing the Japanese to conserve their weakening bomber forces for limited night raids on US forward bases, small numbers of Ki-67s and G4Ms running the gauntlet of P-61 Black Widow and F6F Hellcat radar night fighters.

The Effect of Radio Silence; Neutralization of the Night Fighters

In January, British monitoring of German radio transmissions revealed that the Germans were tracking RAF bomber streams at ranges of up to 350km, far beyond normal ground radar range. Despite the likelihood that the bombers' IFF sets were being triggered, no action was taken. Then in July, test flights at Farnborough with a captured Ju88G-1 intruder night fighter revealed that its *Flensburg* homing set could pick up a bomber's 'Monica' transmissions at 130 miles. The light dawned. Appreciating at last that the bombers' radio and radar were attracting the German night fighters, Bomber Command ordered radio silence (no Monica, very sparing use of H2S/Fishpond, and only emergency R/T and IFF) for main force bombers on subsequent raids. The effect was immediate. On the night of 23 July, only 4 of 629 aircraft raiding Kiel were lost. [R.V. Jones, 1978:586] Although before this, the British had found no real answer to it, the German night fighter force was soon becoming much less effective for other reasons: greater use of spoof raids; effective airborne jamming of the German radars; the capture of the German coastal early warning sites; bombers flying from the Continent, giving less time for interceptions; losses of night fighters deployed against US day bombers; incessant attacks on the German airfields and radars; and the worsening German fuel shortage, which hampered operations and the training of new crews. By October, the German night fighter force was effectively neutralized. On the night of 14 October, only nine bombers were lost out of a huge total of 1,573 aircraft attacking Duisburg and Brunswick.

Bomber Command Operations from Continental Bases; 'Fan Raid' Techniques

By August, RAF heavy bomber raids into Germany were being mounted from Allied-held airfields in France. The shorter range allowed heavier bomb loads, and even successive day and night raids. As the Allied forces advanced, the British introduced mobile Gee, Oboe and Gee-H transmitters on the Continent, repeatedly moving them forward to enable precision raids deeper and deeper into Germany. Eventually, even Berlin was subjected to Oboe-marked bombing.

By assigning different false wind settings, the RAF now often bombed two or more aiming points from one marker centre. If the bombers approached from several different directions, each AP became a curved arc 'aiming line'. On the night of 11 September, 249 RAF Lancasters and Mosquitos attacking Darmstadt implemented such a 'line bombing' fan raid, using two APs, to help spread the bombing over the target area. The bombers approached along seven paths in different directions at different heights, converging in what Darmstadt survivors called *Der Todesfacher* (the Death Fan), releasing the bombs at varying delay times of 3–12 seconds. Darmstadt was devastated by a firestorm which took hold some 30 minutes after the last bomb dropped. Against Brunswick on the night of 14 October, the technique changed to 'sector bombing', each aircraft having its own course and releasing the bombs one at a time at regular intervals to achieve a more uniform density of bombing.

Use of 'Tallboy' Penetration Bombs, and 'SABS'

Tallboy bombs were dropped by 617 Sqdn Lancasters, normally from 18,000ft at night, using the Stabilized Automatic BombSight (SABS) against a dive-marked aiming point. Whereas a 12,000lb HC blast bomb exploded on the surface with a brilliant flash, the 12000lb Tallboy penetration bomb showed only a red pin-point of light as it exploded 90ft below the surface. The SABS required a 10-mile straight run in to the target, making a line of bombers vulnerable to flak and fighters. Also a rapid sequence was desirable, to release the last bomb before the first one exploded and began obscuring the target and/or markers. The approach adopted involved circling a point away from the target and then proceeding on converging courses towards it, at staggered times and heights to avoid collisions and bombs hitting lower aircraft. Unusually, on 7 October the sluice-gates of the Kembs dam on the Rhine were breached by delay-fused Tallboys dropped by six

Lancasters in a low-level daylight raid. To divert the defences, a higher altitude force drew the flak, while Mustangs made gun and rocket attacks on the AA gun emplacements. On the night of 26 November, Tallboys were dropped in a raid on Munich, their first use against a population centre rather than against industrial or military targets.

VII 1945

Bomber Developments

Piston-engined Bombers

With the running down of the war and the transition to turbojet power, 1945 saw a sharp drop in the number of new bomber types appearing. The new piston-engined bombers making their first flights were: the Boeing XB-44 four-engined heavy bomber (USA, May), a B-29 development which eventually became the B-50; and the Myasishchev VB-109 twin-engined bomber (USSR), flown in prototype form only. In France, with the nationalization of the Farman Co., the He274 V1 was renamed the AAS 01A, and flew post-war in December 1945. The prototype of the Japanese Army's Kawasaki Ki-91 four-engined heavy bomber was nearing completion at the end of the war; it had a pressure cabin, and an exceptionally heavy defensive armament of ten 20mm cannon.

Bombers entering service in 1945 included the Consolidated B-32 and Avro Lincoln heavy bombers. Among technology developments, a power boosted side 'formation stick' introduced on B-17Gs helped reduce pilot fatigue in holding a tight formation on a long raid. US advances with fire prevention and fire extinguishing on B-17s and B-24s involved venting of wing tanks and purging with inert gases (CO_2, nitrogen, methyl bromide, and engine exhaust gases). Also in the USA, experiments were made with dropping small bombs from a Sikorsky R-4 helicopter. In Japan, trials began with turbosupercharged engines fitted to G4M3 bombers. In Britain, a Bristol turret with two 20mm cannon was being progressed for the Lincoln. In Germany, the *Mistel* composite aircraft/missile concept was adapted to provide the *Fuhrungsmaschine*, a much-stretched Ju88H-4 manned long-range pathfinder aircraft carrying pick-a-back fashion its own Fw190A-8 manned escort fighter, to be started up and launched when attack was imminent.

Turbojet Bombers

In Japan, the Yokosuka R2Y2 projected attack bomber had a Ne-330 turbojet under each wing, and carried a ventral 800kg bomb; an aerodynamic prototype, the R2Y1 with coupled liquid-cooled engines in the fuselage driving a nose propeller made its only flight on 8 May 1945. In Germany, Ar234 prototypes with experimental laminar flow and crescent planform wings were still under construction on VE-Day. Meanwhile, the cancelled Ju287 six-turbojet heavy bomber was restarted in January 1945; the prototype, in final assembly, was captured by Soviet forces and eventually flew in the USSR. In June 1945, the USAAF ordered prototypes of the Northrop YB-49 flying wing bomber, an eight-turbojet derivative of the XB-35. In Britain, the future twin-jet English Electric Canberra reached the drawing-boards.

British and US Radar-laid Gun Turrets

Since 1943, the USA and Britain had been developing radar-laid tail gun systems for bombers, to achieve automatic, accurate aiming and firing at an enemy fighter approaching from the rear, irrespective of visibility. Each system incorporated: a tail centimetric radar with a lock-on/tracking facility; range, elevation and bearing signalling to the power-operated turret; and gyro-stabilized gun following to give the correct 'lead'. The quadruple 0.303-inch gun British AGLT (Air Gun Layer Turret), code-named 'Village Inn', was developed at TRE. Its radar system incorporated automatic IFF interrogation, but a nose-mounted IR identification system ('Liquid Lunch') was also fitted to bombers to avoid blind-fire AGLT attacks from other bombers. Plagued by technical problems, the AGLT saw limited service on Lancasters late in the European War. The US system was the GE-developed AN/APG-15B, with a scanner in a ball-shaped radome below the triple 0.5-inch gun tail turret. It was introduced on the B-29B Superfortress in April 1945, but it too was to prove troublesome, especially failing to lock-on after searching, and it saw little combat use by the end of the war.

Weapon Developments

The British Terrell Rocket Bomb; US Operational Use
In Britain, the Terrell CP/RA rocket-assisted bomb was developed under Cmdr E.Terrell of the British Admiralty, primarily for use against German U-boat shelters. It was a long, slim 4,500lb weapon incorporating nineteen 3-inch rockets for propulsion to supersonic speed, the rockets being ignited barometrically at 5,000ft. The RAF – committed to the 'Tallboy' – opposed development of the rocket bomb, so the US 8th AF was co-opted to test and use it. A B-17 could carry two, under the wings. Trial drops showed good transonic stability, and little trajectory deviation under rocket thrust. The few operational missions were flown by B-17s of the US 92nd BG under code-name 'Disney', two against the E-boat pens at Ijmuiden in Holland on 10 February and 14 March, the third against the U-boat assembly plant at Farge on 30 March. The bombs were dropped from 20,000ft, some penetrating through 4m of concrete to explode below.

On 14 July, US A-20s made the first use of rocket bombs in the Pacific theatre, with Mk.50s against the Boela oilfields.

The British 'Grand Slam' Earthquake Bomb; the Japanese Ko-Dan Rubber Bomb
When the Germans increased the thickness of concrete protecting major installations in response to the Tallboy, the British developed the full Barnes Wallis bomb, the 25ft 6in long, 22,000lb MC or DP/HE 'Grand Slam'. To carry this largest operational HE bomb of the war, 617 Sqdn Lancasters needed a strengthened u/c, fuselage and bomb-bay main beams, and removal of the bomb doors. After one prior test drop the previous day, a Grand Slam was first used against the Bielefeld viaduct on 14 March 1945. The subterranean explosion caused seven arches of the

viaduct to disappear downwards – a neat demonstration of Barnes Wallis's theory. In total, 41 Grand Slams were dropped by the RAF on German targets. A few US B-29s were modified to carry a Grand Slam under each inboard wing. No operational drops were made, however B-29s carrying a Grand Slam semi-buried in the front bomb-bay were used in post-war bombing tests against German defence structures. The US Smith Corp., manufacturers of the Tallboy and Grand Slam for Britain, also scaled up the Grand Slam to produce an experimental 45,000lb version, almost certainly the largest bomb of the war but not used operationally. [Huskinson, 1949:191] The US 4,000lb Mk.63 unpowered AP bomb also appeared in 1945, too late for operational use; an 8,000lb version was cancelled.

For use against smaller concrete emplacements, the little-known *Ko-Dan* bomb exploited 'Kobayashi's principle'. The front half of the case was of 2mm thick rubber and the explosive charge was in the form of small balls, so that at impact, the whole front of the bomb squashed flat against the target surface, giving a large increase in contact area during detonation. A *Ko-Dan* of 85kg was expected to equal a 250kg conventional bomb, but despite much experimental work, it may not have reached operational use.

Bomb Proximity Fuses

With no gun-barrel discharge acceleration involved, proximity fuses for bombs were easier to develop than those for shells. They were usable to give detonation prior to impact, for maximum blast damage and shrapnel spread, e.g. for AA suppression. The Japanese had introduced a photoelectric fuse in 1944, used on 250 and 800kg bombs to cause detonation 10–15m above ground; it transmitted light pulses and detected the return, and was usable in daylight as well as at night. [USSBS, 1945–49:No.63] In Britain, the No.44 Air Burst Pistol was successfully used with the 500lb MC bomb in night flare attacks on German troop convoys. Other than for air-to-air bombing, the Germans developed at least two bomb proximity fuses. The acoustic BAZ55A was usable when bombs were dropped in sticks, the first bomb detonating on impact, the noise of the explosion then detonating the second bomb in mid-air, and so on. The *Zunder-19* was apparently a radio fuse for single bomb use, and with its relatively high detonation altitude of 30m, may have been intended for chemical bombs. Beginning with 7th AF attacks on Iwo Jima in February 1945, US forces used the AA-shell VT radio proximity fuse in GP, fragmentation and napalm bombs. One USMC Corsair squadron was blown to bits when its VT-fused bombs were armed incorrectly and triggered by the aircraft themselves at release.

US Guided- and Glide-bombs

In the USA, two new radio-guided free-fall bombs appeared, the 1,000lb VB-3 and 2,000lb VB-4 'Razon' bombs. As the added 'R' in the name denoted, these had control in range as well as azimuth. The first homing free-fall bomb, the 1,000lb VB-5 used an optical seeker based on image contrast; another, the 1,000lb VB-6 'Felix' used an IR seeker. 'Dove', the Navy Bomb Mark 64 project for an IR-homing M65 1,000lb GP bomb was also under way in 1945. None of these later guided bombs reached service by the end of the war. Air Force GB-series glide-bombs still under development included the GB-5 with an optical-contrast homing seeker, and the GB-7 with a radar-homing seeker.

The Two US Atom Bombs: Uranium and Plutonium

At Los Alamos, the two types of A-bomb emerged in 1945 with two different designs and shapes, but each equivalent in explosive power to 20,000 tons of TNT. Both types were to detonate in mid-air for maximum ground damage, by completion of three separate circuits triggered respectively by a timer, a barometric device, and quadruple radar altimeters, all carried on the bomb. A transmitter with aerials on the bomb's tail provided telemetry.

The 'Little Boy' uranium bomb was a 9,000lb device, 120 inches long by 28 inches diameter. It used a 'gun' technique, a 5lb cylindrical slug of 235U being fired by an explosive charge along a 52-inch barrel, to break a neutron-absorbing safety shield and insert into a 17lb cylindrical ring of 235U to make up the required critical mass. A polonium-84 device emitted the neutrons to start the chain reaction. There being only sufficient 235U for one bomb, 'Little Boy' would be the first major weapon to be used operationally without a prior test. For the plutonium bomb, the fissionable material was more plentiful, allowing a prior test explosion. This was judged essential because its detonation system was more complex, plutonium reacting more quickly than uranium. To prevent premature disintegration ('fizzle') before reaching the most reactive state, Prof. Neils Bohr and Dr S.H. Neddermayer had devised an 'implosion' technique. A spherical-shaped subcritical mass of plutonium was surrounded by 64 explosive charges which were to be fired evenly and simultaneously, the resulting millions of atmospheres pressure causing the plutonium to compress suddenly to a dense supercritical form able to sustain the rapid chain reaction. Because of its spherical internal design, the plutonium bomb became a bulbous-looking device, 128 inches long by 60 inches diameter, and weighing 10,000lb. It was nicknamed 'Fat Man', apparently after Churchill.

The 'Trinity' A-bomb Test
On 16 July 1945, under code-name 'Trinity', the first ever nuclear explosion took place in a remote area of semi-desert, one-time Apache territory, at Alamogordo, New Mexico. The plutonium bomb, minus its aerodynamic case, was mounted atop a steel framework test tower. At detonation, awed observers noted: the intensity of the flash ('a light not of this World, a light of many suns ...'); the blast wave; then the fireball a mile in diameter rising and changing to an immense mushroom-shaped cloud, followed by a hurricane wind and thunderous roar. The test tower vanished except for stumps, while the sand around ground-zero was transformed momentarily to a white-hot saucer 500 yards in diameter, before cooling to glazed green lumps. The flash was seen in New York. The explosion, heard across several states, was ascribed to 'an ammunition dump blowing up'.

Navigation, Blind Bombing and Countermeasures

Navigation/Bombing System Developments;
'Radarscope' Missions

Two more Gee-H derivatives entered service early in 1945. The 'Loran-H' or 'SHORAN' (SHort RAnge Navigation) system with AN/CPN-2 ground and AN/APN-3 airborne equipment, featured on-board computers linked to the autopilot using the received 'H' signals to control the flight path of the aircraft and automatically release the bombs. 'Rebecca-H', used by 2TAF Mosquitos, was based on the British Rebecca/Eureka radio homing system, using an onboard Rebecca set to determine the aircraft's position relative to two Eureka-H mobile ground beacons.

New US airborne radars of 1945 included: (on B-29s) the AN/APQ-13 ground imaging set, with a ventral radome; (on B-29Bs, B-17s and B-24s) the AN/APQ-7 'Eagle' ground imaging set, synchronizing with the Norden bombsight, and using a wide high-definition scanner in a 17ft span wing-like ventral housing, pivoted for 45-degree scan; (on B-17s, experimentally) the AN/APA-46 'Nosmo' equipment providing for synchronization of H2X radar inputs with the Norden sight; (on B-29s) the SCR-729 radar interrogator system to give the range and bearing of any aircraft interrogated. In Britain, H2S improvements under development included a large (6ft) scanner named 'Whirlygig', and a K-band (1.25cm) Mk.VI version of H2S, code-named 'Lion Tamer'. Neither reached service by the end of the war. The Germans had provided details of the 'Rotterdam *Gerät*' to the Japanese in 1944, but Japanese ground imaging sets had not reached service when the war ended.

In 1944, RAF and 8th AF bombers had begun flying 'radarscope missions', obtaining photos of H2S/H2X radar images of cities, landfall points and navigation way points, for use in future raid planning and crew familiarization. For

D-Day, US B-17s had obtained radarscope photos of much of the northern coastline of France. In 1945, radarscope reconnaissance was exploited by the USAAF in the Pacific theatre, with a first B-29 radarscope sortie over Japan on the night of 4 March 1945, seven B-29s bombing Nagoya from 26,000ft while an eighth one bombed from 7,000ft and then loitered to obtain some 30 good quality radar photos. Beginning on the night of 5 May, radarscope missions were flown by single 'Eagle' B-29B aircraft using the new AN/APQ-7 'Eagle' high-resolution radar.

Countermeasures Developments; Chaff Dispensers; 'Rope' and 'Angels'

US and British chaff dispensers, to overcome the effort and discomfort of manually ejecting bundles of chaff down an aircraft's flare chute in sub-zero temperatures, were introduced early in 1945. The US A-1 automatic dispenser became a standard item on B-17 and B-24 bombers delivered to the ETO. The British 14ft 6in-long Mk.I semi-automatic Window Dispenser, mounted in the bomb bay of Halifax RCM aircraft, was loaded manually with Window bundles in flight and it ejected them at a pre-set rate. The smaller automatic Mk.III fitted into the Mosquito's 100-gallon drop tank.

The principal new Allied airborne jammers of 1945 were both derivatives: 'Airborne Grocer II' for use against *Würzburg* radars, and 'Meerschaum', to counter FuG220 AI radar; neither was operational by the end of the war. In the Pacific theatre, the Japanese had been installing more and more EW and gun control radars on the islands under their occupation. This caused a steadily increasing US countermeasures response. Intelligence missions were flown by Navy PB4Y-2s and a top-secret 'Black Cat' PBY unit, plus USAAF B-24 and B-29s carrying RCM observers and search equipment. The Japanese EW radars operated at exceptionally low frequency, requiring purpose-designed electronic jammers, and chaff strips which were much longer, and therefore bulkier and heavier to carry. Referred to as 'rope' because of their length, the foil strips used were coiled with one end attached to a small square cardboard 'parachute', the coil unwinding as it fell away. The Japanese response was to develop radar sets operating on even longer wavelengths. The principal new offensive use of RCM came with four B-29 RCM conversions, known as 'Angels' or 'porcupines' from their aerials. These aircraft were required to arrive over the target first and remain throughout the bombing, jamming the Japanese R/T communications and searchlight and AA radars. Some of the rope strips used were 400ft long. [Birdsall, 1981:206] The 'Angels' first operated on the night of 1 July 1945, during a raid on Kure.

Ground-attack Developments, Techniques and Operations

Ground-attack Aircraft and Weapons; German Adaptations for Large Bombs
By early 1945, the Soviets were working on the Tupolev Tu-2Sh, a heavy *Shturmovik* version of the Tu-2 twin-engined bomber, with a 57mm anti-tank cannon in the nose; it appeared post-war. In March, construction began on the Henschel Hs132 prone-pilot turbojet-powered dive-bomber, but the prototype did not reach completion. Among modifications for ground attack, some US A-26 Invaders were given an extra eight 0.5-inch guns in underwing packs, plus provision for locking the upper barbette to fire forward under pilot control; this gave a total of 18 forward firing guns. Also impressive, the Japanese devised a unique gun installation on the Yokosuka P1Y1-S *Ginga*, consisting of no fewer than 17 Type 99 20mm cannon in oblique/downward configuration in the bomb bay, 12 angled forward, 5 to the rear. At the end of the war, some 30 aircraft with this installation were being prepared to make attacks on US airfields in the Marianas, to wipe out the B-29 fleet in single, low-level passes. US ground-attack RP innovations included AF use of VT proximity-fused HVAR rockets in Europe, and limited Navy use of the huge 11.75-inch Tiny Tim anti-shipping RP against concrete emplacements in Okinawa. In Britain, Hurricanes were used for firing trials

with the 500lb warhead Long Tom RP.

Of all the combatants, the Germans went furthest in trying to make small fighter-bombers carry large bombs: first a Bf109G with a tall, jettisonable rear undercarriage leg to allow ground clearance for a SC500 bomb; then a few Fw190Gs carrying single SB1000 and SC1000 bombs, with the lower fin cut away to provide ground clearance. Now several Fw190G-1s of NSG20 were adapted to carry the 1,800kg SC1800 bomb, the largest carried operationally by a single-seat single-engine fighter during the war. Although stripped, the aircraft required special tyres and a very long take-off run. On 7 March, the Fw190s dropped 1,800kg bombs in attempts to destroy the US-held Remagen bridge over the Rhine, the attacks being foiled by Allied fighters and flak.

Operation Bodenplatte; Night Jet Bombers; Pathfinder Aircraft

On New Year's Day 1945, the Luftwaffe mounted Operation *Bodenplatte*, its last major ground attack operation of the war. It was preceded by two Ar234Bs making the first jet bomber night raid, dropping bombs on Brussels and Liège as a cover for what was in reality a weather reconnaissance mission for *Bodenplatte*. Some 800 fighters and fighter-bombers, including 20 Me262s, took off in darkness for a surprise dawn attack on 13 British and 4 US-held airfields in France and the Low Countries. Initial navigation was aided by coloured smoke and by pyrotechnic markers fired by AA guns, while searchlights showed the location of airfields for emergency landings. Each unit was guided by Ju88 or Do17 pathfinder aircraft, and flew in radio silence at low level to avoid radar detection. Surprise was achieved. The Germans were to claim 439 Allied aircraft destroyed on the airfields, but on the way there and back around 100 of the German aircraft were shot down by the Luftwaffe's own light flak batteries, whose officers had not been warned of the operation. [Gerbig, 1975:73]

British Attacks Against Railway Tunnels; Napalm

Destroying railway tunnels by lobbing bombs into them at low level had been used on occasion, e.g. by RAF Typhoons to seal a railway gun in its hiding-place near Pont L'Evêque on 18 August 1944. Now, on New Year's Day 1945, RAF Mosquitos were assigned to destroying 15 tunnels in western Germany, mostly with success. The technique used was to approach the tunnel along the railway line at 200ft, releasing a 4,000lb delay-fused bomb to drop into the tunnel mouth. Trial approaches were made first, and in at least one case this brought the bulk of the local population out to watch.

Mosquitos also made the RAF's first operational use of napalm, on the night of 18 April, seven of them each dropping two 100-gallon underwing napalm tanks on Neubiburg airfield under Operation 'Firebash'.

Soviet Use of Deception in Major Offensives; US/Soviet Operation

Despite their now huge numerical superiority, in 1945 the Soviets were making ever more elaborate use of deception in their westward offensives. For the Vistula crossings in January, the VVS deployed over 8,000 aircraft, but concealed the build-up by having air units rapidly flown in stages to forward airfields. Extensive use was made of camouflage for the airfields, and in the 16th Army sector alone, 55 dummy airfields were built, with 818 dummy aircraft. Flights were made into and out of these dummy airfields to aid the deception, and the Germans did indeed mount air strikes on some of them. For the offensive in East Prussia, the Soviets again made extensive use of a concealed build-up, with dummy airfields, and radio stations simulating an Air Army HQ and its units. Later, to begin the assault on Berlin on 16 April, relays of VVS fighters laid and maintained a 240-mile long smokescreen to conceal Soviet troops crossing the Oder at 150 points. Eventually, Soviet fighters and ground-attack aircraft were operating from the German *autobahnen*. On 9 May, Soviet Il-2 *Shturmoviks* and US P-38 fighter-bombers carried out the first and only joint tactical air operation by the two forces, attacking a German armoured column heading West (actually with the intention of surrendering to the Americans). [Piekalkiewicz, 1985:418]

The Soviet VVS ended the war in Europe as the world's most powerful tactical air force. Even so, its loss rate had remained high right to the end; over 500 aircraft were downed in the last few days, mostly by German light flak, the Luftwaffe fighter force having effectively ceased to exist.

Allied Operations in South-east Asia

By 1945, Allied air superiority over Burma was such that despite efforts to camouflage their tanks and troop positions, the Japanese were under incessant attack, notably from cab-rank patrols of Spitfires and Thunderbolts. For close support in the jungle, the RAF had introduced Visual Control Posts (VCPs), with an RAF liaison officer and W/O in a jeep or (in the mountains) on mules, with the forward troops. Features of the campaign included: in January, amphibious landings on Ramree Island, supported by Hurricane-laid smokescreens and Mitchell and Thunderbolt bombing strikes; close 'Earthquake Major' heavy and 'Earthquake Minor' medium bombing operations to dislodge Japanese troops well dug in at the front; spectacular HE and napalm close support attacks, giving ground troops a tendency 'to watch the exhibition rather than to get on with the attack'; night 'Rhubarbs', with aircraft using their landing lights to aid the attacks, Japanese vehicles being now mostly hidden by day with fuel tanks drained to reduce the risk of fire if attacked; in February, night 'Cloak' operations, with Beaufighters dropping dummy paratroops, automatic Very lights, and 'canned battle' flash and noise simulators to distract the Japanese, plus use of aircraft noise to drown troop and tank movements; in March, the use of a Master Bomber to direct bomb and rocket attacks against the earth walls of Fort Dufferin at Mandalay; on 15 March, a 1,600-mile round trip by 40 USAAF P-51s, destroying 26 Japanese aircraft at Don Mouang in Siam; and in May, the parachuting of VCPs, men and equipment behind enemy lines for ground attack near Rangoon. With aircrew lost over the jungle mostly disappearing without trace, some Allied fighter-bombers undertook AJSR (Air Jungle Search and Rescue) sorties when aircraft were missing, to search and drop emergency supplies while rescue was organized.

German Night Ground-attack Operations

With enemy fighters omnipresent during daylight hours, by

early 1945 the Germans had extended the use of Fw190s and Ju87s in *Nachtslachtgruppen* for night ground-attack operations on the Eastern Front and in Italy. Sorties were made singly at low altitude to avoid night fighters, climbing over the target for a dive attack. For front-line operations, flare illumination by ground units was used to mark the target; otherwise operations were carried out under moonlit conditions. Dive-bombing with the Fw190 involved over-flying the target, rolling upside down and pulling through an effective second half of a loop, releasing the bombs at 40 degrees using the Revi gunsight; or more usually, flying to one side of the target and making a banked turning dive so as to keep the target in view all the time. Attacks involved dropping HE bombs, and SD2 and SD4 cluster bombs; and making strafing runs. On the Eastern Front, attacks were made on columns of Soviet tanks crossing the frozen Odessa river, 250kg bombs being dropped to destroy the tanks or break the ice so that the tanks fell through.

Air Support to the Crossing of the Rhine

During March 1945, the Germans assigned available aircraft (including Me262s, Ar234s, Mistel composites, and even V-2 ballistic missiles) to a desperate effort to destroy the US-held Remagen bridge over the Rhine.

Operation 'Varsity', the Allied airborne crossing of the Rhine on 24 March was accompanied by large-scale use of air power. Fighter- and medium bombers cut railway lines in 41 places, the 8th AF attacked all enemy airfields within fighter range of the crossing, and the 8th AF and RAF Bomber Command carried out heavy attacks on rail centres. To protect the air transport armada, RAF Typhoons were assigned to seeking and attacking the local flak positions, which were well camouflaged. The technique adopted was to fly at 2,000ft in spaced pairs along the Rhine; if AA guns opened up at the first pair, the second pair could spot the location of the flashes and puffs of smoke, and dive for a rocket attack. On the day itself, the 8,200 sorties flown between dawn and dusk included many by 2TAF and 9th AF medium bombers, then Typhoons again, against flak positions. But there were around 1,000 AA guns; most survived, and many gliders were hit.

Allied Air Support in Italy

In Italy on 21 March, DAF Thunderbolts, Mustangs and Kittyhawks carried out Operation 'Bowler' at Venice, destroying AA positions and then attacking warehouses and shipping. Precision bombing was essential to avoid damaging historic buildings, so to provide evidence for any enquiry the entire raid was photographed by a PR Spitfire orbiting at 20,000ft. Elsewhere, the Allied offensive against Lugo began on 9 April with bomb carpets laid by 825 heavy and 234 medium bombers, after which 740 fighter-bombers began strikes on small targets. Waves of DAF Spitfires made four strafing runs to force the enemy under cover; on the fifth run, there was no strafing but the enemy remained under cover as the ground assault moved forward. Among other tactics in use in Italy, the RAF introduced a further ground-attack variation: 'Pineapple' operations in which roving Tac/R Spitfires were used to hunt for targets of opportunity, and then call up fighter-bombers to make the attacks. At night, Boston intruders were used to attack targets of opportunity, in part to disguise night supply drops to partisans.

The Soviet Offensive in Manchuria

On 8 August, two days after the Hiroshima A-bomb attack, the USSR declared war on Japan, and 1.5 million Soviet troops began the last great offensive of the war, invading Japanese-held Manchuria. Having a huge superiority in quality as well as quantity of transport and arms, including 4,800 combat aircraft facing barely 300 Japanese combat aircraft, the sweep southwards was rapid. As the ground forces progressed, new airstrips were quickly cleared, and fuel was flown in to support the bombers, fighters and ground-attack aircraft as well as the tanks. The offensive ended when Japan surrendered.

Daylight Bombing

New Allied Techniques: Command Aircraft; Smoke Markers; Radar Direction

In February 1945, the US 8th AF revised its bomber formation yet again, recognizing the near elimination of the German fighter force, but increased strength of the Flak units. The basic Group was changed from 3 squadrons of 12 aircraft to 4 of 9 aircraft, and these were spread further in height to reduce the AA threat. Also in February, the 8th AF began using its Mosquitos as command aircraft on bombing raids, one aircraft carrying the task force commander to the target, to monitor and direct the raid by R/T. Later, a specially lightened B-17 was introduced as a 'Command Scout' staff aircraft. This flew on raids to France on 15 April and Dresden on 17 April, joining each combat box as it crossed the target.

By February, the PFF's daylight marking (including for close support) had improved by the introduction of non-illuminating TIs. The 250lb 'Coloured Smoke' TI ground marker burned for eight minutes, the red, blue, green or yellow smoke remaining visible thereafter until dispersed by the wind. Later a 1,000lb version was introduced. On 2 March, 858 RAF bombers supported the Rhine crossing by attacking German armour at Cologne, using ground marking by Smoke Puffs dropped by Oboe Mosquitos. [Musgrove, 1976:176] For daylight sky marking in overcast conditions, a parachute-dropped 'Skymarker Puff' TI floater ejected coloured powder in mid-air to form a red, blue, green or yellow puff.

One offensive use of the huge US AN/CPS-1 MEW (Microwave Early Warning) ground radar introduced in autumn 1944, was for the tracking of Allied fighter-bombers, enabling voice instruction from a ground controller to direct them to the target area for visual search and attack, and to guide them back to base afterwards. Now in 1945, the shorter ranged (30 miles) but more accurate US SCR-584 radar could be used for blind bombing if need be, a bomb-release instruction being given if cloud prevailed. Most such attacks were made by US 9th AF bombers, but on 8 February RAF Typhoons used the technique for high-level bombing in the Cleve area. [Franks, 1979:197]

The Allied Operation 'Clarion'; US Medium-bomber Operations

On 22 February 1945, the Allies began Operation 'Clarion', the systematic destruction of German road and rail transport. Some 9,000 RAF and US aircraft participated, including heavy, medium, and fighter-bombers, plus covering fighters. Within days around 90 per cent of the German transport capability had been eliminated. The US 9th AF medium bombers alone flew 17,847 sorties in 37 days. Many of the raids were blind, led by B-26 pathfinders, mostly using Oboe but at times relying variously on Gee, SCR-584, Shoran, and even dead-reckoning. [Rust, 1970:163]

Allied Large-scale Daylight Raids; Transport Operations

On 3 February 1945, 937 B-17s and B-24s carried out the first 8th AF raid specifically intended for a residential area, in Berlin; 2,267 tons of bombs killed 23,000 people. With the German day fighter force now all but annihilated, the RAF now also undertook large-scale daylight raids into Germany. On 11 March, some 1,055 Lancasters, Halifaxes and Mosquitos dropped 4,700 tons of bombs in a daylight sky-marked raid on Essen; the only fighters seen were the Spitfire and Mustang escorts. On 12 March, 1,107 Lancasters and Halifaxes dropped 4,851 tons on Dortmund in the heaviest single raid of the war. On 18 March, 1,221 8th AF B-17s and B-24s, escorted by 632 fighters, made the heaviest raid on Berlin, dropping 4,000 tons of bombs. The heaviest 8th AF raid of the war followed on 7 April, 1,300 bombers attacking Dessau. On 18 April, 978 Lancasters, Halifaxes and Mosquitos inflicted huge destruction on Heligoland and Dünne.

With the end of the European war in sight, on 29 April

under Operation 'Manna', Allied bombers began PFF-marked low-level daylight food supply drops to near-starving civilians in occupied Holland. After VE-Day, the bombers were again adopted as transports to bring home Allied POWs in their bomb bays, under Operations 'Exodus' (Europe) and 'Dodge' (Middle East).

Late Soviet Use of Strategic Bombing; German use of Missiles

Only in the last weeks of the European War did the Soviet long-range bomber force, the 18th Air Army, begin mounting large-scale strategic bombing raids on major German centres. The first big daylight raid, by over 500 medium bombers with 108 escort fighters, came on 7 April, attacking Königsberg. Other raids were mounted against Budapest and Berlin. Post-war analysts were to criticize the failure of the Soviets to make concerted attacks on German rear areas, supply routes and industrial centres until long after they had achieved overwhelming air superiority. [Hardesty, 1982:217]

German RSHA plans in 1944, to drop Henschel Hs293 anti-ship missiles to home onto radio transmitters placed by agents at key targets in Britain, had not materialized. But now, in trying to hold up the Soviet advance, Hs293 and Fritz X missiles did get used against land targets, notably against bridges over the Oder in April 1945.

Japanese Difficulties in Outlying Bases

In the Pacific, by 1945 the Japanese were able to mount only token offensive operations, due to a combination of primitive jungle conditions, logistic support curtailed by US Navy blockade, US air strikes, combat losses, and a lack of an Air-Sea Rescue service. Whereas the US forces were well supplied (with earth-moving equipment, vehicles, medicines, pesticides, etc.) and were able to build many more airfields, the Japanese had few bases, had to rely on manual labour (for hiding aircraft in the jungle, filling in bomb craters etc.), and suffered from poor food and sanitation. Japanese bombing raids were few, mounted by day (with A6M escort) and by night (timing the attack for dawn or dusk unless there was moonlight). Losses were high, including from US intruders which followed the bombers home. Having longer-ranged bombers, the USAAF was able to strike at the Japanese bases from airfields beyond the range of Japan's bombers. One Japanese tactic was to pull their bombers back to safer bases, only moving them forward when about to mount a raid. But intelligence and the ubiquitous PR aircraft often enabled a US strike on the forward bases when the bombers had arrived there.

US Advances Against Japan

The US offensive in the Pacific included major landings in the Philippines (Luzon in January, then Corregidor and Mindanao), Iwo Jima in February, and then the huge operation against Okinawa in April; all were supported by large-scale use of land- and carrier-based air power. Unusually, the only major urban battle of the Pacific war, that for the Philippines capital Manilla, was fought without bombing. Mindful of civilian casualties, and despite the US having overwhelming air superiority, MacArthur forbade its use; but 100,000 civilians died in the land fighting.

Meanwhile, the air offensive against Japan itself was increasing steadily, and not just from the B-29s, and P-51s on Iwo Jima. It included on 16 February the first large-scale strategic attacks on land targets by carrier-based air units; US Navy Task Force 58 flew 2,761 sorties in two days, attacking airfields and aircraft factories around Tokyo. On 17 May, P-47 fighter-bombers flew from Ie Shima, Formosa, to attack Kyushu. Elsewhere, as part of the US blockade of Japan, the Alaska-based 11th AF was systematically attacking the 65 canneries and fisheries in the Kurile Islands, which provided food for the people of Japan. By August, only 5 of the plants were active. [USSBS, 1945–49:No.70]

US B-29 Daylight Operations; Jetstream Winds; Air-sea Rescue

USAAF B-29 bombers on daylight raids against Japan normally proceeded to within sight of the Japanese coast, and then circled to build up their formations for the bombing run. Although the bombers were vulnerable to attack while forming up, the Japanese were now critically short of fuel as well as pilots, and waited until the formation made its move and the likely target could be assessed, before scrambling fighters. But thereafter, the bombers were shadowed and fighters summoned to attack. US losses mounted, requiring either escort fighters or night bombing. There was another problem. 'Jetstream' stratospheric winds had been encountered over Europe, blowing high-flying Spitfire and Mosquito PR aircraft off course. Now, over Japan, the B-29 crews were finding winds of up to 200mph at 30,000ft. Bombing accuracy was lost due to excessive speed or drift, or – in runs made upstream, or at reduced altitude – the exposure to flak was increased; second runs over the target were seldom attempted. The effects contributed to the change to lower altitude night bombing.

With ASR a major concern for the B-29 long range overwater bombing raids, a 'buddy system' was implemented whereby if one aircraft was hit or otherwise in difficulties, another aircraft would detach and stay with it, circling if the other aircraft ditched, for as long as fuel reserves allowed, to guide rescue craft. All crews were required to watch for any survivors using flares or mirrors. After a mission, the B-29s flew search missions back over the route taken. The rescues were made by 'Dumbo' PBY-5 amphibians or by surface ships or submarines, including some positioned for 'planeguard' duty. On 27 January, a B-29 raid on Japan was the first to be accompanied by two SB-29A 'Superdumbo' rescue escort conversions. Each carried additional radio equipment and droppable supplies, including a large A-3 ventral lifeboat, life rafts and survival kits. The crew included an extra radio operator to communicate with downed crewmen and rescue ships.

Iwo Jima: Escort Fighter Operations; Sweeps

After a conventional bombardment (the Lethridge plan to 'sanitize' it with chemical bombs and shells having been rejected), on 19 February 1945 US forces invaded Iwo Jima. The heavily defended island was half way between the B-29 bases in the Marianas and their targets in Japan. Its occupation enabled elimination of the Japanese radar early warning station, and the provision of both an emergency landing field for B-29s and a forward base for P-51 escort fighters. The first of 2,251 B-29s to make an emergency landing there did so on 4 March. P-51s arrived on 6 March. The first escorted B-29 daylight mission against Japan came on 7 April, 95 P-51s from Iwo Jima accompanying the raid on Musashino. For such raids, escort assembly was achieved by squadron lead aircraft dropping parachute flares and smoke bombs to indicate the assembly point. But the Iwo Jima P-51s were to fly only ten escort missions, the B-29s continuing to operate mainly at night and in bad weather, bombing by radar. When by June, the Japanese fighter force could offer little opposition to large-scale daylight B-29 raids, the P-51 escorts were able to drop down low for strafing attacks. On 16 April, P-51s from Iwo Jima made the first of 33 sweeps over Japan, attacking airfields, factories and transport targets; usually a formation of P-51s was guided there and back by a B-29 'navigation ship'.

The Hiroshima A-bomb Raid

In May 1945, the US 509th Group moved to Tinian Island in the Marianas. Training now included lone high-altitude flights over Japan, to accustom the Japanese to single B-29 overflights apparently on weather or reconnaissance missions and not justifying defence action. In July the 'Little Boy' bomb, without its 235U 'ring', was secretly transported to Tinian by the cruiser USS *Indianapolis*. The ring was taken separately, by a 509th transport aircraft. On 25 July, incoming US President H.Truman formally ordered the dropping of A-bombs on Japan. On 5 August, the 'Little Boy' 235U bomb was hoisted from a special pit into B-29 'Enola Gay' (named after Tibbets' mother). With Tibbets in command, the aircraft took off in the early hours, preceded by three weather-scout B-29s, and followed by two further B-29s, carrying monitoring and photographic equipment, plus several SB-29 rescue aircraft. The bomb was armed in flight. Most crew members were not told of the nature of the weapon until close to the target. All were given dark polaroid goggles for protection against the flash; and reportedly, Tibbets carried cyanide pills for all crew members, should the aircraft be brought down over Japan. [Thomas and Witts, 1977:300] At 8.15 a.m. on 6 August 1945, the first operational drop of an A-bomb was made, over the Japanese city and military base of Hiroshima. The bomb, decorated with impolite graffiti, was released at 30,000ft, aimed using the Norden sight. As it fell away, the escorting scientific monitoring B-29 (named 'The Great Artiste' and flown by Maj. C. Sweeney) dropped three canisters on parachutes. These contained sensors and telemetry equipment to transmit data to recording equipment carried by the aircraft.

In Hiroshima, an air-raid warning had been followed by an 'All Clear' when only three aircraft materialized. Many people were caught in the open. The bomb exploded at 1,850ft altitude, destroying 62,000 buildings, and killing or mortally wounding some 80,000 people, one third of whom were soldiers. The B-29s themselves were hit violently by two shock waves (one direct, one reflected from the ground), each fully visible travelling at the speed of sound. The flash, fireball and mushroom cloud were witnessed at the nearby Kure naval station, and quickly reported to Tokyo where Capt. Yasui of the Naval Bureau of Aeronautics surmised that an atomic bomb had been used. Some 16 hours after the attack, US radio confirmed that an A-bomb had indeed been used.

The Nagasaki A-bomb Raid; and After

A proposed air leaflet campaign to warn Japanese cities of future A-bomb attacks had not been implemented, when on 9 August, the 'Fat Man' plutonium bomb was dropped on Nagasaki, after the primary target Kokura was found to be obscured by cloud. The dropping aircraft was B-29 'Bock's Car', flown by Maj. Sweeney. Again the bomber was accompanied by 'The Great Artiste' (flown by the displaced Maj. F. Bock) and a photographic plane.

Two more plutonium bombs were being prepared on Tinian, with drops tentatively scheduled for 13 and 16 August (Tokyo being a likely target for one of them), but Truman halted their use. Japan surrendered on the 14th.

Night Bombing

Increased Effectiveness of British Night Bombing;
Mosquito operations
By January 1945, the declining German defences, increasing experience of bomber crews (thanks to lower losses), the forward movement of blind bombing transmitters, and the refined marking techniques had all helped to increase the effectiveness of the British night raids on Germany. On 19 January, Speer noted that, 'the attacks which take place so often at night now are considerably more effective than daylight attacks, since heavier bombs are used and an extraordinary accuracy in attacking the target is reported'. [Webster and Frankland, Vol.III, 1961:235]. With few area targets left having combustible buildings, Bomber Command's bomb loads were now mostly HE again. But a post-war study found that 18 per cent of British bombs (and 12 per cent of US ones) dropped on Germany at this period failed to explode, mostly due to structural failure. The RAF's night bombing reached its zenith on the night of 14 February, in an elaborate group of operations involving extensive use of countermeasures and diversions. A total of 1,193 bombers mounted three separate main force raids, one on Rositz and two on Chemnitz, plus seven different diversionary operations. Two groups of Window-dropping Mosquitos emerged through an intensive jamming screen, followed by two of the main force streams heading in different directions before converging again. The third main force stream was itself preceded by Window-dropping Mosquitos, and the other diversions included three more Mosquito spoof raids. Because of the complex diversions, few German night fighters reached the bomber streams and the overall loss rate was 1.3 per cent.

In January 1945, the previously almost invulnerable Mosquito bomber, without tail radar, began experiencing losses at night to Me262 day fighters attacking visually by searchlight. To provide warning, the RAF flew some Mosquito intruders, having tail warning radar, amongst the bombers on one raid. An unusual feat was achieved on the night of 21 March when 118 LNSF Mosquito sorties were flown from Britain to bomb Berlin. Of the aircraft used, 20 made the round trip once, were serviced, refuelled and bombed up again in record time, and made a second round trip that same night, with a different crew.

The Dresden Raid and Aftermath; the First Soviet Night Strategic Raid

On the night of 13 February 1945, 786 Lancasters carried out what became one of the most controversial raids of the war, dropping 2,640 tons of bombs on the historic East German city and rail centre of Dresden. Initially, the attack used Wanganui blind bombing, but the 10/10 cloud gradually cleared as the raid progressed, allowing more effective coverage. Dresden had been selected as a priority target by the Allied Chiefs of Staff to cause maximum disruption of German support to the Eastern Front, but it was crowded with refugees fleeing the Soviet advance. The immense destruction included central and residential areas, and all of Dresden's 19 hospitals, while next morning US P-51s strafed refugees and rescue workers alike. The RAF's night raid was followed by US 8th AF daylight attacks on Dresden, on the 14th (316 bombers), 15th (211 bombers), 2 March (406 bombers) and 7 April (572 bombers), the latter aimed at the marshalling yards. The overall death toll is uncertain, perhaps 35,000. The attacks on Germany's cities had reached 'a scale which might have appalled Attila or Ghenghis Khan' [Richards and Saunders, Vol.3, 1975:271] and reports of Dresden's devastation and deaths led in Britain to censorship, misrepresentation, and a political distancing from the RAF's area bombing. US disassociation followed, even though the USAAF area bombing of Japanese cities was now getting under way. Then with only days to go in the European War, on 26 April the Soviet Air Force mounted its first large night strategic bombing raid, 563 medium bombers of the 18th Air Army flying from bases in Poland to attack Berlin.

RAF 'Tiger Force' Preparations
With the end of the war in Europe, and the completion of
POW repatriation, the RAF began preparations for
transferring part of Bomber Command for operations in the
Far East. The proposed No.5-Group 'Tiger Force' was to
consist of 12 squadrons of Lancasters and one of Mosquitos,
plus maintenance and airfield construction units. The force
was to be based on Okinawa, for bombing attacks on Japan
beginning on 1 October, including the use of Tallboy and
Grand Slam bombs. Crew training and aircraft tropicalization were still under way in Britain when Japan
surrendered.

*The US Change to Night Area Bombing of Japanese
Cities*
By early 1945, the USAAF was rethinking its bombing
policy against Japan. Dispersed Japanese industry offered
few valuable targets for precision bombing; the bombing
accuracy being achieved in precision daylight raids from
32,000ft was unsatisfactory; and the B-29 loss rate was
running at over 6 per cent. Since November 1944, the 21st
BC had been attempting precision raids against nine priority
targets. But with none of them yet destroyed, on 3 January a
trial fire-bombing raid was mounted against Nagoya by
almost 100 B-29s, the fires failing to coalesce. On 20 January
LeMay replaced Brig. Gen. H.S. Hansell as C. in C. of the
21st BC. LeMay pursued precision bombing but mounted a
fire raid on Kobe on 3 February, another on Tokyo on 23
February; neither was decisive, despite the largely
wood-built Japanese houses. A more positive approach was
thought necessary. Noting Intelligence reports that Japanese
cities had few medium AA guns protecting them from
attacks at lower altitude, LeMay ordered a change to night
area fire-bombing from intermediate altitude (8,000ft),
enabling three times the bomb load to be carried. In the
ETO, the USAAF had argued that a change to night
bombing would represent a major upheaval, needing
extensive retraining. Now, in the Pacific, such a change was
implemented with little difficulty. The first night raid was
made by 170 B-29s against Tokyo on the night of 25
February. With Japanese night defences minimal, the B-29s

were stripped of their defensive armour and all except tail guns in order to increase the bomb load still further. But in a night attack on Nagoya on 11 March, B-29 tail gunners carried additional ammunition for use against ground searchlights. On later missions, this defence suppression role was extended. Some B-29s, retaining all guns and full ammunition but with reduced bomb load, flew at below 3,000ft just ahead of the main force, to shoot out searchlights.

The new 'Eagle' B-29B high-altitude night bomber had only tail guns fitted, but these used the AN/APG-15B gun laying radar. The B-29B flew its first mission, a radarscope sortie, on 5 May. The B-29Bs typically bombed individually, with altitude separation on three converging tracks. If an aircraft was found by a radar-directed searchlight, it dropped 'rope' and used full throttle to accelerate and so leave the flak bursts behind. In July 1945, some B-29B crews began painting the undersides of their aircraft black. After it was found that Japanese searchlights tended to follow only unpainted aircraft, a dark paint scheme was generally adopted.

Limited US Use of Night Precision Attacks

In Europe, the US 9th AF's 410th Bomb Group began precision night bombing operations on 1 February, using black-painted medium bombers and RAF-type pathfinder techniques. But after four such raids, further ones were judged unnecessary. The last of the four, against the Hildesheim marshalling yards on 24 February, used the evolved tactics: flare illumination (103 flares dropped by 7 B-26s); target marking using red, green and yellow TIs (14 TIs dropped at low altitude by two A-26s – the Master Bomber and Master Marker); individual bombing of the TIs from medium altitude (34 A-20s dropping 500lb GP bombs), under instruction from the Master Bomber.

In the Pacific, advocated by Gen. H.H. Arnold, the USAAF made a few attempts at precision night bombing attacks on Japan by B-29 heavy bombers using pathfinder techniques. In particular, use was made of proximity flares, dropped using ground-imaging radar, enabling visual marking of specific targets by M69 incendiaries for the main force to aim at. The first such raid was on the night of 24 March, 250 B-29s attacking the Mitsubishi factory at Nagoya, but cloud prevented accurate marking. After several further smaller attempts, LeMay reverted to area bombing.

The Tokyo Firestorm Raid; Homing and Observation Aircraft

On the night of 9 March, 334 B-29s, dropping 2,000 tons of incendiaries, attacked Tokyo in 'the most devastating air attack in history, not excluding the attacks on Hiroshima and Nagasaki'. [MacIsaac, 1976:106] A US pathfinding innovation was first used on this raid. As an aid to inexperienced crews, several 'homing aircraft' were employed to precede the main force by 20 minutes and loiter over the target area to provide homing signals to guide main force aircraft to it. These aircraft were fully armed B-29s, carrying extra fuel plus a dedicated radio and radio operator, but no bomb load. The attack itself was made by marking with M47 incendiaries and using a fan approach to improve coverage. The raid was hugely destructive, later crews aiming not at the fires but at black areas among the fires. Some 15 square miles of Tokyo, almost four times the area to be devastated by the A-bomb at Hiroshima, were destroyed in a great firestorm caused by the clustered, napalm-filled M69 incendiaries. The US bombers were tossed and raised by the violent thermal updraughts, crews could feel the intense heat, and some vomited at the stench of burning flesh. The death toll was 78,660 in the official Japanese estimate, probably nearer 130,000 in reality. Fourteen B-29s were lost to AA. The raid was watched by Gen. T. Power in a loitering observation B-29, carrying full armament but no bombs.

Further fire-bombing raids followed, against Nagoya on 11 and 18 March, Osaka (by radar) on 13 March, and Kobe on 16 March; the 21st AF then ran out of bombs, but only temporarily. Japanese civilian morale declined, and mass evacuations began, when on 27 July the Americans started dropping leaflets given prior announcements of their next targets.

Summing Up

Ground Attack

Against most predictions of the mid-1930s, ground attack and especially close support operations became one of the war's most important uses of air power. It took various forms, from the Soviet light night harassment bombers, to the RAF's wide-roaming rocket-firing Beaufighters and Mosquitos, and even the use of heavy bombers against troop concentrations.

At the outbreak of the European war, only the Germans had acquired an effective close support capability, used spectacularly in the German army's early Blitzkrieg offensives. After Barbarossa, the Soviets acquired the aircraft and eventually the communications for close support, and used it on a large scale. For their part, the British and the Americans gradually changed from outright opposition to major commitment, and developed ground attack to a high peak of effectiveness which came to be relied on. Late in the war, Allied ground troops were reluctant to move forward without prior heavy air attacks ahead of them. [Carrington, 1987:194]

The main vehicles for ground attack were: first the dive-bomber adopted by the Germans, relying on altitude, plus a steep dive for accuracy; then the Soviet *Shturmovik*, relying on armour for survival; and finally the fighter-bomber, relying on speed in sweeping low-level passes. Later in the war, all of the combatants were using fighter-bombers to great effect, at the Front and against targets of opportunity. The weapons used also changed, with a steady increase in installed gun firepower, the German and Soviet introduction of hollow-charge bombs, and British and US use of RPs.

While the Germans were the real pioneers, the Western Allies contributions to close support were various: improved communications, cab-rank system, moving bomb line, etc. But the bulk of the German army and the Luftwaffe were destroyed on the Eastern Front, where although the Soviets excelled with the rapid staging to forward airstrips and in the use of deception, if German reports are accepted the main Soviet characteristic was the sheer weight of air power implemented rather than the finesse used. But despite heavy use of their overwhelming air superiority on both fronts, the Allies seldom equalled the early German success rate on the ground.

Bombing Technology and Tactics

The technology of bombing had seen steady advances during the war, with the bombers themselves; new, bigger and more specialized bombs; improved bombsights; new navigation and blind-bombing aids; target illumination and marking; and electronic warfare support. Techniques and tactics varied as the war progressed, and depended markedly on enemy defence capability in the different war theatres. Only Britain and the US used fleets of heavy bombers for strategic bombing. Only Britain used very large HE bombs.

Despite the effects of weather, defence action, decoys, etc., the Allied area bombing of towns using HE and incendiaries in combination, had been brought to a high level of destructiveness, even if its military value had remained questionable. Precision low-level and dive-bombing strikes had often been very efficient also. Medium- and high-level bombing against defended key targets had mostly become effective, if still relatively wasteful. Specialist bombs and improved bombsights helped, but it had often needed a large force and many bombs to take out a bridge or a building, giving much peripheral destruction. The new guided bombs (Azon, Fritz-X) offered an improvement, perhaps with wire guidance to avoid jamming.

In daylight operations, accurate visual bombing was often prevented by overcast cloud, requiring resort to blind bombing. Also, despite US expectations, and improved armament, armour and self-sealing tanks, the day bomber – even the formidable B-29 – had remained vulnerable to fighters. The key to deep penetration daylight bombing came with the US development of the long-range single-seat fighter. Vital as an escort, the P-51 was available in numbers early enough for sweeps and strikes against the Luftwaffe's bases to neutralize the Me262. In night bombing, the RAF's difficulties in finding and marking the target were progressively overcome, the difference in accuracy compared with day bombing virtually disappearing; bombing accuracy became a matter of clear weather versus overcast, rather than day versus night. But the invulnerability of night bombers had disappeared much earlier. In the escalating electronic war of radar and countermeasures, the night fighters had not been prevented for long from finding the RAF's bombers, which had limited defence and inadequate night-fighter intruder protection.

Strategic Bombing: Cost, Morale and Production

An operational bomber fleet needed a large manufacturing, supply, training and support infrastructure. It was expensive in manpower, materials and money, not least because the operational losses were frequently also high, with young crews having to face regularly a frightening ordeal, and with a life expectancy measured in months, if not weeks; RAF Bomber Command alone lost 47,293 aircrew killed on operational missions.

But despite the expenditure, effort and lives, the war's strategic bombing never became quite the winning weapon its advocates had promised. In line with earlier fears and expectations, much of it was directed against population centres. This reflected both the difficulties in hitting small, key targets; and assumptions that casualties and 'de-housing' would undermine the enemy's morale and disrupt his war production. True, there were early adverse reactions to bombing among people unprepared for it: millions in Calcutta and Rangoon fled, and Mussolini quickly complained that his citizens had 'given proof of moral weakness'. But civilians, including in Italy, mostly learned to stand up well to the bombing of their cities. The 'terror raids' were apt to bring defiance, demands for retaliation, and motivation for war production. But morale wavered locally under the heaviest raids, and in Germany and Japan, right at the end.

The RAF and USAAF inflicted the heaviest bombing, but

tended to overestimate its effectiveness. The 'diminishing returns' factor (bombs being wasted on the rubble from previous raids) often ruled out repeat attacks that might have been more decisive. As it was, many who fled from the bombing returned to live and work among the ruins. The British bombing destroyed mainly central urban areas, whereas most industry was on the periphery. Factories shown as ruined in PR photos were assumed to be a total loss, but the tools mostly survived and often the rubble was quickly cleared and assembly lines restarted in the open. Some production went underground, some into private homes. Thus, despite the devastation, arms production increased, especially in Germany, only declining when communications became chaotic in the last months.

The Bombing of Britain

The first strategic bombing campaign of the war was also the smallest and least effective. The Luftwaffe dropped a total of 74,172 tons of HE and incendiaries on Britain, including the V-weapon warheads, killing 64,000 civilians. But despite the destruction caused, mostly in the night blitz of 1940–41, the results were indecisive. Damage (and dispersal of production) did cause a small drop in British aircraft production in the winter of 1940–41. But jamming of the German blind bombing aids, and their inaccuracy, made most precision attacks on key targets ineffective, while the size and bomb load of Germany's medium-bomber force was inadequate for saturation bombing. Although the Germans had no prior experience to follow, critics were to argue that the bombing policy was misguided; Britain's Achilles' heel was its reliance on maritime supply, and its defeat might have been obtained by diverting Luftwaffe bomber capacity to supporting the highly effective U-boat operations against Allied shipping.

The Bombing of Germany

The RAF and USAAF dropped 955,000 and 395,000 tons of bombs respectively, on Germany during the war; of these, 430,000 and 80,000 tons respectively fell on populated areas, killing 590,000 civilians. Critics of the Allied bombing, especially the (mainly British) area bombing, have pointed to the increase in German war production despite the bombing, and argued that – morality aside – it was perverse to devote such huge resources to attacking German civilians instead of the military; and that it starved other aspects of the war effort, even prolonging the war by delaying provision of *matériel* for the invasion. [Rumpf, 1963:210] Supporters of the bombing claimed that it: provided a 'second front' to support the USSR when there was no other way of doing so; tied down two million people in Germany on AA defence; forced the Germans to build fighters and AA guns rather than bombers and artillery, to keep large fighter forces in Germany, and to divert vital resources to 'retaliation weapons'; forced the dispersion of industry, aggravating Germany's labour shortage and reducing quality (through poor materials and manual work instead of mass production); and ensured that even at its peak, German war production did not reach World War One levels. Others point to the consequences for the Axis powers of their inability to mount strategic air strikes against the sources and supply lines from US and Soviet production centres; and to the more obviously decisive US bombing of Japan. But greater concentration on the destruction of rail and oil targets, once it became possible in 1943, would probably have brought earlier and serious damage to the German war output. Speer himself believed Germany was even more vulnerable to attacks on its chemical industry. As it was, real damage was eventually done in 1944 by the bombing of German oil installations and by long range US fighters and fighter-bombers destroying the Luftwaffe and ground transport.

The Bombing of Japan

The early Japanese expansion had served to establish a remote defence perimeter, to keep US bombers out of range of Japan. As a result, the bombing offensive against Japan was smaller and shorter than that against Germany. Of the total of 656,400 tons of bombs dropped by all forces in the Pacific theatre, US forces dropped 153,000 tons on Japan, 98,000 tons being incendiaries. The raids on Japan, which killed 392,000 civilians, only began in late 1944, when the Japanese economy was already in decline due to the US naval blockade. Early attacks on the shipbuilding and aircraft industries, plus six major urban/industrial areas, gave way to the area bombing of cities. This destroyed 2.2 million dwelling-houses, (excluding 0.6 million pulled down to provide fire breaks), compared with 3.6 million in Germany. Again, there was some increase in war production; and plans to move much of it underground were in progress. But the bombing brought surrender without the need for invasion: the A-bombs and the Soviet invasion of Japanese-held Manchuria seem to have been the 'last straws'. Unlike Germany, Japan had a head of state capable of a rational decision to end the suffering.

Eastern Front Bombing
The air war on the Eastern Front differed from that elsewhere in that the air power on both sides was used almost exclusively in direct support to the huge land war. On both sides, most aircraft losses were to enemy AA.

The Germans had expected a quick blitzkrieg victory without needing long-range bombing, but had grossly underestimated the strength and resilience of the Soviet armed forces, Soviet industrial capacity, and their own supply difficulties. The German medium-bomber force had been weaker at the start of *Barbarossa* than at the start of the Battle of Britain, and was steadily frittered away by diversion to ground attack and transport operations. A German view is that '... the reason for Germany's defeat at the hands of the Russian giant was the fact that she made no attempt to carry out strategic air warfare'. [Faber, 1979:219] Expediency had overruled; Germany had become fully stretched in a multi-front war.

The Soviet air effort was far greater, increasing steadily as the war progressed. But although increasing air superiority gradually allowed a greater range of options away from pure expediency, it was Stalin's will that the air power usage remained largely the same; mostly close support, with few offensive fighter sweeps, limited interdiction in the enemy's rear, mostly at small scale (no saturation bombing), and almost no strategic bombing except at the end. In line with this policy, it seems the Soviets made little effort to develop advanced navigation, marking and bombing aids themselves, or to make much use of equipment (e.g. the Norden sight) supplied under Lend-Lease. Even the long-range ADD 'confined itself to cooperation with the Red Army'. [Baumbach, 1986:159] The Soviets dropped a total of 660,000 tons of bombs during the 'Great Patriotic War'.

CW/BW: The Weapon in Reserve

Only the Japanese made much use of chemical weapons during the war, and only against the Chinese who were unable to retaliate. Hard evidence for German and Allied use of CW or BW in the war remains scant, although late in the war, blight on Japanese rice crops and Colorado beetles in Germany were both ascribed to US secret BW drops. [Harris and Paxman, 1982:99].

By and large, chemical and biological warfare had remained among the great secrets of the war, contingencies to be used for retaliation if necessary. They had absorbed large resources, chemical weapons in particular being stockpiled in every theatre, to a total of 0.5 million tons. The US alone ended the war with over 100,000 aircraft spray tanks. It seems CBW was not used largely because: the ground war was much more mobile than in 1914–18, making contamination a problem for the user; air delivery made CBW a strategic element, not just a battlefield one, hence the threat of its use against civilian populations was far greater, and the results of escalating into CW were far less predictable. The Germans (with tabun) were best equipped for a CW offensive, e.g. in repelling the Normandy landings. But they overestimated Allied CW technology, noted the prevailing west wind, and thought their own Army – dependent on horses for transport – very vulnerable to poison gas attacks. The Dyhrenfurth nerve gas plant fell into Soviet hands at the end of the war; it was dismantled and restored to full production in the USSR.

The Atomic Bomb: Post-war Problem

The US use of A-bombs against Japan in the ultimate form of Allied area bombing, was justified publicly in terms of avoiding a million US casualties in an invasion of the Japanese homelands. But the chiefs of the US armed forces – Marshall (Army), King (Navy) and Arnold (Air Force) –

had all resisted the use of the Bomb [Kurzman, 1986:364], at least without a prior demonstration to the Japanese; and LeMay believed that a few more weeks of conventional bombing would finish Japan anyway, albeit with greater civilian casualties than the two A-bombs would give. But political factors overruled. The Hiroshima and Nagasaki attacks made plain to the world the destructiveness of the new weapons. A marriage of nuclear weapons with the ballistic missile had already been foreseen, and once the Soviet aim of acquiring nuclear weapons was appreciated, US work on far more powerful thermonuclear weapons restarted. The world was headed for an arms race, and a dangerous military stalemate in which the human race stood little chance of surviving much beyond local 'conventional' wars.

Bibliography

Air Ministry, *Wings of the Phoenix – the Air War in Burma* (HMSO, 1949)
   The Rise & Fall of the German Air Force 1933-1945 (Arms & Armour
   Press, 1983)
Alexander, J., *Russian Aircraft Since 1940* (Putman, 1975)
Allen, H.R., *Who Won the Battle of Britain?* (Arthur Barker, 1974)
Anderton, D.A., *B-29 Superfortress at War* (Ian Allan, 1978)
Arcangelis, M. de, *Electronic Warfare – from the Battle of Tushino to the
   Falklands and Lebanon conflicts* (Blandford Press, 1985)
Argyle, C.J., *Japan at War 1937-1945* (Arthur Barker, 1976)
Banks, D., *Flame over Britain* (Sampson Low, undated)
Barker, R., *The Thousand Plan* (Chatto & Windus, 1965)
Baumbach, W., *Broken Swastika – the Defeat of the Luftwaffe* (Robert
   Hale, 1986)
Bennett, D.C.T., *Pathfinder – a War Autobiography* (Frederick Muller,
   1958)
Bethel, N., *The War Hitler Won – September 1939* (Futura Publications,
   1976)
Bidwell, S. and Graham, D., *Fire Power – British Army Weapons &
   Theories of War 1904-1945* (George Allen & Unwin, 1982)
Bishop, E., *Their Finest Hour – the Story of the Battle of Britain 1940* (Pan
   Books, 1972)
Birdsall, S., *Saga of the Superfortress* (Sidgwick & Jackson, 1981)
Blue, A.G., *The B-24 Liberator* (Ian Allan, 1976)
Bowyer, C., *Pathfinders at War* (Ian Allan, 1977)
   Guns in the Sky – the Air Gunners of WW2 (J.M.Dent & Sons, 1979)
   Bomber Barons (William Kimber, 1983)
   Royal Air Force Handbook 1939-45 (Ian Allan, 1984)
Bowyer, M.J.F., *Air Raid! – The Enemy Air Offensive Against East
   Anglia, 1939-45* (Patrick Stephens, 1986)
Boyd, A., *The Soviet Air Force since 1918* (Macdonald & Janes, 1977)
Brickhill, P., *The Dam Busters*, rev. edn (Evans Bros, 1977)
Carrington, C., *Soldier at Bomber Command* (Leo Cooper, 1987)
Chisholm, R., *Cover of Darkness* (Chatto & Windus, 1953)
Clark, R.W., *War Winners* (Sidgwick & Jackson, 1979)
Clarke, R., *We All Fall Down – the prospect of Biological and Chemical
   Warfare* (Allen Lane, 1968)
Clayton, A., *The Enemy is Listening* (Hutchinson, 1980)
Coffey, T.M., *Decision over Schweinfurt* (Robert Hale, 1978)
Collier, B., *The Defence of the United Kingdom* (HMSO, 1957)
Condon, R.W., *The Winter War – Russia v. Finland* (Pan/Ballantine,
   1972)

Cooksley, P.G., *Flying Bomb* (Robert Hale, 1979)

Cooper, A.W., *Bombers over Berlin – the RAF Offensive, Nov.43-Mar.44* (William Kimber, 1985)

Costello, J., *The Pacific War*, rev. edn (Pan Books, 1985)

Cross, R., *The Bombers* (Bantam/Transworld, 1987)

Crowther, J.G. and Whiddington, R., *Science at War* (HMSO, 1947)

Cruickshank, C., *The Fourth Arm – Psychological warfare, 1938-1945* (Davis Poynter, 1977)

Deighton, L., *Fighter – the True Story of the Battle of Britain* (Jonathan Cape, 1977)

Blitzkrieg (Jonathan Cape, 1979)

D'Este, C., *Bitter Victory* (Collins, 1988)

Douglas-Hamilton, J., *The Air Battle for Malta* (Mainstream Publishing, 1981)

Eggleston, W., *Scientists at War* (Oxford University Press, 1950)

Erickson, J., *The Road to Stalingrad* (*Stalin's War with Germany, Vol I*) (Weidenfeld & Nicolson, 1975)

Faber, H (Ed.), *Luftwaffe – an analysis by former Luftwaffe Generals* (Sidgwick & Jackson, 1979)

Farago, L., *The Game of the Foxes* (Hodder & Stoughton, 1972)

Fetzer, L.(Trans.) and Wagner, R. (Ed.), *The Soviet Air Force in World War II* (Doubleday, N.Y., 1973)

Fleming, P., *Operation SeaLion* (previously *Invasion 1940*) (Pan Books, 1975)

Francillon, R.J., *Japanese Aircraft of the Pacific War* (Putman, 1970)

Franks, N., *The Greatest Air Battle – Dieppe, 19 August 1942* (William Kimber, 1979)

Typhoon Attack (William Kimber, 1984)

Freeman, R.A., *Mighty Eighth War Diary* (Janes, 1981)

Mighty Eighth War Manual (Janes, 1984)

Fuller, J.F.C., *The Second World War 1939-1945* (Eyre & Spottiswoode, 1948)

Galland, A., *The First and The Last* (Methuen, 1959)

Gelb, N., *Scramble – a Narrative History of the Battle of Britain* (Michael Joseph, 1986)

Gerbig, W., *Six Months to Oblivion – the Eclipse of the Luftwaffe Fighter Force* (Ian Allan, 1975)

Goulding, J. and Moyes, P., *RAF Bomber Command and its Aircraft, 1936-1940* (Ian Allan, 1975)

Green, W., *The Warplanes of the Third Reich* (Macdonald & Janes, 1970)

Gunston, B., *Night Fighters – A Development and Combat History* (Patrick Stephens, 1976)

Halpenny, B.B., *To Shatter the Sky – Bomber Airfield at War* (Patrick Stephens, 1984)

Hardesty, Von, *Red Phoenix – The Rise of Soviet Air Power 1941-45* (Arms & Armour Press, 1982)

Harris, R. and Paxman, J., *A Higher Form of Killing – The Secret Story of Gas and Germ warfare* (Chatto & Windus, 1982)

Hartcup, G., *The Challenge of War – Scientific and Engineering*

Contributions to World War II (David & Charles, 1970)
Hastings, M., *Bomber Command* (Michael Joseph, 1979)
Haswell, J., *The Intelligence & Deception of the D-Day Landings* (Batsford, 1979)
Hersh, S.M., *Chemical and Biological Warfare – America's Hidden Arsenal* (McGibbon & Kee, 1968)
Hogg, I.V., *German Secret Weapons of World War II* (Arms & Armour Press, 1970)
    Anti-Aircraft – A History of Air Defence (Macdonald & Janes, 1978)
Hough, R., *The Longest Battle* (Weidenfeld & Nicolson, 1986)
Horne, A., *To Lose A Battle – France 1940* (Macmillan, 1969)
Howard-Williams, J., *Night Intruder* (David & Charles, 1976)
Huskinson, P., *Vision Ahead* (Werner Laurie, 1949)
Irving, D., *The German Atom Bomb* (Simon & Schuster, N.Y., 1967)
Johnson, B., *The Secret War* (BBC Publications, 1978)
Johnson, B. and Cozens, H.I., *Bombers: The Weapon of Total War* (Methuen, 1984)
Jones, G.P., *Night Flight – Halifax Squadrons at War* (William Kimber, 1981)
Jones, L.S., *US Bombers* (Aero Publishers, Inc., Fallbrook, Calif., 1974)
Jones, R.V., *Most Secret War* (Hamish Hamilton, 1978)
Jones, W.E., *Bomber Intelligence* (Midland Counties Publications, 1983)
Kemp, N., *The Devices of War* (Werner Laurie, 1956)
Killingray, D., *The Atom Bomb* (Geo. G. Harrap, 1970)
Kilmarx, R.A., *A History of Soviet Air Power* (Faber & Faber, 1962)
Kinsey, G., *Aviation – Flight over the Eastern Counties since 1937* (Terence Dalton, 1977)
    Bawdsey – Birth of the Beam; The History of RAF Stations Bawdsey and Woodbridge (Terence Dalton, 1983)
Kurzman, D., Day of the Bomb – Hiroshima 1945 (Weidenfeld & Nicolson, 1986)
Lawrence, W.J., *No.5 Bomber Group, RAF* (Faber & Faber, 1953)
Lewis, P., *The British Bomber since 1914* (Putman, 1980)
Longmate, N., *The Bombers: The RAF Offensive against Germany 1939-1945* (Hutchinson, 1983)
MacIsaac, D., *Strategic Bombing in World War Two* (Garland Publishing, N.Y., 1976)
Maitland, A., *Through the Bombsight* (William Kimber, 1986)
Mason, F.K., *Hawker Aircraft since 1920* (Putman, 1961)
Masters, D., *German Jet Genesis* (Janes, 1982)
Mayer, S.L. (Ed.), *The Russian War Machine* (Arms & Armour Press, 1977)
Messenger, C., *The Art of Blitzkrieg* (Ian Allan, 1976)
    The Tunisian Campaign (Ian Allan, 1982)
Middlebrook, M., *The Nuremberg Raid* (Allen Lane, 1980)
    The Peenemünde Raid (Allen Lane, 1982)
    The Schweinfurt-Regensburg Mission (Allen Lane, 1983)
Middlebrook, M. and Everitt, C., *The Bomber Command War Diaries* (Viking, 1985)

Mondey, D., *American Aircraft of World War II* (Hamlyn Publishing Group, 1982)

Munson, K., *Aircraft of World War II* (Ian Allan, 1972)

Murray, W., *Luftwaffe – Strategy for Defeat, 1933-45* (Geo. Allen & Unwin, 1985)

Musgrove, G., *Pathfinder Force – a History of 8 Group* (Macdonald & Janes, 1976)

Nayler, J.L. and Ower, E., *Aviation: its Technical Development* (Peter Owen, 1965)

Nemecek, V., *The History of Soviet Aircraft from 1918* (Collins, 1986)

Nowarra, H.J., *Heinkel He111 – a Documentary History* (Janes, 1980)

Nowarra, H.J. and Duval, G.R., *Russian Civil and Military Aircraft 1884-1969* (Fountain Press, 1971)

Okumiya, M. and Horikoshi, J. with Caidin, M., *Zero! The story of the Japanese Navy Air Force, 1937-45* (Cassell, 1957)

Olmsted, M., *Aircraft Armament* (Sports Car Press, USA, 1970)

Ordway, F.I., III and Sharpe, M.R., *The Rocket Team* (Heinemann, 1979)

Overy, R.J., *The Air War 1939-1945* (Stein & Day, N.Y., 1981)

Owen, R., *The Desert Air Force* (Hutchinson, 1948)

Parry, S.W., *Intruders over Britain* (Air Research Publications, 1987)

Pawle, G., *The Secret War, 1939-45* (Geo. G. Harrap, 1956)

Piekalkiewicz, J., *The Air War 1939-1945* (Blandford Press, 1985)

Pile, F., *Ack-Ack: Britain's Defence Against Air Attack during the Second World War* (Geo. G. Harrap, 1949)

Postan, M.M., Hay, D. and Scott, J.D., *Design and Development of Weapons* (HMSO & Longmans Green, 1964)

Potter, J.D., *Fiasco – the Breakout of the German Battleships* (Heinemann, 1970)

Powis-Lybbe, U., *The Eye of Intelligence* (William Kimber, 1983)

Price, A., *The Bomber in World War II* (Macdonald & Janes, 1976)

    Instruments of Darkness: The History of Electronic Warfare, rev. edn, (Macdonald & Janes, 1977)

    Focke Wulf 190 at War (Ian Allan, 1977)

    Blitz on Britain 1939-1945 (Ian Allan, 1977)

    Luftwaffe Handbook 1939-45 (Ian Allan, 1986)

Ramsey, W. (Ed.), *The Battle of Britain, Then & Now* (Battle of Britain Prints International, 1980)

Rawlings, J.D.R., *Coastal, Support & Special Squadrons of the RAF and their Aircraft* (Janes, 1982)

Rawnsley, C.F. and Wright, R., *Night Fighter* (Collins, 1957)

Reit, S., *Masquerade – the Amazing Camouflage Deceptions of World War II* (Robert Hale, 1979)

Renaut, M., *Terror by Night* (William Kimber, 1982)

Rhodes, R., *The Making of the Atomic Bomb* (Simon & Schuster, USA, 1986)

Richards, D. and Saunders, H.St.G., *Royal Air Force 1939-1945*, 3 Vols (HMSO, 1975)

Robinson, A. (Ed.), *Aerial Warfare – an Illustrated History* (Orbis, 1982)

Rose, S. (Ed.), *CBW - Chemical and Biological Warfare* (Geo. G. Harrap, 1968)

Rumpf, H., *The Bombing of Germany* (Frederick Muller, 1963)

Russell, F., *The Secret War* (Time-Life Books, 1981)

Rust, K.C., *The 9th Air Force in World War 2* (Aero Publishers, Fallbrook, Calif., 1970)

Saward, D., *Bomber Harris - the Authorised Biography* (Cassell, 1984)

Sawyer, T., *Only Owls and Bloody Fools Fly at Night* (William Kimber, 1982)

Shores, C.F., *Second Tactical Air Force* (Osprey, 1970)
Duel for the Sky (Blandford Press, 1985)

Siefring, T.A., *US Air Force in World War II* (Hamlyn Publishing Group, 1977)

Smeaton, A., *The Russo-German War, 1941-45* (Arthur Barker, 1971)

Smith, B.F., *The Shadow Warriors* (Andre Deutsch, 1983)

Smith, J.R. and Kay, A., *German Aircraft of the Second World War* (Putman, 1972)

Smith, P.C., *Pedestal: the Malta Convoy of August 1942* (William Kimber, 1970)
The Stuka at War (Ian Allan, 1971)
The History of Dive Bombing (William Kimber, 1981)
Jungle Dive-Bombers at War (John Murray, 1987)

Stahl, P.W., *KG200 - The True Story* (Janes, 1981)
The Diving Eagle - A Ju88 Pilot's Diary (William Kimber, 1984)

Stewart, A., *Hurricane - the War Exploits of the Fighter Aircraft* (William Kimber, 1982)

Streetly, M., *Confound & Destroy - 100 Group and the Bomber Support Campaign* (Macdonald & Janes, 1978)

Sweetman, J., *Operation Chastise - The Dams Raid, Epic or Myth?* (Janes, 1982)
Schweinfurt - Disaster in the Skies (Pan Books, 1971)

Taylor, E., *Operation Millennium* (Robert Hale, 1987)

Terraine, J., *The Right of the Line: The RAF in the European War, 1939-45* (Hodder & Stoughton, 1985)

Terrell, E., *Admiralty Brief* (Geo. G. Harrap, 1958)

Thomas, G. and Morgan-Witts, M., *Ruin from the Air - the Atomic Mission to Hiroshima* (Hamish Hamilton, 1977)

Thompson, J.W., *Italian Civil & Military Aircraft* (Aero Publishers, USA, 1963)

Thompson, R.W., *D-Day - Spearhead of Invasion* (Pan Books, 1972)

Toland, J., *The Rising Sun - The Decline and Fall of the Japanese Empire, 1936-45* (Cassell, 1971)

Townsend, P., *Duel of Eagles* (Weidenfeld & Nicolson, 1970)
Duel in the Dark (Harrap, 1986)

Turnill, R. and Reed, A., *Farnborough - The Story of RAE* (Robert Hale, 1980)

Tute, W., *The North African War* (Sidgwick & Jackson, 1976)

Uebe, K., *Russian Reactions to German Air Power in World War 2* (USAF Historical Studies, No.176)

USSBS Reports (United States Strategic Bombing Survey, Washington, 1945-9)

Verrier, A., *The Bomber Offensive* (Batsford, 1968)

Wagner, R., *American Combat Planes* (Macdonald, 1960)

Wakefield, K., *The First Pathfinders – The Operational History of Kampfgruppe 100, 1939-41* (William Kimber, 1981)

Webster, C. and Frankland, N., *The Strategic Air Offensive Against Germany, 1939-45*, Vols I, II and III (HMSO, 1961)

Whaley, B., *Codeword Barbarossa* (MIT Press, 1973)

Whiting, C., *The 3-Star Blitz – the Baedeker Raids and the start of Total War (1942-43)* (Leo Cooper, 1987)

Wilson, D., *When Tigers Fight – the Story of the Sino-Japanese War, 1937-45* (Penguin, 1982)

Winfield, R., *The Sky Belongs to Them* (William Kimber, 1976)

Winterbottom, F.W., *The Ultra Secret* (Weidenfeld & Nicolson, 1974)

Wood, D., *Target England – the Illustrated History of the Battle of Britain* (Janes, 1980)

Wood, D. and Dempster, D., *The Narrow Margin* (Hutchinson, 1961)

Wragg, D.W., *The Offensive Weapon: the Strategy of Bombing* (Robert Hale, 1986)

Yass, M., *Hiroshima* (Wayland Publishers, 1971)

Zuckerman, S., *From Apes to Warlords – the Autobiography 1904-46* (Hamish Hamilton, 1978)

Index